A Star Is Born
and Born Again

A Star Is Born and Born Again:

Variations on a Hollywood Archetype

by James Stratton

BearManor Media
2015

A Star Is Born and Born Again:
Variations on a Hollywood Archetype

© 2015 James Stratton

All rights reserved.

For information, address:

BearManor Media
P. O. Box 71426
Albany, GA 31708

bearmanormedia.com

Typesetting and layout by John Teehan

Published in the USA by BearManor Media

ISBN—1-59393-819-5
978-1-59393-819-2

For
J. Paul Stratton
and
Mildred Eileen Naragon

Table of Contents

Acknowledgements..............................ix

1   Hollywood Looks at Hollywood 1

2   *What Price Hollywood?* (1932) 39

3   *A Star Is Born* (1937) 69

4   *A Star Is Born* (1954) 111

5   *A Star Is Born* (1976) 217

6   Conclusion 261

Works Cited 273

Index 277

Acknowledgments

I could not have written this book without the generous assistance of Robin Cresto and Matt Severson. Their enthusiasm, professionalism, and friendship are gifts for which I am hugely grateful. Joanne McGee's sincere support over many years has been equally important; her comments and advice are always in mind. Special thanks as well to Roberto Rangel for encouragement, patience, and understanding—especially during the conversations when I was "writing" in my head.

It is difficult to express how indebted I am to Jan Denman and Robert Bertholf. As teachers, role models, and friends, they helped to set and steer a life's direction. Thanks to them for opening so many doors.

Ben Ohmart at BearManor Media is the best publisher anyone could ask for. His support, commitment, intelligence, and energy are exceptional. Congratulations and gratitude to John Teehan for his wonderful work in designing and setting the book. I would also like to thank each of the following people for all that I have learned from them: Richard Stratton, Marsha Stratton, Patricia Kondan Davis, Bryan Olivas, Anais Wenn, Serafina Bathrick, Betty Ulicny, Irene Weeks, Stuart Kaminsky, and Peter Wollen. Special thanks as well to Maggie, Dashiell, Jacy, Domo, and Rufus, whose unconditional love and loyalty continue to inspire and teach.

All photos courtesy the Collections of the Margaret Herrick Library. Sincere thanks to Faye Thompson and all the other incredible staff members there. Photograph credits and acknowledgments: 20th Century-Fox, Metro-Goldwyn-Mayer, Paramount Pictures, Warner Bros., RKO Radio Pictures, United Artists, and Selznick International Pictures. All images are reproduced for the purposes of critical analysis and remain the copyright of those companies. Special gratitude to each of them for the support of film scholarship.

Parenthetical notations of authors and/or page numbers refer to the Works Cited section at the end of the book. I am grateful to each of those sources for information and insight.

Finally, I would like to pay tribute to the incredible talents of Judy Garland and James Mason, whose Esther Blodgett and Norman Maine motivated this whole project in the first place.

"It's the most unprofessional, God-awful business anywhere: Hollywood. Porn is much more respectable. No shady power plays. People are nicer."
– porn star James Deen

"The movie business is cyclical. Some guys are up, some guys are down."
– actor Matt Damon

"Hollywood is wonderful. Anyone who doesn't like it is either crazy or sober."
– writer Raymond Chandler

1

Hollywood Looks at Hollywood

Searchlights sweep the wide night sky as vintage limousines deposit men in tuxedos and women in silver gowns on the carpeted threshold of a Chinese theater. A worried man with a cigar watches a screen test and decides to give that naïve kid from the Midwest her career-making break. Or, less happily, a once promising writer slouches through one studio gate after another in a desperate but unsuccessful search for either a loan or a little hack work. We know the moments, we know the movies.

Since its inception as a sun-blessed outpost far from the east coast Edison patent enforcers, Hollywood has been telling stories about itself. Primed by studio publicity departments and fan magazines such as *Photoplay, Motion Picture,* and *Modern Screen,* the public rapidly developed an insatiable interest in all things Hollywood. Just as the Independent Moving Pictures Company had increased ticket sales by showcasing Florence Lawrence as a named, featured actress (and arguably the film industry's first movie star), the amorphous new California studios also found it profitable to give especially photogenic or talented performers a star build-up complete with fanciful biography, artfully composed fan photos, public appearances, and assuredly "inside" magazine profiles. Even when scandals involving sex, substance abuse, and murder snaked their way into the headlines, moviegoers seemed to become even more fascinated by Hollywood and its glamorous citizenry. Stars continued to fill theater seats, earned ever larger salaries, and endorsed everything from cigarettes to playing cards. Making fortunes for the studios, they piled up huge personal fortunes, as well. Magazines documented their lavish mansions, expensive cars, and exotic pets. Opulence and excess became signifiers of stardom.

Always eager to extend its brand and market its opulent self as product, Hollywood inevitably embraced the novelty of completely self-referential films. Studios set stories in Hollywood and populated them with actual stars playing themselves. The boundary between real and fictional characters was blurred intentionally. In fact that gauzy, possibly porous, separation between the material world and the filmic experience always had been one of silent cinema's earliest points of speculation. Everyday events (e.g., the arrival of a train at La Ciotat in the famous fifty second Lumière Brothers film of 1896) appeared so realistic on screen that some audiences apparently shrank back in a spontaneous reflex reaction. In 1901, Robert W. Paul, British inventor and film pioneer, used the act of film perception as the basis of a comic short. Titled *The Countryman and the Cinematograph* (also known as *The Countryman's First Sight of the Animated Pictures*) and shot at Paul's one-set, trick photography studio in Muswell Hill, the film revolves around the responses of a country yokel, a stereotypical mainstay of British and American theater, who is watching moving pictures for the first time.

Only a fragment of the brief film survives, but that existent footage, coupled with Paul's catalogue description, indicates how the narrative worked. The countryman, dressed in a black broad-brimmed hat and a long white worker's duster, stands to the left of the frame in front of his music hall box and views three short films projected on a screen to the right. In the first segment, a young woman in a ballet skirt dances on a revue stage; in the second, a railroad engine (a reference to the Lumière short) steams into a station and frightens the rube back into his box; and in the final segment, a country couple sit down together on a bench. The man, who is dressed exactly like the countryman, slips his arm around the maiden and inspires an energetic, perhaps jealous, response from the countryman. The point of the film is the unsophisticated pantomiming of the country viewer, who seems to take for real and synchronous everything he sees on the screen. The creator of one of cinema's earliest examples of a film within a film (precursor to Buster Keaton's 1924 *Sherlock, Jr.* and Woody Allen's 1985 *The Purple Rose of Cairo*), Robert Paul was also one of the first filmmakers to show his work commercially and one of the original "studio executives," paying Britain's first professional film actor Johnny Butt a nominal fee to appear in *Trilby Burlesque*, a dance clip from a popular London stage production.

One year later, Edwin S. Porter, who worked for Thomas Edison and soon would direct the twelve-minute early Western film *The Great Train Robbery*, "remade" Paul's short as *Uncle Josh at the Moving Picture Show*

(1902). A less generous and more cynical historical view might see it as the notoriously competitive Edison and Porter "stealing" the "Countryman" story idea. In either case, Porter's film, which exists in its entirety and is readily available online for viewing, is an exact copy. Uncle Josh, a dark-suited country bumpkin, jumps out of his theater box in excitement to watch three short films being projected on a white sheet. The three shorts are from the Edison catalogue: *Parisian Dancer*, *The Black Diamond Express* and *The Country Couple*. The action of each segment follows that of the Robert Paul film. In the opener, a woman in a long dress and bonnet lifts her skirts and performs an abbreviated can-can. After several additional high kicks, she cartwheels off stage. Throughout her dance, Uncle Josh jumps around on the left edge of the frame in a rough imitation of her moves; the projected image screens simultaneously on the right. The middle sequence has the Black Diamond train engine rounding a curve and advancing directly toward the camera. In exaggerated fear, Uncle Josh hops into his box and out of the frame. The final bit is a more developed narrative. A young country maiden with a pail enters the left side of the projection and a farmer in hat and vest enters the right. Setting aside his rake to help her draw water from a well, he gets hit on the head by the handle of the pump. She helps him to his feet and the two of them embrace. Up until this point, Uncle Josh has been laughing at the pratfalls, but, perhaps mistaking the young woman for his wife or daughter, he suddenly becomes agitated, takes off his coat, rolls up his sleeves, and jumps into the screen for a fight. As the sheet collapses, Uncle Josh discovers an angry kinetoscope operator projecting images—Wizard of Oz-like—behind it. The film ends with the collective anarchy that will become the go-to conclusion for American slapstick comedy; Uncle Josh and the projectionist wrestle each other to the floor.

Uncle Josh, like Happy Hooligan, was a recurring character for early Edison productions, played in film by Charles Manley and on cylinder recordings by Cal Stewart. Among other titles in the silent movie series are *Uncle Josh's Nightmare* (1900) and *Uncle Josh in a Spooky Hotel* (also 1900). Interestingly, both Paul's "countryman" and Porter's Uncle Josh are baffled by where the observable real world ends and the illusory world of cinema begins, but, unlike the projectionist from Keaton's film and Tom Baxter in Allen's film, neither actually jumps the divide and merges with the projected images.

As Hollywood continued to foreground film illusion and to make movies about movies, the newly crowned stars became both more credible and more fascinating at the same time. King Vidor's 1928 silent *Show*

Marion Davies and William Haines perform slapstick on an open-air set.

People, popular upon release and mostly forgotten now, is a revealing example. Peggy Pepper (Marion Davies) drives cross country from Georgia to Hollywood with her father to make it in the movies. Despite some initial setbacks, she meets actor Billy Boone (William Haines), who gets her a part doing slapstick in one of his low-budget comedies. She quickly becomes a success for Comet Studio but yearns to be a "real" actress in sophisticated motion pictures, a wish soon fulfilled when she signs a contract with the appropriately titled High Arts Studio. Changing her name to the pseudo European but still alliterative "Patricia Pepoire," she reaches even higher stardom in the serious, dramatic parts she feels born to play. That success, however, goes to her head and she turns away from Billy, the Comet comedy troupe and anything that reminds her of the old seltzer-spraying days.

When her arrogance makes her performances stilted and lifeless, the public (often flattered by Hollywood for its astute judgment) begins to withdraw its support. On the day she is to marry co-star and fake aristocrat André Telefair (Paul Ralli), Billy crashes the festivities and, in a gag reminiscent of one of his comedies, sprays Peggy with some soda water, tosses a pie at André, and halts the wedding. In the final scene, Peggy is working with director King Vidor (playing himself) in a war picture much like Vidor's own hit *The Big Parade*. Unbeknownst to Billy, she has persuaded Vidor to give him a part. As the camera rolls, Billy momentarily freezes when Peggy enters in character, but he quickly recovers to play smoothly off her spontaneity. After Vidor calls "cut," the old pals keep kissing, committed to each other and to the kind of "natural" acting the film has been championing all along.

Show People builds a comic contrast between authenticity and pretentiousness. Telefair calls himself André de Bergerac le Comte d'Avignon, but Billy reveals in a title card that "Andy used to serve me spaghetti" at a nearby restaurant. Peggy and her maid (well-played by Polly Moran) are continually putting on airs. Peggy has wolfhounds and a Rolls Royce and curls her upper lip into a crazed chipmunk grimace to show haughtiness. The maid walks with an affected prance and, by way of the titles, says things such as "Pardon my depravity but that terrible comedian person is downstairs." When Peggy as Pepoire is required for location shooting, she arrives with a limousine and entourage and has perfume sprayed because the director's breath disturbs her.

Peggy interrupts filming on the studio factory line.

The on-location filming of Peggy's costume drama is one of several "behind the scenes" glimpses of Hollywood at work. Coincidentally, Billy's Comet Studio troupe shows up at the same time and place to disrupt the serious atmosphere with a surreal Mack Sennett-like chase shot from the back of an open-air jalopy. On Peggy's first day in a studio, she stumbles onto two different sets, interfering with the action and spoiling the camera angles. In a remarkable deep focus shot, Peggy and Billy wait for an interview at High Arts and through the floor to ceiling window behind them we can watch an outdoor rain scene as it is prepared and filmed. Most of *Show People*'s action occurs in studios, and its dream factory ambiance fits perfectly with the gauzy image of Hollywood being pushed in fan magazines and publicity releases.

Adding to a moviegoer's enjoyment of Haines and Davies is the aficionado's delight in recognizing all the real celebrities that Peggy encounters during her Hollywood adventures. In the film's studio lunch scene, fans can spot Renée Adorée, George Arthur, Karl Dane, Douglas Fairbanks, John Gilbert, William S. Hart, Leatrice Joy, Rod La Rocque, Mae Murray, Louella Parsons, Aileen Pringle, Dorothy Sebastian, Norma Talmadge, Estelle Taylor, and Claire Windsor—all playing themselves. Gilbert and Eleanor Boardman appear in a film clip (from *Bardelys the Magnificent*) within the movie, and Gilbert shows up one more time outside the High Arts Studio. Charlie Chaplin contributes a very funny bit as part of the audience exiting the sneak preview of Peggy and Billy's first co-starring comedy. Chaplin asks both of them to sign his book of autographs; Billy quickly complies but Peggy is unaware that it's Chaplin and keeps ignoring him. "Who is that little guy?" her title card asks. To her extreme dismay, she finds out only after Chaplin has departed and is waving at her from his chauffeur driven car. Also turning in cameos are the well-known writer Elinor Glyn and matinee idol Lew Cody, who have an extended conversation with each other in the High Arts front lobby. Finally, in a self-effacing bit of Russian doll casting, Marion Davies (as herself) pulls up to High Arts in a sporty automobile and runs off across the lawn with a tennis racket. When told who it is, Peggy (as any practiced lip reader can observe) responds, "Oh, I don't like her."

As they will in all self-reflexive Hollywood movies, the real-life references resonate in several different ways. Distributed by Metro-Goldwyn-Mayer and co-produced by Irving Thalberg and Davies herself, the film is above all an advertisement for the extensive MGM star roster and the studio's sumptuous production values. Billing itself in the 1930s and 1940s as the studio with "more stars than there are in heaven," MGM here is

The stars appear as themselves in Vidor's MGM film.

overwhelming the audience with one celebrated performer after another. At MGM, *Show People* is saying, you get big talent and lots of it. For the knowledgeable moviegoer, the film also works as a kind of narrative *à clef* complete with insider reference jokes. Peggy's faux-French "Pepoire" screen name suggests Renée Adorée's persona, and that lip pucker for high drama is similar to a gesture used by Mae Murray. Her slapstick to theatrics transition recalls Gloria Swanson's rise from Mack Sennett comedy performer at Keystone to Cecil B. DeMille dramatic actress at Paramount. The character of André Telefair is probably a parody of Swanson's French nobleman husband or of John Gilbert. Viewers who understand the jokes get to feel that much closer to the Hollywood elite, as if they are privileged accomplices keyed in to the codes.

The Peggy Pepper story also constitutes a kind of meta commentary on Marion Davies's career. Like Peggy, Davies first reached stardom in a series of light comedies and then switched to less successful costume dramas, such as *Yolanda* and *When Knighthood Was in Flower*. The presence of Hearst newspaper syndicate columnist Louella Parsons in *Show People's* banquet scene surfaces Marion Davies's link to William Randolph Hearst.

Marion Davies as Patricia Pepoire referencing various Hollywood careers including her own.

Parsons is there because Hearst had powerful connections at MGM and throughout Hollywood due to his ownership of newspapers, magazines, and even a film company, Cosmopolitan Pictures. Looming unseen over the movie's financial context, Hearst produced many of Davies's silent and sound films at Cosmopolitan Pictures and released them for a while through MGM (until a disagreement with Irving Thalberg over Davies's failure to be cast in *Marie Antoinette* led him to Warner Bros.). It was Hearst who steered Davies into the unpopular costume dramas alluded to in *Show People* and who became her business and romantic partner. Although they never married because of his wife's refusal to divorce him, Hearst and Davies lived together until his death and entertained all the major Hollywood players at their various lavish residences, these strong social alliances providing another reason for the extensive and impressive guest appearances in *Show People*.

Perhaps the most interesting way to read the movie star cameos is to note how they highlight issues of perception and illusion inherent in the viewing of fiction films. We are aware of the masks actors don when they portray different characters and we accept the artifice. Seeing them out of costume and in everyday situations, we look for gestures and expressions that are there in the acting but also there in reality—that is, behavior that is not technique-driven but is intrinsic. Does Douglas Fairbanks always show off his nimble athleticism? Does Charlie Chaplin grin nervously and turn his mouth up and down at the corners? If the answers are yes, does that mean the "acting" is any less skillful? Or does it mean these performers never remove the masks and never behave in real life without some remnant of their screen persona still attached?

Whatever the truth, the idea that movie stars might actually be "accessible" on the streets of Hollywood accounts for the popularity of these films (and for part of the growth in Hollywood's population, as well). The name itself was talismanic. Five years before *Show People's* release, Paramount had produced a now lost and legendary 1923 comedy directed by James Cruze called *Hollywood* with a similar story line involving a young girl traveling to Hollywood with her grandfather to make it in the movies. Appearing in brief cameos as themselves are more than thirty major celebrities, such as Fatty Arbuckle, Mary Astor, Noah Berry, William Boyd, Chaplin, Ricardo Cortez, Bebe Daniels, Cecil B. DeMille, Douglas Fairbanks, Sid Grauman, William S. Hart, Nita Naldi, Jack Holt, Pola Negri, Mary Pickford, ZaSu Pitts, Will Rogers, Gloria Swanson, Ben Turpin, and Lois Wilson. Partly an exercise in reparative public relations, the film was released in the midst of several Paramount employee scandals, such as actress Olive Thomas's suicide, director William Desmond Taylor's murder, actor Wallace Reid's drug-related death, and comedian Arbuckle's multiple trials for the rape and manslaughter of aspiring actress Virginia Rappe. Although he was finally acquitted, Arbuckle's career was ruined and the sensational newspaper coverage called the whole community's morals into question. In defensive contrast, *Hollywood* proudly displays a long worthy roster of hard-working, respectable professionals and even includes Arbuckle among the "regulars."

The play for respectability seemed to work. Rob Reel, reviewing *Hollywood* for *Chicago American*, wrote, "It is the real, wholesome, enterprising and amazingly successful Hollywood that is shown. Romance, yes. But that which is legitimate and fine." Reel's considered use of "wholesome" and "legitimate" is specifically meant to distinguish *Hollywood's* content from the movie capital scandals being reported in various popular magazines. The film's storyline has familiar characters and plot conventions. Angela Whitaker (Hope Drown in her only starring role) is a movie-crazy

Another Hollywood hopeful admires the stars in James Cruze's lost film, *Hollywood*.

girl from a small Midwestern town, who decides to go to Hollywood to break into pictures and earn much needed money for her penniless family. Accompanying her on the journey is her apparently infirm and ailing grandfather Joel Whitaker (Luke Cosgrave). Although she is pretty and photogenic, Angela has no luck at the studios; her grandfather, however, is cast by a director in need of a particular-looking old man, and he soon becomes a big success. As his ailments vanish, Grandfather Whitaker adapts easily to the Hollywood lifestyle, taking up a reckless game of golf and having his name and phone number printed on his cigarettes. Concerned with the changes in her grandfather, Angela sends a letter back home asking for help.

In response, Angela's grandmother, mother, and boyfriend Lem Lefferts (George K. Arthur) soon arrive in Hollywood and are themselves fortuitously cast in movies. Cecil B. DeMille hires the two women as pioneer wives in a picture with Grandpa Joel, and Lem is signed by William S. Hart after the cowboy star sees Lem in a fight and decides he would make the perfect, two-fisted tough guy co-star for his next movie. Angela, meanwhile, continues to come up empty-handed. During one interview, studio casting directors ask her if she has any experience, and she tells them yes, only to have them reply that they are looking for someone with no experience at all. Eventually, Angela and Lem marry, and Angela gives birth to twins Doug and Mary (named, obviously, after married Hollywood mega-stars Douglas Fairbanks and Mary Pickford). When the twins and even the pet parrot all are offered parts in the movies, Angela finally decides it is all right to be the pretty "civilian" in a family of working actors.

Hollywood was a major production by one of Paramount's favored directors, James Cruze. A former silent film actor and medicine show performer, Cruze had directed several films starring either Arbuckle or Wallace Reid and would go on to make *The Covered Wagon* (1923), *Merton of the Movies* (1924), *The Pony Express* (1925), *Old Ironsides* (1926), *The Great Gabbo* (1929), and *I Cover the Waterfront* (1933). Louise Brooks, who worked for him in *The City Gone Wild* (1927), claimed that he knew exactly what he wanted in a scene, shot fast, and drank continuously throughout the day. Like many successful silent directors, Cruze had formed a collaboration with a preferred cinematographer and that

An elaborate scene from the much searched-for *Hollywood* suggests the picture's visual richness.

partner, Karl Brown, was on the team with him for *Hollywood*. The story was by the prolific Frank Condon and had been published a year earlier in *Photoplay*. Condon also had provided the stories for *The Knickerbocker Buckaroo* (1919), *Crazy to Marry* (1921), *The Man Who Saw Tomorrow* (1922), and *Sixty Cents an Hour* (1922). Thomas Geraghty, who wrote some seventy silent and sound films during his twenty-two-year Hollywood career, contributed the screen adaptation.

Existing photos from the Paramount stills collection reveal that the film had a substantial budget and impressive production values. A deep-focus fantasy sequence shot under a billowing columned canopy, for example, features fountains, staircases, arched footbridges, and a couple hundred extras dressed as everything from chorines to sultans. Costumes here and in the various studio department scenes are lavish. Action sequences, like Lem Lefferts's nightmare aboard the train to Hollywood, are packed with striking detail. Opening at New York's Rivoli Theatre in July, 1923, the movie was hugely successful and equaled the box office record set there a year earlier by Rudolph Valentino's bullfighter movie, *Blood and Sand*. Reviews were overwhelmingly positive, as well. Robert Sherwood, in *The New York Herald*, remarked, "'Hollywood' represents the turning point in the life of the silent drama—100 percent entertainment. A momentous production, and we sincerely trust none of our readers will fail to see it." "By laughing at himself and his crowd," said *Photoplay*, "Mr. Cruze has turned out a rattlingly good film." Reviewers especially liked the cameos performed by the stars, bits like Will Rogers using a lasso to hurry some reluctant actors into a train, Pickford and Fairbanks emerging from their fabled Pickfair estate, and Jack Holt struggling under a huge pile of fan letters.

Some twenty years later during the war effort, Hollywood stars are appearing as themselves in ways even more accessible and more civic-minded. In Warner Bros.' 1944 *Hollywood Canteen* (directed by Delmer Daves), Bette Davis and her movie star pals operate a screen version of the real armed forces recreation center that was located from 1942 to 1945 at 1451 Cahuenga Boulevard in Hollywood. It is not a documentary, of course, but a fictionalized account of the nights a soldier and his buddies spend on leave at the Canteen. The stars (all from the Warner Bros.' stable for obvious reasons) play themselves. Bette sweetly calls the celebrities by their first names and refers to her Canteen co-founder John Garfield as "Johnny." Barbara Stanwyck flirts from behind a refreshment counter, Joe E. Brown stuffs doughnuts into his mouth, Jane Wyman gives chatty

Bette Davis and Joan Leslie fraternize with regular soldier Robert Hutton at the Hollywood Canteen.

tours of the place, Ida Lupino speaks French, Peter Lorre calls out Sydney Greenstreet for acting too creepy, Jack Carson busses tables, Roy Rogers rides in and out on Trigger while singing a song, and S.Z. Sakall lets servicemen pinch his famously chubby cheeks.

Hollywood Canteen serves up the illusion of transcending the illusions. We apparently are being privileged to see the stars as they truly are and as they interact with ordinary people. So accessible are the celebrities that the soldier portrayed by Robert Hutton is able to begin a requited romance with real life actress Joan Leslie. As he rides off to deployment on the obligatory departing train, it is Joan Leslie playing Joan Leslie who waves tearfully from the platform. More attuned to the conventional separation between audience and film performer than the producers, Ann Sheridan was presumably offered the Leslie part but refused to take it, arguing that nobody would believe such a mingling of star and commoner could really happen.

In 1960, Columbia tried the "stars as themselves" gimmick again with George Sidney's *Pepe*, in which Cantinflas as Pepe comes to Hollywood to track down a beloved white stallion that has been sold to hard-drinking film producer Ted Holt (Dan Dailey). During the course of the movie's three-plus hours, Pepe encounters over thirty major personalities, including Bing Crosby, Tony Curtis, Bobby Darin, Sammy Davis Jr., Jimmy Durante, Zsa Zsa Gabor, Judy Garland (voice only, singing the Oscar-nominated song "A Far Away Part of Town"), Greer Garson, Ernie Kovacs, Peter Lawford, Janet Leigh (in a humorous reference to *Touch of Evil* and *Psycho*), Jack Lemmon (in drag as Daphne from *Some Like It Hot*), Dean Martin, Donna Reed, Debbie Reynolds, Edward G. Robinson, and Frank Sinatra. Nominated for seven Academy Awards, *Pepe* did not do well at the box office and was mostly disparaged by critics. The all-star real-life cavalcades now have more or less disappeared, although Robert Altman's *The Player* featured cameos by about sixty celebrities, and actors still occasionally play ironic, self-deprecating caricatures of themselves like Neil Patrick Harris in the Harold and Kumar movies, Bill Murray in *Zombieland*, John Malkovich in *Being John Malkovich*, and James Franco, Seth Rogen, Jonah Hill, Jay Baruchel, Craig Robinson, and Danny McBride in *This Is the End*.

Even with no real-life stars popping up along the way, the transformative journey to Hollywood has been a key narrative trope in films about finding success in the movies. When "Hollywood" appears in the title, the word immediately suggests a sunnier, more extravagant take on the American dream, the inflated vision of fame and wealth that drives the main characters(s). Arrival in this golden place, we know, will provide the opportunity to redefine oneself. *Going Hollywood* (MGM, 1933, directed by Raoul Walsh) and *Hollywood Hotel* (First National, 1937, directed by Busby Berkeley) are illustrative. In the first film, Sylvia Bruce (Marion Davies in by now a signature role) gives up small-town teaching and goes to California, where she transforms herself into a star and wins singing sensation Bill Williams (Bing Crosby) away from a favorite Hollywood target—a selfish and conceited foreign temptress (played by Fifi D'Orsay).

In the latter film, a dense plot finds St. Louis singer and sax player Ronnie Bowers (Dick Powell) coming to Hollywood where, after treachery and disappointment, he teams with waitress/stand-in Virginia Stanton (Rosemary Lane) to wheedle a chance to perform on a popular radio show and ultimately sign a lucrative studio contract. The movie's big "Hooray for Hollywood" airport production number, with Benny Goodman's orchestra playing on a fleet of convertibles, celebrates Hollywood as the place "where any office boy or young mechanic can be a panic" and where "any shop girl can be a top girl." It is exactly that chimera of success, writes Carey McWilliams in his landmark *Southern California: An Island on the Land*, that explains how "motion pictures have attracted perhaps more people than they have ever employed and more capital than they have ever invested" (page 340). Movie making, he continues, "provided the community with precisely what it needed, payrolls, purchasing—a simulated industrial base. Like the region itself, this key industry is premised upon improvisation, a matter of make-believe, a synthesis of air and wind and water" (page 340).

Interest in the mechanics of this make-believe industry, in the actual process of assembling a movie, also permeates some of the stories Hollywood tells about itself. More so than in the star cavalcade pictures, these films devote substantial narrative time to how studios operate and how technology and personnel interact. Buster Keaton's 1928 *The Cameraman* (MGM, directed by Keaton and Edward Sedgwick), which follows Buster's accident-prone quest to become a newsreel cameraman, may be the most well-remembered silent film treatment of a movie technician, but, as early as 1914, Mack Sennett produced a comedy short called *A Film Johnnie* (Keystone Studios, directed by George Nichols) that featured a young Charles Chaplin making his way to Keystone Studios to find the beautiful actress he has fallen in love with on the screen. Before Charlie disrupts its production, we see a film being shot on one of the open-air sets and we see crew members going about their tasks. Fatty Arbuckle and Ford Sterling appear as themselves.

Nine years later, producer Sennett expanded the idea of a film looking at film production with the 1923 comedy feature *The Extra Girl* (Pathé, directed by F. Richard Jones); Mabel Normand portrays Sue Graham, another small town girl, who comes to Hollywood to become a film star. Along with Keystone's rural-like location on what is now Glendale Boulevard in Silver Lake, the film shows viewers a studio in full operation complete with film set, actors, cameras and cameramen, production people and a pianist/violinist combo to create "atmosphere" for the actors. Director Mack Sennett and Billy Bevan appear briefly in cameos. Reversing the rise to fame theme played out two months earlier with the release of *Hollywood*, Normand's character fails miserably with her screen test and settles for a job in the wardrobe department instead.

The conventions of silent filmmaking and the challenges of early sound recording are famously satirized in MGM's 1952 *Singin' in the Rain* (directed by Gene Kelly and Stanley Donen). Kelly is Don Lockwood, a former vaudevillian cum stuntman, who climbs through the

Benny Goodman and his Orchestra send Dick Powell off on a ballyhooed journey to the movie capital in the 1937 *Hollywood Hotel*.

ranks at Monumental Pictures to become a star of adventure movies. Like many actual male silent actors who made it big, his popularity stems from an ability to move gracefully in front of the camera and to seem like a regular American guy. When Monumental pairs him with ditzy but conniving Lina Lamont (Jean Hagen in a rightfully acclaimed comic part) for a series of romantic swashbucklers and costume dramas, the couple becomes a major sensation. The scenes at Monumental capture the creative looseness of the silent days as well as the factory model they initiated: on-set orchestras for mood and inspiration; the fluid, overlapping roles of employees; the simultaneous, assembly-line shooting on multiple stages; continuous product advertising through events like the radio coverage of movie premieres.

One evening at a party, studio head R.F. Simpson (Millard Mitchell) shows a Vitaphone talking picture short, which everyone disparages but which soon becomes the new norm. To keep up with the success of *The Jazz Singer*, Simpson decides to turn the latest Lockwood and Lamont project, *The Dueling Cavalier*, into a talkie. Although playing the technical challenges for laughs, the film again is insightful about historical context, showing us the dialogue coaches, the bulky sound recording equipment, the uncertain microphone range, and the reduced camera mobility of the transition period. These mechanical problems combined with the stars' archaic acting style and Lina's irritatingly shrill voice mean disaster for *The Dueling Cavalier's* sneak preview. Audience members openly mock the performance and the sound slips out of synch. But it is the sound recording process itself that gives Don's pal Cosmo (Donald O'Connor) the idea of reshooting the movie as a musical to be called *The Dancing Cavalier* and with Lina's speaking and singing to be dubbed by Don's talented new girlfriend Kathy Selden (Debbie Reynolds).

The idea of a likable unknown covering for an unbearable star is borrowed from *Hollywood Hotel,* where Ronnie Bowers dubs the singing for Alex Du Prey (Alan Mowbray). Just as true credit is ultimately resolved in *Hollywood Hotel*, Kathy Selden gains recognition and stardom when Lina pushes R. F. Simpson (previously protective of the studio's most ill-tempered property) too far and he, Don, and Cosmo raise a curtain be-

Gene Kelly and Jean Hagen humorously confront the challenges of early sound films in *Singin' in the Rain.*

hind Lina's premiere night lip-synching to reveal Kathy performing for real. The joke foregrounds some of the actual procedures (e.g., dubbing and singing to playback) that are used in the recording of sound for motion pictures.

As a period piece musical, *The Dancing Cavalier* suggests Lubitsch's *The Love Parade* and Mamoulian's *Love Me Tonight*. Other historical references include the chorine production numbers (*Broadway Melody*, *Ziegfeld Follies*, Busby Berkeley movies) and characters like the "Zip Girl" (based on "It" girl Clara Bow) and screen vamp Olga Mara (Pola Negri). Along with the incandescent primary color images and Gene Kelly's titular dance in the rain, what viewers most remember about *Singin' in the Rain*, however, is the exuberance and camaraderie of shooting movies. The studio makes all things possible, sorting out talent and rewarding creativity.

It is this carnival-like energy of Monumental Pictures that also animates more recent films whose subject is the making of a film, movies like Fellini's *8½* (1963), Paul Mazursky's *Alex in Wonderland* (1970), Truffaut's *Day for Night* (1973), and Richard Rush's *The Stunt Man* (1980). Although not set in Hollywood, the Fellini and Truffaut films deify the director as auteur in the same way the two American movies do. In *8½*, famous film director Guido Anselmi (Marcello Mastroianni as a fictive stand-in for Fellini himself) is suffering a creative block during production of his latest film, some kind of science fiction and contemporary drama mash-up filled with thinly veiled autobiographical references. Guido scouts locations, approves sets, endures interviews, casts actors, shoots screen tests, and views footage but ultimately abandons the film while simultaneously embracing all the contradictions and creative fantasies of his life. *Alex in Wonderland* is Mazurksy's MGM-distributed homage to Fellini's film. Donald Sutherland portrays Alex Morrison, a hot young Hollywood director with one feature to his credit and an inability to settle on his next project. Like Guido, he struggles with producers, family problems, self-doubts, and a hyperactive imagination prone to staging improbable movie scenes. Mazursky plays a slippery Hollywood producer and Fellini appears in a cameo as himself.

Francois Truffaut directs *Day for Night* and acts in it as the director of the film within the film. *Day for Night* (English translation of the term "la nuit américaine," which refers to the process of using special lighting, film stock, and filters to shoot action in daylight so that it appears to be happening at night), opens with a crowd scene outside of a Paris metro entrance and then halts suddenly to reveal the episode as a climactic moment in a melodrama called *Meet Pamela* that director Ferrand (Truffaut) is shooting on the set of a studio in Nice. The director's voice intrudes, a camera crane swings into view, and crew members race around redressing the set. The scene is shot again with running voice-over commentary from Ferrand instructing the actors and extras how to move and how and when to interact with one another. Faced with budget and insurance constraints, tortuous romances among cast and crew, and the death of one of his key actors, Ferrand strives at first to do his best possible work and then later to just finish the film on schedule.

Another director, Peter O'Toole as imperial Eli Cross, is the star of *The Stunt Man* (20th Century Fox), the story of a WWI action movie being shot on location at San Diego's Hotel del Coronado (also the setting for Billy Wilder's 1959 *Some Like It Hot*). In arguably the best American movie ever made about the production of a film, Eli swoops in and out of scenes on camera booms and helicopters, controlling the lives of his actors and continually blurring the lines between appearance and reality. Among his puppets are an insecure actress and a fugitive from the police, whom Eli agrees to harbor if he takes the place of Eli's ace stunt man killed in a filming accident which the fugitive may or may not have caused.

As mentioned previously, what all of these films have in common with one another, with *Singin' in the Rain* and with current critical favorites, such as *The Artist* (2011, directed by Michel Hazanavicius) and *Hugo* (2011, Paramount, directed by Martin Scorsese) is awestruck admiration for the process of making movies. Actors may behave like children in real life, but they are also mercurial artists who can be guided by godlike directors to create magic. For the few frantic months that a film is in production, uniquely talented individuals come together as a chaotic extended family set loose in a technical wonderland to play with what Orson Welles supposedly once described as "the biggest electric-train set any boy ever had." Or, as Eli Cross says in describing his toys, "If God could do the tricks we do, he'd be a happy man." Under the influence of this wizardry, bad behavior is forgiven and differences are resolved to such a degree that the films often end in collective celebrations like the ringmaster-led, linked-hand dance around the abandoned space ship set in *8½*, the crew's spirited acknowledgment of the successful final stunt in *The Stunt Man* or the chain of comic farewells in *Day for Night*.

A recent variation in the self-referential film production story is the mostly historical account of the making of a specific real movie from Hollywood's past. *My Week with Marilyn* (2011, BBC Films and the Weinstein Company, directed by Simon Curtis), for example, chronicles the challenges Laurence Olivier (Kenneth Branagh) faced directing and co-starring with Marilyn Monroe (Michelle Williams) in the production of *The Prince and the Showgirl*. Told from the point of view of the young third assistant director, who spent the eponymous seven days with the then Mrs. Arthur Miller, the film focuses on the star's gentle, childlike nature, as well as her insecurities and doubts that led to major delays in shooting. When the film is finally completed, all those involved, including Olivier, seem to think the turmoil was worth the moments of magic that Marilyn delivers on screen.

There is a different kind of behavior to forgive in *Hitchcock* (2012, Fox Searchlight, directed by Sacha Gervasi) and *The Girl* (2012, BBC/HBO, directed by Julian Jarrold), two varyingly factual accounts of how Alfred Hitchcock's alleged lechery impacted the filming of *Psycho* and *The Birds* respectively. In *Hitchcock*, the acclaimed director (Anthony Hopkins) belittles his wife Alma (Helen Mirren) and makes suggestive advances to Janet Leigh (Scarlett Johansson) while fighting censors and deciding to self-finance *Psycho* rather than submit to studio executives. In *The Girl*, Hitchcock (played this time by Toby Jones) becomes so sexually obsessed with leading lady Tippi Hedren (Sienna Miller) that her eventual rejection leads him to retaliatory acts of mental and physical cruelty that play out in the filming itself. The scene in *The Birds* where Hedren as Melanie Daniels is attacked by birds upstairs in the Brenner house is faithfully rec-

From above, magisterial director Eli Cross (Peter O'Toole) commands his film crew like a general in *The Stunt Man*.

reated (just as is the *Psycho* shower murder in *Hitchcock*) to show Hedren confined on a cramped set and buffeted with birds continually thrown at her by prop men. But even with Hitchcock portrayed in both films as a boorish predator, the filmmakers would have us marvel at the finished products. Hitch may have been a little creepy but look what he was able to do in *Psycho, The Birds,* and *Marnie.*

In *Shadow of the Vampire* (2000, BBC Films, directed by E. Elias Merhige), *Nosferatu* actor Max Schreck is a real vampire who kills crew members, but the footage is great. Would-be leading ladies like Paulette Goddard and Tallulah Bankhead are lied to and manipulated in *The Scarlett O'Hara War* (1980, Warner Bros. Television, directed by John Erman), but the final apotheosis of Vivien Leigh as Margaret Mitchell's heroine in the revered *Gone with the Wind* makes the mistreatment seem almost necessary. *RKO 281* (1999, HBO, directed by Benjamin Ross) deals with the ego, chaos, and intimidation surrounding a film production that just happens to be *Citizen Kane*. The message of all these movies about actual movies, and a point to be expanded later, is that the filmic end justifies the messy "making of" means.

A similar emphasis on the complicatedly creative people involved in film production occurs naturally in the star bio pics. Like the bandleader and baseball player biographies of the 40s and 50s, the earliest films about movie stars tended to be hagiographic. *The Story of Will Rogers* (Warner Bros., 1952, directed by Michael Curtiz), for example, features Will Rogers Jr. as his decent, down-to-earth father and Jane Wyman as the devoted wife. Opening on shots of the "Will Rogers Shrine of the Sun", various buildings and parks named for Rogers and a horse mounted statue, the film emphasizes the actor's humanitarianism and virtue. Partly from fear of lawsuits, the 1951 *Valentino* (Columbia, directed by Lewis Allen) sanitizes the movie idol's life story and portrays him as a talented, hardworking performer with a strong sense of pride and a chivalric protectiveness toward women. Reflecting the late 60s demise of the Motion Picture Production Code, subsequent versions of Valentino's life like *The Legend of Valentino* (1975, Spelling-Goldberg Productions, directed by Melville Shavelson) and *Valentino* (1977, United Artists, directed by Ken Russell) made up for the white wash by alleging ambiguous sexuality, bigamy, a criminal past, and an early career as a gigolo.

As censorship has lessened and audience tastes have changed, comedians, legends, and romantic teams have all been treated in the same sensationalistic way. Their screen biographies have been guided by the

The life of Will Rogers becomes a lesson in simple American values in *The Story of Will Rogers*.

headlines of fan magazines and have transitioned abruptly from success to crisis and sorrow. Among these Sturm und Drang tales are *The Buster Keaton Story* (1957, Paramount, directed by Sidney Sheldon), *W.C. Fields and Me* (1976, Universal, directed by Arthur Hiller), *Chaplin* (1992, Carolco Pictures, directed by Richard Attenborough), *Frances* (1982, Universal, directed by Graeme Clifford), *Mommie Dearest* (1981, Paramount, directed by Frank Perry), *James Dean* (2001, Turner Network Television, directed by Mark Rydell), *Gable and Lombard* (1976, Universal, directed by Sidney J. Furie), *Liz and Dick* (2012, Lifetime, directed by Lloyd Kramer) and many others. The more lurid elements of the star biographies are mirrored in the fictional melodramas that Hollywood conjures about itself. There is a clear link, for example, between a film like *Harlow* (1965, Paramount, directed by Gordon M. Douglas) and a film like *The Legend of Lylah Clare* (1968, MGM, directed by Robert Aldrich). The broadly drawn, tragically lost leading ladies could almost be interchangeable.

Melodrama, writes film scholar Susan Hayward in her book *Key Concepts in Cinema Studies*, "dreams of the unobtainable—emotions, including hope, rise only to be dashed, and for this reason the melodrama is ulti-

Faye Dunaway's portrayal of Joan Crawford in *Mommie Dearest* is less than flattering.

mately masochistic" (page 205). Think of classic self-reflexive Hollywood melodramas such as *Sunset Boulevard* (1950, Paramount, directed by Billy Wilder) or *The Barefoot Contessa* (1954, United Artists, directed by Joseph Mankiewicz) and the pattern is confirmed. Norma Desmond (Gloria Swanson) desires a rekindled career and romance with young screenwriter Joe Gillis but shoots Gillis when he attempts to leave her and loses her sanity instead. Maria Vargas (Ava Gardner) rises from nightclub dancer to great film star but cannot find love until the mysterious Count Vincenzo Torlato-Favrini rescues her one night from boorish company and whisks her away to be married. Their happiness is temporary. The count is impotent from a war injury, and when Maria becomes briefly involved with another man, the count shoots her before she can confess her pregnancy and beg forgiveness. The conflated quest for stardom and for love which climaxes in the irrevocable loss of one or both recurs frequently in the inside Hollywood melodrama. Again Hayward is instructive: "Melodrama plays out forbidden longings, symptomatic illness and renunciation" (page 205).

Realized dreams become tragic ironies, and reaching "success" becomes charged with peril. The theme has deep roots. In the bizarrely over-the-top *Souls for Sale* (1923, Goldwyn Pictures, directed by Rupert Hughes), a newly-minted star almost loses her life. Remember "Mem" Steddon (Eleanor Boardman) jumps train on her wedding night and finds herself on the desert location set of a movie where she gets work as an extra and attracts the romantic interest of both the director Frank Claymore (Richard Dix) and the star Tom Holby (Frank Mayo). Meanwhile Mem's husband Owen Scudder (Lew Cody) is revealed as a serial murderer who kills his wives for insurance money. After he himself is fleeced by a fake English noblewoman, Scudder shows up in Hollywood to find Mem on the brink of fame. In a feverish climax that takes place on an outdoor circus set, the jealous Scudder tries to kill Claymore with the propeller of a wind machine, fights with Holby and finally dies saving Mem from the lethally out of control machine. Even in a melodrama as dubious as this one, several movie celebrities including Erich von Stroheim, Jean Hersholt, Barbara La Marr, Chester Conklin, and the ubiquitous Charlie Chaplin appear in cameos as themselves. The bluntly obvious message of *Souls for Sale* is that navigating Hollywood entails danger to self and to romance.

There is similar fallout from movie fame in *Show Girl in Hollywood* (1930, First National Pictures, directed by Mervyn Le Roy). Dixie Dugan (Alice White) goes to Hollywood on the promise of a movie role that doesn't materialize. However, since her once and future boyfriend Jimmy Doyle (Jack Mulhall) sells his musical play to a studio and advocates for her, she gets her big chance anyway. The problem is that she falls under the influence of a slick director who turns her into a temperamental star and almost destroys her career.

In a really extreme melodrama, the lead actress can lose her life, not just her love. Built around melodrama's "doubling" device, *The Legend of Lylah Clare* finds Kim Novak (just like she did in *Vertigo*) helplessly duplicating her own death. Revealed via multiple conflicting flashbacks, Lylah Clare (Novak) is a tempestuous Garbo/Dietrich-like screen queen who, on her wedding might, either falls or is pushed to her death from the heights of an absurdly free-floating, non-banistered staircase inside her baroque mansion. So devastated is husband and director Lewis Zarken (Peter Finch) that he cannot make another picture for the next couple of decades until dying agent and wannabe producer Bart Langner (Milton Selzer) discovers young Lylah look-alike starlet Elsa Brinkmann (also Novak) and convinces Zarken to direct her in a film based on Lylah's life. Transcendingly coarse studio executive Barney Sheean (Ernest Borgnine) agrees to finance the project although he continually reminds everyone, "I make movies, not films," a creative position made satirically even clearer by his initials "BS" stamped on all the studio property and equipment.

Along with key structural elements of melodrama—characters altering their identities, environment determining destiny, mood replacing motivation—Aldrich also gives us the oversize personalities of the genre. There are the four principals plus Rossella Falk as dialogue coach and Lewis's lesbian companion, Valentina Cortese as flamboyant costume designer Countess Bozo Bedoni, and Coral Browne as a bitchy, wooden legged Louella Parsons-like gossip columnist. There is also the requisite scene of Elsa walking on Hollywood Boulevard and passing Mann's Chinese Theater. With her last name changed to Campbell, Elsa is molded and manipulated to such extremes that she invariably becomes the long-dead Lylah. Catastrophe and loss are soon repeated.

Fedora (1978, United Artists, directed by Billy Wilder) also deals with tragic duplication. Reworking the ageing star motif of Wilder's *Sunset Boulevard*, *Fedora*'s improbable plot follows the attempts of washed-up Hollywood producer Barry "Dutch" Detweiler (William Holden) to lure the perennially beautiful Garboesque screen goddess Fedora (Marthe Keller) out of retirement to star in his new adaptation of *Anna Karenina*. Regret over a seemingly unavoidable tragedy in the past guides the narrative voice of many melodramas and is often achieved, as it is here, through an extended flashback. The film opens á la Tolstoy's climax with Fedora throwing herself under a train at Paris's Gare de Mortcerf and mourners gathering for her funeral. Among them is Detweiler, whose voice-over narration lays out the events of the previous weeks and his sorrow over not doing more to save Fedora.

Detweiler had tracked down Fedora in Corfu, where she lived in seclusion with bitter Countess Sobryanski (Hildegard Knef), protective personal secretary Miss Balfour (Frances Sternhagen), plastic surgeon Dr. Vando (José Ferrer), and a chauffeur named Kristos (Gottfried John). Although Fedora is eager to star in Detweiler's film, her entourage insists she is too ill and unstable, and when Detweiler tries to help her escape the villa in Corfu, he is knocked unconscious by Kristos. A week later, he awakens from a coma to learn of Fedora's death. At the funeral, Detweiler confronts the Countess, who admits that she is actually Fedora and that her daughter Antonia had been impersonating her for years after Dr. Vando disfigured her face during an experimental treatment. The charade crumbled, she explains, when Antonia as Fedora fell in love with Michael York and threatened to tell him the truth. To protect the "legend of Fedora," Antonia is hauled off to Paris where she ultimately escapes and

On another melodramatic staircase, Kim Novak as Elsa Brinkmann embodies the late Lylah Clare.

kills herself at the train station. Despite the preposterous story, there is a stylistic assuredness about the film coupled with a respect for Fedora's grueling commitment to her image—to the illusion of movies. Detweiler's preservation of Fedora's secret (sealed as well when the "Countess" dies six weeks after the funeral) is his way of protecting and saluting the old Hollywood he was part of and where he first met Fedora, just as Wilder's melodrama celebrates the lush camera movements, lavish sets, and dense, flashback-driven narratives of classic Hollywood moviemaking.

To better understand the ideological underpinnings of the self-referential Hollywood melodrama it is helpful to look again more closely at *The Barefoot Contessa* and *Sunset Boulevard*. With a few notable exceptions, such as Aldrich's other Hollywood insider exposé *The Big Knife* (1955, United Artists), in which Jack Palance as movie star Charlie Castle harbors a scandal-making secret, gets blackmailed by a ruthless studio boss, betrays a friend, loses his wife, and quietly takes his own life, the victimized central characters in Hollywood melodramas are women exploited in various ways by scheming men. Joe Gillis works on Norma Desmond's wretched Salome comeback screenplay and serves double duty as her kept lover

Gloria Swanson on location as Norma Desmond in *Sunset Boulevard*.

for the money and the perks. At least four different men have proprietary interest in Maria Vargas. Business tycoon and would-be movie producer Kirk Edwards (Warren Stevens) wants her as leading lady and romantic possession, Edward's rival Alberto Bravano (Marius Goring) wants her as stolen trophy, Count Favrini (Rossano Brazzi) sees her as an answer to his lonely isolation, and even the sympathetic writer-director Harry Dawes (Humphrey Bogart) needs her as a way back into the movie business.

The power structure confronting each woman is overwhelmingly patriarchal. Whether Norma will make a new picture is a question to be decided by top male executives represented by producer-director Cecil B. DeMille. And although DeMille is politely solicitous, it is clear that no decision-maker at Paramount has any intention of ever putting Norma Desmond in a studio product again. Similarly, Maria Vargas's livelihood and even her personal safety are controlled by whichever alpha male rises to the top. As actresses working during the decline of Hollywood's "Golden Age," both Norma and Maria are alienated from the means of production—Norma because of her expendable age and Maria because of class and education. Silent star Norma Desmond made a lot of money for the moguls ("Without me, there wouldn't be any Paramount studio," she reminds a gate guard), but with her exchange value depleted, she is irrelevant inventory. Maria trades on her beauty but lacks the knowledge to independently manage her business affairs. The narrative thrust for both characters is the progressive loss of control. Their careers, happiness, romances, security, Norma's sanity, and Maria's life increasingly move beyond their grasp. To reinforce the inevitability of collapse, the *mise-en-scène* (as it does in all melodrama) works on an inflated thematic level. Norma's ornately claustrophobic mansion, Kirk's expensive yet arid house, and the Count's austere villa reduce options for any kind of healthy open future.

Archetypal elements begin to emerge in the films considered here so far. As in any genre, the Hollywood-based melodrama recycles a set of characters who have become easily recognizable. Foremost is the studio boss, usually played as a heavy and motivated mostly by profit margin. Rarely pictured in domestic settings, the chief seemingly lives in the studio and sees people as properties to be used, traded, and maximized. The ageing white face of post-industrial capitalism, he sells entertainment with no pretense of art or social message. Rod Steiger's Stanley Shriner Hoff in *The Big Knife*, Ernest Borgnine's Barney Sheean in *The Legend of Lylah Clare*, Michael Lerner's Jack Lipnick in *Barton Fink* (1991, Circle Films/Working Title Films, directed by Joel Coen), and Kevin Spacey's Buddy Acker-

Maria Vargas (Ava Gardner) pauses on foreboding steps belonging to the mysterious Count Favrini (Rossano Brazzi) in *The Barefoot Contessa*.

man in *Swimming with Sharks* (1994, Trimark Pictures, directed by George Huang) are prime examples. Coded as Jewish, the characters reflect biographical shards from real-life moguls Jack Warner, Louis B. Mayer, Harry Cohn, and others. Each is beyond redemption. Hoff blackmails, extorts, and plans murder. Sheean and Ackerman cruelly berate associates and employees in public. Jack Lipnick forces a misled writer to create scripts that will intentionally never be produced, telling him, "If your opinion mattered, then I guess I'd resign and let you run the studio. It doesn't and you won't, and the lunatics are not going to run this particular asylum." Created by screenwriters with real resentments over studio politics, the villainous bosses are both easily interpreted payback and also narrative counterpoint to make the hard-fought achievements of the writers and directors look just that much more significant, authentic and "artistic."

In orbit around the head of the studio are various executives, assistants, and agents. Closest to the center are producers, such as the one played by Kirk Douglas in *The Bad and the Beautiful* (1952, MGM, directed by Vincente Minnelli). Douglas's Jonathan Shields, as revealed in three extended flashbacks by the director, actress, and writer he has conned and betrayed, is a ruthless charlatan. He is also a consummate judge of talent and instinctive master of the filmmaking process. This success with his pictures and with the careers of those involved may or may not temper the bad behavior. As a human being, producer Griffin Mill (Tim Robbins) in Robert Altman's comedy melodrama *The Player* (1992, Avenue Pictures/Spelling Entertainment) is worse. He murders a writer he thinks is blackmailing him, gets away with the crime, and then marries the dead man's girlfriend. But like Jonathan Shields, Griffin Mill also has a feel for movies. By proposing a different ending, he salvages a film in production and gets named the new head of the studio.

Circling along far distant trajectories are agents and publicity people. Agents are the most venal. Money is their sole motivation. They either convince their clients to stay in lucrative yet damaging professional relationships (Everett Sloane as Nat Danziger in *The Big Knife*) or they abandon clients who no longer generate revenue for them (Lloyd Gough as Joe Gillis's agent in *Sunset Boulevard*). The agents' standard bite on those they sign for "10% of everything" has long been a punch line target for comics and writers. Other sycophants feeding off celebrity also come off badly in the melodramas. Publicity departments, such as the one managed by studio boss Raymond Swan (Christopher Plummer) and his emotionless assistant, Walter Raines (Roddy McDowall) in *Inside Daisy Clover* (1965, Warner Bros., directed by Robert Mulligan), manipulate the truth to burnish studio properties. Swan and his lackeys force their new singing star, Daisy Clover (Natalie Wood), to commit her vagrant mother to a mental institution to preserve Daisy's sunny image as America's sweetheart. Complicit in all the distortion are the lurid gossip columnists, who repeatedly show up like Harpies to inflate a story or expose a secret.

Along with fictional characterizations, such as Coral Browne's physically and morally challenged rumormonger in *The Legend of Lylah Clare*, the columnists sometimes inexplicably appear as negative versions of themselves (see Hedda Hopper's shrilly sensationalistic reporter cameo in *Sunset Boulevard*).

The principled heroes of the melodramas are the writers and directors. Joe Gillis notwithstanding, the screenwriters are motivated by literary ambitions loftier than the crass commercialism of their producers who, in Jack Warner's infamous words, disdain them as "schmucks with Underwoods." Often, the writers come to Hollywood reluctantly after success in "high culture." James Lee Bartlow (Dick Powell from *The Bad and the Beautiful*) is a pipe-smoking college English professor, who has written a bestseller that producer Jonathan Shields wants to make into a film. Persuaded against his will to write the script, Bartlow not only feels alienated from Hollywood's glamorously phony distractions but also loses his wife when Shields sends her off with a notorious playboy to keep Bartlow free from her constant interruptions. After the runaways are killed in a plane crash, Bartlow leaves Hollywood and returns to academia, where he writes a second even more highly celebrated novel. Barton Fink (John Turturro) is lured to Hollywood upon the success of his serious Broadway drama, *Bare Ruined Choirs,* and is promptly assigned by the studio to write a wrestling movie. Unable to work, Fink gets mixed up with an irritable producer, an alcoholic, Faulkner-like novelist screenwriter, and a neighbor in his decaying hotel, who turns out to be a serial killer named Madman Mundt (John Goodman). By the film's end, Fink has awakened with a dead secretary in his bed and narrowly escaped a hotel fire set by Mundt. In a final iteration of the violated writer trope, Barton is rejected by the studio chief for writing a "fruity" picture about "suffering people" and told that he will remain employed but unproduced so that everyone can see what a complete loser he is. Nicholas Ray's *In a Lonely Place* (1950, Columbia) gives us another besieged writer in Dixon Steele (Humphrey Bogart), who is violently self-destructive and proclaims, "I won't work on something I don't like." (It also gives us the speed record for Hollywood stereotypes. Within its opening minutes, we are introduced to autograph hounds, a worried agent, a smarmy maître d', a washed-up alcoholic actor, an arrogant son-in-law studio exec, a fur-clad actress on the make, a cultured director, and the fiery Dix Steel himself).

Directors also almost always come off sympathetically. *The Barefoot Contessa's* Harry Dawes (Bogart redux) is the only man who does not try to possess Maria Vargas and who actually tries to understand her. Happily married, he is driven not by ego but by the desire to do good honest work. Making what is hopefully an authentic movie similarly motivates the directors in films as disparate as *Two Weeks in Another Town* (1962, MGM, directed by Vincente Minnelli), *All About Eve* (1950, 20th Century Fox, directed by Joseph Mankiewicz) and *Contempt* (1963, Embassy Pictures, directed by Jean-Luc Godard). Although never taking an absolute position on who is the real author of a Hollywood film, the melodramas invariably showcase the director as key decision-maker on the set.

As seen repeatedly, the stars are female and are usually viewed by the men who employ them as damaged goods. They range in age from young girls like Daisy Clover fighting to build a career to ageing actresses like Margaret Elliot (Bette Davis) struggling to still find work (*The Star*, 1952, 20th Century Fox, directed by Stuart Heisler). In between, at twenty-something, there is the Marilyn Monroe-like Rita Shawn (Kim Stanley) in *The Goddess* (1958, Columbia, directed by John Cromwell). Stressed and under enormous pressure, the women suffer from a barrage of scandalous problems: bankruptcy, alcoholism, sexually ambiguous husbands, sycophantic families, dwindling offers, paranoia, and even arrest. Given all its frenzied excess, however, the melodrama is often extremely perceptive on issues of gender and class. The actresses in Hollywood-based melodramas confront a double standard. At forty plus years, Margaret Elliot is considered too old to be a leading lady and is only offered character parts, a dilemma not shared, for example, by the similarly aged male actor in *The Big Knife*. Like Norma Desmond and Fedora, she is painfully aware that her stardom has a rigidly enforced shelf life. (This emphasis on an actress's age appropriateness for starring roles reflects real Hollywood practice as well. Bette Davis, at age 54, was playing Baby Jane. Cary Grant, at age 54, was romancing Sophia Loren in *Houseboat*.) Daughters of the working class, the actresses are determined to transcend their pinched beginnings and gain admittance to a world of money and privilege. All of them—Daisy Clover, Elsa Brinkmann, Maria Vargas, Margaret Elliot, Rita Shaw—struggle to retain those riches they earn. And unlike the male executives, who exploit them and who are schooled in asset management and diversified investment, they generally fail.

Just as Italian Renaissance comedy, which influenced theatrical traditions throughout Europe, utilized many of the tropes and characters of tragedy, so, too, do comedies about Hollywood use the melodramas' stereotypes. Venal or incompetent producers and studio executives, for example, abound in *Never Give a Sucker an Even Break* (1941, Universal, directed by Edward F. Cline), *Silent Movie* (1976, 20th Century Fox, directed by Mel Brooks), *S.O.B.* (1981, Paramount, directed by Blake Edwards), *Postcards from the Edge* (1990, Columbia, directed by Mike Nichols), *Wag the Dog* (1997, New Line Cinema, directed by Barry Levinson), and *Tropic Thunder* (2008, Red Hour Films, directed by Ben Stiller). The villains interfere with the artistic visions of directors who stumble

Directors like *The Barefoot Contessa's* Harry Dawes (Humphrey Bogart) usually are portrayed positively in self-referential Hollywood films.

through various comic obstacles before finding a measure of success. Several comedies focus on the making of a specific, troubled movie. Christopher Guest has written and directed two such films. In *The Big Picture* (1989, Columbia), a recent student Academy Award winner struggles to make his first feature, a chamber drama set inside a cabin during the winter. Plagued by corporate sharks, he loses his deal but ultimately salvages his integrity and his career. In *For Your Consideration* (2006, Castle Rock Entertainment), a group of second-rate actors gets caught up in hearsay Oscar buzz during the shooting of an independent film called *Home for Purim* set in the American South during the 1940s. As expectations get stoked by fatuous entertainment reporters, the film increasingly becomes both more pretentious and more commercialized, with the Jewish holiday frame ultimately scrapped and the title changed to *Home for Thanksgiving*. When the tinsel settles, there are no awards and the actors go back to their marginal careers, including the lead actor's gig as the hot dog-costumed spokesperson for kosher frankfurters.

Get Shorty (1995, Jersey Films, directed by Barry Sonnenfeld), *Bowfinger* (1999, Imagine Entertainment, directed by Frank Oz) and *The Deal* (2008, Muse Entertainment Enterprises, directed by Steven Schachter) are satires about the comic machinations involved in financing a film. In all three movies, hapless but for once likable producers try to make budgets and players come together. Scripted from an Elmore Leonard novel, *Get Shorty* follows loan shark cum movie-producer Chili Palmer (John Travolta) as he navigates rival mobsters, temperamental actors, a debt-ridden B-movie producer, and a beautiful actress to finance and shoot a movie based on his own life. Penny Marshall, Harvey Keitel, Jane Fonda, and Sonnenfeld himself make guest appearances. In *Bowfinger*, low-rent film producer Bobby Bowfinger (Steve Martin) is promised a distribution deal for his movie *Chubby Rain* if he can get action star Kit Ramsey (Eddie Murphy) to star in it. When the pretentious and paranoid Ramsey refuses, Bowfinger shoots Ramsey's' scenes with guerrilla actors and hidden cameras. Among the satirical targets are Scientology (Ramsey belongs to a religious group called Mind Head and believes in aliens), action blockbusters, "creative financing," and Eddie Murphy's own scandalous private life. *The Deal*, based on Peter Lefcourt's comic novel, features an equally conniving yet ingratiating producer named Charlie Berns (William Macy), who transforms his nephew's Benjamin Disraeli biographical script into an action espionage film titled *Ben Disraeli: Freedom Fighter* starring an African American martial arts enthusiast recently converted to Judaism. After the star is kidnapped during filming in South Africa, Berns moves the crew to Prague and films his nephew's original script without informing the current studio heads—an under the radar project that goes on to win an Oscar for Best Picture. Quality, the film argues, is often produced accidentally.

The unstable actors of *Bowfinger* and *The Deal* are eclipsed in craziness by the badly behaved stars of several other cult comedies. In *What Just Happened* (2008, Magnolia Pictures, directed by Barry Levinson), a producer played by Robert DeNiro is plagued by one film project where his star (Sean Penn) and pet dog get murdered in a climactic barrage of bullets and another where Bruce Willis (as himself) refuses to cut his full beard for the non-hirsute featured role. In *State and Main* (2000, Fine Line Features, directed by David Mamet), a movie company has to move its film location from one small New England town to another when the star (Alec Baldwin) gets in trouble for his romantic interest in underage local girls. *Living in Oblivion* (1995, Sony Pictures Classics, directed by Tom DiCillo) concerns a similar crisis-ridden location shoot where director Nick Reve (Steve Buscemi) contends with pompous lead actor Chad Palomino (James LeGros) constantly changing his blocking and prickly dwarf actor Tito (Peter Dinklage) rejecting his lines. Tim Burton's comic biopic *Ed Wood* (1994, Touchstone Pictures) introduces us to the infamous transvestite shlockmeister as he wrangles a cast that includes a psychic, a chiropractor, an unintelligible professional wrestler, and an ageing Bela Lugosi (Martin Landau) weakened by depression and morphine addition. With their veiled as well as direct references to specific real actors, all of these films imagine a past and present Hollywood often at the mercy of childlike egos wielding way too much power.

For every subgenre of the self-referential Hollywood drama—anatomy of a specific production, star biopic, travails of location shooting, etc.—there is a corresponding comedy. Woody Allen's films about moviemaking cover similar territory. *Stardust Memories* (1980, United Artists) is his take on *8½*, a black and white reverie in which director Sandy Bates (Allen) attends a film festival honoring his work and reflects on his relationships and the demand of his fans that he continue to make comedies rather than the new "serious" pictures he has been producing. In *Hollywood Ending* (2002, Kennedy/Marshall Company), erstwhile directing prodigy Val Waxman (Allen) has lost his touch and is reduced to making tacky television commercials to support himself. Fired from a current project, he gets an offer from his ex-wife and her new studio exec boyfriend to direct a big-budget film on location in New York. Just

In *Sunset Boulevard*, Cecil B. DeMille and the business of making movies are treated with great reverence.

before production begins, Waxman is struck by a psychosomatic blindness which he and his friends try to disguise as he proceeds to shoot the film anyway. Literally and figuratively, the role of a director's "vision" in constructing a film becomes the central thematic issue.

Authorship is just one of many shared themes that the comedies and dramas pursue together. Several recurrent motifs, developed as binary oppositions, comprise the message and meaning of these films. The blurred boundary between reality and illusion is charted in *The Stunt Man* as well as in *Wag the Dog*. To be recognized for making "high" rather than "low" art motivates both Barton Fink and the director of *For Your Consideration*. When this hubris also infects the actors, the results look like the earnest thespians of *The Bad and the Beautiful* and *Two Weeks in Another Town* and the deluded prima donnas of *Bowfinger*, *Tropic Thunder*, and *The Deal*. A dividing line is drawn continually between those who want to send a message and those who want to make money.

It is in the melodramas with their stark dichotomy of rewarded talent overshadowing neglected talent and ego confounding collaboration where Hollywood pretends to be most critical of itself. These "exposés" proclaim a litany of abuses. Sparked by greed and jealousy, tyrannical studio heads crush the creativity of young idealists. Veteran talent, once it can no longer be exploited, is callously abandoned. The surest way to success is to steal credit rather than cement friendships. On closer consideration, however, the melodramas are not really so defamatory. The filmmaking process itself is never denigrated. The medium is not messaged as defective. There may be vain and unprincipled filmmakers, but a successful finished product is worth the personal challenges. Even in a melodrama as otherwise bitter as *Sunset Boulevard*, the history and craft of the movies are revered. During the scene where Norma Desmond returns to Paramount, Cecil B. DeMille passes god-like among the studio technicians and equipment. His time is precious and his work is meaningful. Cynical as he has become, Joe Gillis, under the influence of unsullied Betty Schaefer, believes that a good film, an authentic film, can still be produced. That desire to get the right vision on celluloid and to keep final cut control of a film propels the suicidal film producer of *S.O.B.* and the paranoid writer of *In a Lonely Place*.

The notion that filmmaking is a significant endeavor finds its most elegant expression in *Sullivan's Travels* (1941, Paramount, directed by Preston Sturges). Convinced that his popular but shallow comedies are a waste of his talent, director John Sullivan (Joel McCrea) goes out on the road disguised as a hobo to gather material for a truly "serious" film. Through a series of accidents and misunderstandings, he ends up arrested and confined to a labor camp. It is there, during the screening of a Walt Disney cartoon which convulses the oppressed prisoners with laughter, that he sees how movies can positively influence people's lives. The same testimonial to Hollywood's importance occurs in *Hollywood Canteen* when American soldiers fighting in the jungles of New Guinea are cheered by a Joan Leslie movie being projected during a storm with its sound on the blink. Amid flashes of lightning, the drenched faces reflect a mixture of joy and longing. For all their skewering of the negative stereotypes, the films in which Hollywood looks at Hollywood have a core belief in the artistic and social value of moviemaking itself.

This, then, is the context in which to initially understand the "star is born" films. Fashioned partly from real life biography and borrowing successively from each other, they share many of the characters and themes of the inside Hollywood narratives. There are powerful moguls, venal publicity directors, alcoholic stars, and hopeful ingénues. Realistic, behind-the-scenes footage provides insight into how studios operate and how movies are produced. Like the comedies and melodramas, the "star is born" films seem at first to be critiques of Hollywood but are actually celebrations of the creativity, chaos, and collaboration of the movie industry. To this tradition, they contribute a new formula with links to classical mythology and to popular folklore. They also offer up top directors, first-rate writers, the two most talented female pop singers of their generations and, in the case of George Cukor's restored 1954 *A Star Is Born*, a near masterpiece.

2

What Price Hollywood?
(1932)

Taking a title cue from the Laurence Stallings/Maxwell Anderson anti-war play *What Price Glory* and the 1926 Raoul Walsh film adaptation, George Cukor's *What Price Hollywood?* (1932, RKO/Pathé) strikes the same accusatory tone. With an added punctuation mark, it emphasizes the question that the film itself proceeds to answer: how great a personal sacrifice will be paid in making it big in the movies? By the time all the collateral damage has been sorted out, we see that the cost can be extreme but that the reward is probably worth it.

Reflecting solid insider knowledge of the film industry, *What Price Hollywood?* is based on an original story by Adela Rogers St. Johns. In a prime position to know exactly what she was talking and writing about, St. Johns was born in Los Angeles in 1894 and graduated from Hollywood High School in 1910. She reported for William Randolph Hearst's *San Francisco Examiner*, interviewed movie stars for *Photoplay*, contributed short stories to *Cosmopolitan* and *The Saturday Evening Post,* and wrote over a dozen screenplays, including *Old Love for New* (1918), *Inez from Hollywood* (1924), *Children of Divorce* (1927), *Scandal* (1929), *The Great Man's Lady* (1942), and *The Girl Who Had Everything* (1953). Her connections were wide and her Hollywood knowledge, shared later on TV talk shows and in documentaries, was deep. Credited with the script itself are Gene Fowler, Rowland Brown, Ben Markson, and Jane Murfin, all of whom, especially Fowler and Brown, had extensive careers in pictures. Among their other writing credits are Fowler's *Twentieth Century* (1934) and *A Message to Garcia* (1936), Brown's *Quick Millions* (1931) and *John-*

ny Apollo (1940), Markson's *Picture Snatcher* (1933), and Murfin's *Roberta* (1935), *The Women* (1939), and *Dragon Seed* (1944).

The script was especially important to producer David O. Selznick, working for RKO at the time and long interested in making a realistic film about Hollywood. It was Selznick, in fact, who had bought the original Adela Rogers St. Johns short story. As head of production at RKO, Selznick assigned his friend George Cukor (also under contract at RKO) to the picture and cast Constance Bennett in the lead. Although he was also supervising over twenty other pictures being filmed at RKO in 1932, Selznick devoted particular attention to *What Price Hollywood?* and made certain that it had the best production values the studio had to offer. Highly regarded Charles Rosher, who would shoot five films for Selznick at RKO, was brought on as director of photography. The first cinematography Oscar winner (along with Karl Struss) in 1928 for *Sunrise*, Rosher had started in silent films as a newsreel photographer and was one of the first cameramen to arrive in Hollywood from New York in 1911. He later moved over to MGM, working there from 1942 to 1954 and earning another Oscar for *The Yearling*. For the music score, Selznick selected his favorite composer, Max Steiner, who was then serving as music director at RKO. Ultimately composing over 300 film scores during his fifty-year career, Steiner was nominated for twenty-four Academy Awards and won three. Even after he left RKO for a long-term contract at Warner Bros., Steiner continued to compose for Selznick's independent productions, most notably in 1939 for *Gone with the Wind*. Cukor, Rosher, and Steiner were proof of just how seriously Selznick took this insider film about Hollywood.

What Price Hollywood? opens on an extreme long shot of Los Angeles at night, looking northward across the basin up to the Hollywood hills. The city's lights glitter and beckon, filling the entire frame in an iconic image that will be duplicated in two of the three *A Star Is Born* films. This is Hollywood as bejeweled Promised Land, drawing toward it all the dreamers who have ever imagined themselves on a movie screen. Emblazoned across the center of the dark hills is the word "Hollywood," not the famous sign, which, at the time, still advertised the real estate development known as "Hollywoodland," but large lettering on the film itself. The credits follow, mounted on billboards and accompanied by a popular song medley that climaxes with "Happy Days are Here Again." Hollywood's upbeat, Depression-era allure as transformed into consumer cachet is conveyed through post-credit shots of a woman's hands flipping through the pages of a glossy movie magazine. When she lands on an advertisement for Sheer Silk stockings endorsed by rising star Glinda Golden, a subsequent medium shot shows her putting on the very same stockings. Next, a headline challenges her to "Follow Hollywood Star Styles," and the unidentified woman (still viewed from the neck down only) wriggles into one of the body-hugging dresses displayed in the photo layout. Finally, reading that "Hollywood Stars Prefer 'Kissable Lipstick,'" she applies the recommended product while the camera slowly tracks back to reveal Constance Bennett puckering her lips and adjusting the coverage. A brief check in the mirror and she's back to the magazine where she lingers on a portrait of Garbo and Gable, folding back the page to put her own face next to Gable. In a passable imitation of Garbo, Bennett air kisses the photo, murmurs "My dahling, how I love you, I love you I do," and hurries off to work. (Given Adela Rogers St. Johns' rumored romance and child with Clark Gable, the swooning over him is especially interesting.)

Bennett, as Mary Evans, is a waitress at the Brown Derby Restaurant, the original hat-shaped one on Wilshire Boulevard. Wise-cracking and brash, she wields her server's tray like a battle shield. Before their movie careers take off, the Esther Blodgetts of the first two *A Star Is Born* films will also spend time serving food for a living. Where those Esthers are demure and tentative, however, Mary Evans is aggressive and determined.

The original Brown Derby Restaurant is one of many real Hollywood locations used by Cukor.

Batting down the advances of a slimy press agent who promises to help her "go into pictures," she ignores his threat to call the manager Nick and says, "Sure call him over and tell him about that seventeen-year-old girl you put in pictures." When an egotistical second-rate actor demands an immediate order of cold cuts, she mutters, "a lot of ham." Best known later for her comic turns as sophisticated socialites in movies like *Topper* (1937) and *Merrily We Live* (1938), Bennett plays Mary Evans like one of those streetwise, working class spitfires perfected by Glenda Farrell and Joan Blondell over at Warner Bros. Mary knows exactly who she is and where she is going. "You'll see me in pictures some day," she promises two elderly female customers who compliment her on her looks and personality. Darting from table to table, she continually overhears bits of industry gossip and even an advance notice of possible casting trends. For the benefit of a tall, dark and profile-blessed chef, she passes on the news that "Latin types are coming back again" and smiles bemusedly when he claims that he has been vindicated by American women who "want sophisticated love." What Mary wants is a break, and it seems to arrive in the form of hugely successful director Maximilian "Max" Carey (Lowell Sherman).

Mary Evans (Constance Bennett) is a working girl who knows how to take care of herself.

Drunk as usual, Carey has stopped by the Derby en route to the premiere of his most recent picture. Just outside the entrance, he politely greets an old woman selling gardenias and responds to her flattery by purchasing all the flowers and sending her home in his chauffeur-driven car. Like just about everyone else at the Derby, the flower lady is movie-crazy, and before exiting she asks Carey to keep her in mind for his next film, insisting that she could be "another Marie Dressler." Well known for his gags, Carey threads his way through the crowded restaurant, handing out gardenias to the various patrons he encounters.

With the narrative economy of classic Hollywood cinema, the film has already briskly established Carey's most significant personality traits: his talent, his lack of pretense, his humor, and his alcoholism. All four qualities will remain in play throughout the movie, with Carey's wittiness particularly emphasized here in the beginning. Careening toward a table, he bangs into a masculine-dressed woman, mumbles "pardon me old man," does a double take, and then asks "Who's your tailor?" A magnet for sycophants, Max is approached and hustled for "a full-page ad for the new picture" by the same unpleasant agent who harassed Mary. "Every hour you are out of jail," Carey tells him, "you're away from home." Undeterred, the agent sits down uninvited and keeps pitching until Carey dismisses him with a gardenia in a glass of water and the observation that "I bet they count the silver every time you eat here." It is this shared caustic humor, particularly as aimed at Hollywood phonies, that links Mary and her would-be director. Her subsequent come-on is acceptable to Max and to us because she delivers it with candor, as well as restraint. Reminding a co-worker that "I gave you Wally Beery last week," she takes over as Max's server. "I'm looking for a break," she tells the other waitress, "and I'm going to get it."

When Carey jokingly asks, "What's a pretty girl like you doing around here?" Mary immediately responds, "Waiting to meet a big director like you." She further compliments Carey by insisting "You got a lot on the ball," but it is her nonchalant acceptance of his order for six glasses of water that most impresses Max. Like Walter Brennan's Eddy in *To Have and Have Not* admiring Lauren Bacall's Slim after she plays along with his "Was you ever bit by a dead bee?" routine, Carey gives her the rummy seal of approval. Because she is such a "good sport," he asks her to accompany him to the movie premiere.

The more outrageous Carey's behavior becomes the more tightly Cukor anchors the action in real locations. To keep the story credible, he plays out events amid the Hollywood landmarks where they could conceivably have occurred. In a transition from the restaurant set to the actual Brown Derby exterior, Carey appears before the doorman and asks him to hail a cab. A better idea, an opportunity for another gag, arises when he sees an older motorist trying to hand crank his dilapidated jalopy and purchases the vehicle ("If she turns over, I'll buy it") for $50. Again, Mary is game. Not only does she walk out on her job, but she also agrees to ride along on the front seat as Carey drives off to the opening.

Cukor cuts immediately to Grauman's Chinese Theatre and lets the gag play out at Hollywood's most iconic locale. Carey and Evans lurch up to the red-carpeted entrance in a cloud of smoke and a din of grinding gears. Fans and invitees are equally amused; several rapidly edited medium close-ups show faces turning toward the commotion and bursting into laughter. Quickly intercutting the entire sequence, Cukor includes high angle overheads of cars, crowds, and lights and gives the proceedings the feel of a slightly grainy newsreel. In keeping with the media carnival atmosphere, a radio announcer describes the action and introduces us to the film's third major character—movie studio executive Julius Saxe (Gregory Ratoff).

As a stand-in for malapropism-prone moguls like Sam Goldwyn and Harry Cohn, Ratoff creates here the same dyspeptic, heavily accented Middle European (read Jewish) producer that he will revise nearly two decades later for the Max Fabian role in *All About Eve* (1950, 20th Century Fox, directed by Joseph Mankiewicz). "Say a couple words over the microscope," Saxe tells Max as he invites him to join the broadcast. After he informs the audience that he owes his success to "beef, iron, and wine," Max lets loose a Bronx cheer and then introduces Mary as the "Duchess of Derby." Matching Max's playfulness, she vamps for a while in an English accent before signing off with "Mr. Carey is waiting… there's nothing so exasperating as waiting on people." A beat and then, sans accent, she adds, "I ought to know." Julius Saxe, or Saxey as Mary will call him later, is not all that amused. Throughout the picture, Saxe's attitude toward Max will remain ambivalent; tolerant as long as he is directing successful films, he will be less than fully supportive when Max hits the skids.

Cukor exits the premiere with a fade-out and then fades in on an anonymous newspaper column titled "You Ask Me!" Used repeatedly throughout the film, this device operates on multiple levels. Most fundamentally, like spinning headlines and front-page collages, it is a narrative convention of classic Hollywood cinema used to advance the story and reveal character motivation. "Who was that devastating blonde with

Mary impersonates the "Duchess of Derby" with Max Carey (Lowell Sherman) at her side and Julius Saxe (Gregory Ratoff) on the far right.

Max Carey," it asks in this initial instance, "who knocked 'em cold over the radio at the Chinese opening?" As a projection forward, the column cues us to the probability that Mary soon will have the same major impact on moviegoing audiences. Investigative in tone, it further promises to "uncover" real facts and information concerning Hollywood. Its "voice" fits with the question mark of the opening credit and the fact that the film's alternate title was *The Truth about Hollywood*. Like Mary's perusal of the fan magazine, the column emphasizes again the public fascination with all things Hollywood, an interest that, as suggested by the surging premiere crowd contained behind the ropes, may be potentially unstable and even dangerous. Finally, the column is a humorous critique of the hyperbolic style of writing about movies that then predominated and with which a veteran newspaperwoman like Adela Rogers St. Johns would have been very familiar. (Coincidentally, in 1987, satirical author Paul Rudnick, using the pseudonym Libby Gelman-Waxner, began writing a series of hilarious movie reviews and columns titled "If You Ask Me.")

Seemingly prompted by the column's inquiry, the newsprint dissolves to a high-angle, extreme long shot of a Hollywood mansion nestled in verdantly landscaped hills. The camera tracks forward and then dissolves to a continuing tracking shot as it pushes ahead into a dark heavily curtained bedroom. This penetration of unknown space, this forward track to unravel a mystery or accumulate information, becomes in the 1930s and 1940s an expressive stylistic tool mastered in various ways by Welles, Ophuls, Hitchcock, and Renoir. Cukor uses it in *What Price Hollywood?* to visually parallel the investigative thrust of the newspaper excerpts and the narrative itself. As the camera ends on a medium shot of a ringing telephone (another intrusive communication device), Max reaches out of bed and tosses the receiver off its hook. He is in bad shape. Still clothed in his formal shirt, shorts, and one sock, he stumbles into the bathroom, where he opens the medicine chest to retrieve a bottle, looks twice in the mirror, and drops the bottle onto the tiled floor. Written across the front of his starched shirt is a note from Mary summarizing her casting details. Unable to focus, Carey asks his black servant James to check his feet for broken glass and to read what he calls the "fan letter." "Mary Evans. 5 feet

Max discusses the note on his shirt front with his servant James (Eddie Anderson).

4 inches. 102 pounds. Complexion blonde," recites James before including the phone number and the postscript: "sings and swims, rides horseback." The writer herself, James adds, is asleep downstairs. While he mulls the information, Carey pours a drink from the bottle James has brought on a tray and then, flashing an exaggerated frown, marks the bottle with James's pencil to show how much liquor is left. The scene ends comically when Carey leaves to put on a dressing gown and James returns the bottle to an upholstered portable bar after first taking a long swig himself, erasing the level mark, and penciling in a new line. Like the Brown Derby and Grauman's Chinese episodes, the drinking here is still treated as humorous physical shtick, opportunities for Sherman to roll his eyes, grimace, overly enunciate words, and determinedly hold himself erect. The tone will begin to darken later.

Once again, Cukor uses an inquisitive moving camera as he tracks forward on Mary, who is wrapped in a fur blanket and asleep on a downstairs couch. There is, it appears, more to uncover about the previous night. "What's new?" asks Carey by way of gently waking her. After telling Carey that she's "been out on your veranda," she further decides, "Gee, its swell up here on the mountain. So, so fresh," an appraisal that lends her an air of innocence to balance her caginess and hold out hope for Max's own rejuvenation.

A summary of the pair's previous hours together follows in stages. First, Mary informs Carey that he "just passed out in the middle of the picture that's all." Unsure how they connected, Carey asks, "Just where and how did I meet you?" Reviewing their Brown Derby encounter, she somewhat cryptically adds, "I gave up my job for you, palsy walsy." Her hard edge suggests that streetwise Mary may be planning to extort the director.

Next, she explains how she and a cab driver carried Max up the mountain and that "all you did was yodel." When Max marvels that she couldn't leave him, she very directly replies, "I'm looking for a break in pictures. I thought you might give me a chance." Again there is the hint that Mary intends to leverage Max's foggily remembered behavior into a major career demand, a threat re-enforced when she repeats, "all's I need is a break." But she honestly reveals that Max never attempted to force himself on her and that she hopes only that he might "write a letter" for her. If Cukor's tale of Hollywood privilege is to sustain audience sympathy, we need to identify with the often abrasive Mary, and so her fair play comes as a relief to Max and to us here. "I'll do better than that. You're a great kid," he says, the term of approbation signaling that she has won Max's trust and his fatherly rather than romantic interest in her. The budding loyalty between the two is also indicated by Mary's attempt to get Carey to slow down on his early morning drinking. "What and be bored all the time?" he responds in a partial clue as to what underlies the alcoholism.

As he sends her home, Max instructs Mary "to come around the studio tomorrow and come on my set." Thrilled, she gives Max an affectionately appropriate kiss on the cheek and, alone in the frame, he attempts to answer her off screen yodel with one of his own. In a kind of scenic coda that we will come to expect, the gossip column reappears and announces, "Max Carey stole the Derby's prettiest waitress. What for? Oh, same old story. Going to put her in pictures." Even though the columnist implies a typical Hollywood sexual liaison, we have seen the true motivation; the "realities" of the running commentary and of the actual narrative will continue to advance in different directions.

Slowly and somewhat shakily, as if mounted on a truck, the camera dollies in toward a studio soundstage. Four successive dissolves foreshorten both the distance and time to the stage's entrance while the camera continues to track forward. The effect is of barriers peeling away as we breach private territory. It is an impressive, almost flashy, shot for the normally unobtrusive and seamless Cukor. The building is Soundstage 10, and a cut takes us inside, where the camera continues to track behind Mary, our representative now in this chaotic wonderland, as she makes her way toward Carey's set. Sober and businesslike, he is directing a sound check and at first does not recognize her. After she re-introduces herself, he sends her off to make-up and wardrobe to prepare for a scene that will be shot later that evening. Her role: to float down a staircase, flirtatiously quip "Hello, Buzzy, you haven't proposed to me yet tonight," and then freeze at the sight of an off-screen corpse. Full of her usual confidence, she tells an assistant who has praised her appearance, "What'd I tell you. I'm good."

Dissolve to a tight medium long shot of the set, camera on left side of the frame, staircase in middle, lighting equipment on the right. Carey provides Mary some last minute instructions and the scene begins. She is terrible. Her walk is awkward, her speech mechanical, and her expressions exaggerated. Taken aback by her disastrous debut, Carey focuses his full attention on her, giving her perceptive and detailed direction. "Come down easily… don't put your hand on the rail… not on your heels… don't

What Price Hollywood? (1932) • 49

Max gives Mary direction in her first bit part.

clinch your hands," he tells her. There is a highly believable, almost documentary-like feel to the scene, as if we are watching a real director give advice, an authenticity stemming partly from the fact that Lowell Sherman, like Welles, Huston, and von Stroheim, both acted in and directed Hollywood films. Among Sherman's directing credits were *She Done Him Wrong* (1933, Paramount) with Mae West, *Morning Glory* (1933, RKO) with Katharine Hepburn, and *Broadway Through a Keyhole* (1933, 20th Century Fox).

Despite Max's best efforts, the performance continues to be unacceptable, and he tells a crew member that he's going to need another actress. "I wasn't very good, was I?" Mary agrees. The final scene has Mary clocking out and exiting the studio turnstile—an emblematic revolving door image that evokes the cyclical disposal of would-be talent and the recurrent collapse of many Hollywood dreams.

Back at her boarding house by way of a dissolve, Mary feigns success for the landlady, who advises her not to sign a studio contract because she "might do better freelancing." Climbing the steps, she stops to consider the advice Max gave her about the bungled scene, which she now practices over and over again. By coupling her repetition of the Buzzy line and of Carey's advice with repeated close-ups of her feet running up and down the steps, Cukor deftly elides time and brings us to a final triumphant shot of Bennett gracefully descending the stairs, tossing off the dialogue, and aiming a glaringly intense stare toward the unseen body. A multilayered scene, where a good actress portrays a bad actress transformed into a good actress, it is the kind of bravura performance that "woman's director" Cukor was famous for eliciting from his female stars.

In less screen time than it took for Mary to finesse a studio audition, her break is now realized. With James the servant acting on the phone as intermediary, Mary informs Max that she has mastered the part and asks for a second chance. He communicates his agreement with an off-screen yodel.

A close-up call sheet insert (another print artifact of real Hollywood) indicates that Mary has been added to the cast. Wandering around the studio after she has filmed her scene, she stumbles into a screening room, where Julius Saxe, Max Carey, and various department reps are watching dailies. She causes such a disruption that Saxe, unaware who she is, has her ejected from the theater (Janet Gaynor and Judy Garland also will clumsily interrupt studio dailies in their *A Star Is Born* roles). When Mary's scene appears on the reel, Saxe is smitten with her performance and immediately decides to give her the full studio treatment. Seven-year contract. Publicity campaign as "America's pal." Starring roles. Full attention from the department technicians. "I'm in pictures," Mary marvels as it all begins to register. "Well don't blame me," cynically responds Max, who through all the uproar has been slouched down in his seat, smoking calmly and reminding Saxe that it was the director and not the producer who "discovered" this new talent. For Saxe, this is an opportunity to tell Max that he used to be years ahead of other directors but that he is losing his edge. The constant retakes and schedule delays are all because of whiskey. What pictures need then, responds Max, are "light wine and beer."

In reality, there is nothing all that striking about Mary's performance. It is not like the scene in Cukor's *A Star Is Born* where James Mason watches Judy Garland sing in an after-hours nightclub and we can share his excitement over her amazing talent. Mary's "discovery" is more about chance and about the studio system's ability to take a pleasant-looking cipher and build a product around it. As David Thomson observes in *Showman: The Life of David O. Selznick*, "Bennett is an empty beauty; she is skin and cosmetics turned into glossy armour" (pages 135-136).

What Price Hollywood? (1932) • 51

Mary interrupts Saxe's screening of dailies.

Mary's subsequent rise to stardom is revealed in the first of several montages that Slavko Vorkapich specially designed for the film. A Serbian-born painter and filmmaker, Vorkapich co-directed the short experimental films *The Life and Death of 9413: A Hollywood Extra* (1928) with Robert Florey and *Forest Murmurs* (1947) with John Hoffman. He also created the special effects montage sequences for films, such as *Viva Villa* (1934, MGM, directed by Jack Conway), *San Francisco* (1936, MGM, directed by W.S. Van Dyke), *Three Comrades* (1938, MGM, directed by Frank Borzage), and *Meet John Doe* (1941, Capra Productions, directed by Frank Capra). In this sequence, a close-up of Mary's face is superimposed with stars and fireworks. A tiny background figure of Mary slowly widens to fill the foreground and disappear off frame. Behind her a large star burns in increasing brightness. Over all of this are theater marquees advertising her pictures—*Love's Holiday*, *Revenge is Sweet*, *Playing Around*. Finally, a last superimposition brings multiple split images of clapping hands and more fireworks. A slow fade-out concludes her transition to fame. The star is born.

The Brown Derby scene was structured to suggest Max and Mary as intended love interests, but the real meet-cute romance begins at the

Santa Barbara Polo Field. It always comes as a jolt in Hollywood films of the 1930s and 1940s to suddenly shift the action outside for a scene shot in daylight at a real location. Gone are the atmospheric shadows and deep tonal contrasts of the studio, and in their place a flat, almost glaring brightness. A different reality, an x-ray-like sensitivity, seems to intrude, exposing the characters to harsher examination as they interact with more mundane challenges and personalities. Such is the case here. On location for a film and now an established star, Mary seems rather peevish and spoiled. She reacts angrily upon hearing that one of the wealthy society polo players she is watching has announced that he is "fed up with Hollywood blondes." When he accidentally strikes her with a polo ball (a variation on a favorite introductory device of classic Hollywood cinema: the accidental meeting of hostile romantic opposites), she strides across the field to publicly berate him. The player introduces himself as Lonnie Borden (Neil Hamilton), urges her to hit him back, which upon a dare she does, and then invites her to dinner. Like a child recovering from a tantrum, she continues to add expensive demands and conditions concerning menu, location, and entertainment to the dinner invitation. Borden agrees to each of them. "By midnight you'll have forgiven me," he predicts. "By midnight I'll have forgotten you," she counters.

During her tirade, Mary shouts directions at her black maid. "Bonita, bring me a cigarette," she commands with the same regal haughtiness that Mae West invokes with her famous "Beulah, peel me a grape" line from *I'm No Angel* (1933, Paramount, directed by Wesley Ruggles). There is an uncomfortable, not so subtle, racism in *What Price Hollywood?*, as revealed in the treatment of Carey's servant and Mary's maid. James (Eddie Anderson) speaks with an exaggerated dialect and filches Max's liquor. Bonita (Louise Beavers) is easily excitable and in need of constant supervision. On one level, the treatment is simply representative of the pervasive racist stereotyping in most Hollywood films of the era, and on another level, the characterizations further manifest attitudes in this particular director and actress—Max's casual cynicism and Mary's controlling egoism.

Mary's less than likable side continues for a while longer. As the food grows cold and the orchestra members grow restless, Lonnie Borden waits futilely for her to arrive at the lavish private dinner he has arranged at her hotel. Finally she sends a note: "You know what you can do with your dinner—eat it." The message is signed "Just another Hollywood blonde." Enraged by such bad manners, Borden breaks into her hotel room and carries her kicking, screaming, and dressed in bed clothes to the dinner, where he force feeds her caviar and directs the orchestra to play the funeral march she has sarcastically requested.

As expected, by the end of the evening they have fallen for each other, with Mary declaring she has "never had such a divine dinner." Because the film is more about Hollywood than romance, their courtship moves rapidly. Fade-out on the couple dancing in the hotel dining room, and then fade-in on her showing her engagement ring to Julius, who immediately sees publicity potential in a society wedding to a handsome millionaire.

Neil Hamilton is a curious choice for the love interest. Beginning his career as a shirt model for magazine ads, he brought a similarly well-groomed yet somewhat stiff look to his film roles. He appeared in the original silent *Beau Geste* (1926, Paramount, directed by Herbert Brenon) and the original *Dawn Patrol* (1930, First National, directed by Howard Hawks). Often playing prissy socialites, such as Harry Holt in the 1932 and 1934 Tarzan movies, he worked mostly in low-budget productions during the 1940s and 1950s before a late-career resurgence as Police Commissioner Gordon in the ABC television series *Batman* (1966-1968). For *Since You Went Away* (1944, Selznick International Pictures, directed by John Cromwell) he is seen in a picture frame as Claudette Colbert's absent

Neil Hamilton as Mary's wealthy socialite husband Lonnie Borden. Max and Saxe look on as surrogate fathers of the bride.

wartime husband, a disembodied image of domestic bliss. Lonnie Borden represents a similar kind of stability for Mary, a refined and sophisticated patrician among the parvenu glitterati of Hollywood.

Max is much less thrilled than Saxe about the impending marriage. "It'll never last," he announces. "What won't last?" asks Lonnie. "A movie star's marriage and my liver," replies Carey. The reason behind Max's opposition is not readily apparent. So strong is his contempt for Hollywood that he could not possibly be worried that Mary's marriage might negatively affect box office. Neither does he like Borden enough to be concerned that it is the husband who might get hurt by this union. What is much more likely is that Max has his own suppressed love for Mary, a romantic possibility that the film seemed at first to suggest and that would make the eventual decline that she witnesses even more painful for Max to bear. The von Sternberg/Dietrich-like symbiosis between Max and Mary keeps him motivated, and Lonnie is clearly a threat.

The wedding is a staged event resembling the Grauman's Chinese premiere. "Produced" by Saxe, it is held at the First Methodist Church of Beverly Hills (another of the film's authentic locations) and covered extensively by the press. As Cukor's camera tilts down off the church's exterior facade, the wedding party, in which both Saxe and Carey seem to act like fathers of the bride, starts to descend the steps. A large newsreel camera dominates the right side of the frame, and a crowd of onlookers surges behind the security ropes. When Mary follows Saxe's instruction to "throw the flowers to your fans," the mob goes wild. Cukor cuts rapidly between multiple shots of grasping hands and shouting faces. People rush forward directly into the camera. The compositions are tight medium shots and close-ups that fill the frame and convey constricted space. Mary is assaulted, her veil ripped from her face, and she must be escorted back inside the church. For Saxe, however, the melee is a wonderful sign of her popularity. "We broke all the house records for this church," he exclaims as if reviewing a sellout theater performance. But the role of the crowd is darker than the punch line indicates. As it will in *A Star Is Born*, the crowd represents the hysteria underlying Hollywood's energy and the unpredictability of media-controlled public opinion. The intrusions into Mary's personal life will start to become more virulent, foreshadowed here by the newspaper photographer, who pushes open the church window and snaps a photo of Borden embracing her.

The strain that the marriage will endure is also telegraphed when Saxe tells the couple that they will need to postpone their honeymoon for retakes on Mary's latest picture. "Dahling," he tells her, "release dates are not waiting on honeymoons." In a clear sign that their lives have become fodder for public titillation, a newspaper headline proclaims, "Mary, Lonnie Lose Honeymoon." Then, as the narrative again speculates on Max's true feelings, the "You Ask Me!" insert asks, "Was Max Carey burned up over the marriage of his favorite star to an eastern millionaire?"

Mary's return to the studio allows Cukor (who will sign the first of several long-term MGM contracts the following year) to show what the world of moviemaking means to her and to him. Like MGM house colleagues Vincente Minnelli, Clarence Brown, and Mervyn LeRoy, Cukor concentrated on *mise-en-scène* to fashion a personal style. In contrast to the spacious uncluttered sets of Max's and Mary's homes, Cukor fills the studio shots with objects, equipment, and movement. Show business is a whirl of activity with visual details that occupy every inch of Cukor's frame. As the filming of Mary's cabaret scene opens, crew members pass across the foreground, middle ground, and background of the image. She, in chanteuse costume, is mid-center, attended to by Bonita and technicians. A piano cuts into the left side of the frame and a large light stand lines the right side. Nightclub tables ringed with guests in evening clothes spread out in front of the stage on which she stands. Cukor cuts to a light operator and then to a sound machine. Layered off-screen voices rise au-

Mary's wedding, shot on location, is marred by intrusive reporters and hysterical fans.

Cukor again foregrounds the filmmaking process as Max directs Mary's performance as a French entertainer.

dibly on the soundtrack. Finally, an assistant director calls out the familiar "Quiet everybody, this is a take," and Bennett (in surprisingly good French) begins to sing "Je Vous Aime."

We experience the scene as it is being shot. Only Bennett's back is visible as Max and his camera dolly forward toward her and toward us. In a cut to a side angle, Max's camera is on the right and Mary continues to perform in an angled long shot. While she finishes the song, Cukor intercuts medium close-ups of her playing to the crowd and shots of the microphone boom, the microphone itself, the sound booth operator adjusting controls, and technicians observing from the scaffolding overhead. Also intercut are reaction shots of Lonnie waiting on the set and watching his wife perform. Upon the conclusion of her song, Max claims it would have been better if she'd "forget about [her] husband" for a while. By way of demonstration, he acts out the performance he wants, but she ignores him to chat with Borden, insubordination that angers Max and leads to an argument between all three and to her abrupt exit from the set. Exceptionally well-directed, the sequence captures the studio's creative chaos and anticipates the even more striking visual distinction between on-stage and off-stage behavior that Cukor will draw in his 1954 version of *A Star Is Born*.

The "You Ask Me!" column that follows the studio incident has upped its level of vitriol. "What director who discovered a famous blonde star," it asks, "had a little argument with her brand new husband when he visited the set? And why?" The source seems to be a jealous insider actively trying to sow discord and to damage relationships, an example of the ruthlessness that the film catalogues as part of its alleged critique of Hollywood. Tensions continue when the action shifts to a story conference at Mary's house. Present are Mary, Lonnie, Bonita, Julius, Max, and a team of writers.

In a long shot, Saxe strolls around the edge of an on-location swimming pool, where the group has gathered to discuss ideas. A cut on movement takes him to a badly matched studio set. "If you cannot tell it in fifty words, it's not a good story," Saxe declares in rejecting alternatives to the film he is pitching. Neither Mary nor Max wants to make that film. "I don't think I should have a baby in every picture," she protests. In a witty pre-Production Code retort, Saxe answers, "Well, Mary, this baby is different. You are getting married first." Similarly unimpressed with the sto-

Max, Mary, Saxe, and Lonnie participate in a contentious story meeting around the swimming pool of what is only too obviously a studio set.

ry, Max tells Saxe that if he makes "one more mythical kingdom" movie, he is going to become "a mythical producer." Each time that Lonnie offers an opinion, he is quickly dismissed by either Saxe or Carey. "What does he know about pictures?" Saxe says when Lonnie agrees with his wife's critique. Even a simple suggestion that she sit in the sun is ridiculed by Max, who claims knowingly that "her skin can't take the sun." Nothing is resolved and the conversation ends comically as Bonita "auditions" for Max by singing "All of Me" and he pulls her into the pool.

Interior spaces (Max's living room, Mary's hotel room) are reserved for personal intimacy, and that's where she retreats to study her Emily Post manual so that she can better fit into Lonnie's world. Class differences between them, emphasized by contrasting accents, vocabulary, clothing, and gesture, will continue to generate problems. After Mary agrees that her house is a bit too ostentatious, he tells her it doesn't really matter because only studio people ever see it. In defense, she argues that her friends are "kind and human" and "not so doggone superior" as his society acquaintances. Moving even deeper into the protected interior (like the wedding day escape into the church's private chambers), she runs to their bedroom, where Lonnie eventually apologizes and she promises, "You won't be ashamed of me."

Just as the wedding was tarnished by the cancelled honeymoon, this reconciliation is immediately disrupted by the arrival of a gossip columnist, whose interview request Mary feels obliged to fulfill. Instead of "playing tennis with the Reinharts," Lonnie is dragged to the interview, where the prying female writer asks a series of increasingly tawdry questions, such as whether they share a "blind, passionate, oomph kind of love" and whether they have "separate bedrooms." When the columnist asks for a photo of his "magnificent physique," Lonnie stalks off, telling her instead to take a picture of his "appendix in a bottle."

The narrative seems to be making a case for Lonnie to abandon the marriage. He has been stripped of his privacy, referred to as Mr. Evans, denied his personal interests, insulted by Mary's friends, and cut off from his usual social contacts. However, having seen Mary's hard work, humor, and sense of fairness, the viewer continues to identify with her in light of Borden's snobbishness. Besides, Cukor's exuberant, deep focus compositions have made her studio world appear much more interesting and exciting than social engagements with the Reinharts.

While the film grows darker with turmoil between Mary and Lonnie, so too does the attitude toward Max's drinking turn more serious. Up to now, Carey has been portrayed as a mostly comic figure, a hard-drinking but competent professional who, like Nick Charles in *The Thin Man* series, navigates his privileged life with a constant buzz and a rapier wit. Julius Saxe is one among several, however, growing tired of Max's antics. In response to Max's latest weeklong bender and absence from his picture, Saxe has decided to fire the director. "It will break his heart if you do," argues Mary, "and if I don't" answers Saxe, "it'll break my heart. And my pocketbook." Despite Saxe's opposition, she is determined to search through Hollywood's seedier locales until she finds her friend and mentor.

The collapse of Mary's marriage and the collapse of Max's career, documented in detail by the gossip column, proceed swiftly now along the same narrative arc. "Hollywood is laying bets on where a certain blonde star will find her errant director," reads the "You Ask Me!" copy. "The young lady has spent the past two days unsuccessfully combing the speakeasies and dives of Los Angeles." Lonnie reads the column while lying in bed and angrily tosses it onto the floor. "You might think of me and appearances," he admonishes her. Although she tries to placate him, she insists on supporting Max and vows, "I'm not going to let him down." As if on cue, Carey stumbles into their backyard and calls out the yodel which has served as in-joke and bond between them.

Squeezing some last laughs out of Max's drunkenness, Cukor works out a physical gag involving lighted matches. In close-up, Max lights a cigarette, glances to his right, and does his standard double-take, while the camera tracks out to reveal him in direct eye-line proximity to the naked buttock of a garden statue. When Lonnie and Mary refuse to let him in, he sets fire to the newspaper (perhaps containing the "You Ask Me!" column) in his coat pocket and threatens to burn the house down. Admitted inside and put to bed momentarily by Bonita, Max awakens and intrudes on the intimate space of the bedroom to try to give some inebriated "advice" to both Mary and Lonnie. The column, the intrusion, the intoxication are all too much for Lonnie, who storms into the bathroom and dresses to leave. "I'm going as far away from Hollywood and all its inmates as I can get," he announces. In one of the Hollywood critiques the film simultaneously delivers and undermines (since it comes from someone even Mary has dismissed as a "stuffed shirt"), Lonnie angrily tells his wife, "You live in a world where people are cheap and vulgar without even knowing it." Misfit Max and loyal Mary are left to each other, yet there is no screwball comedy triumph to it. "What out of work director," taunts the Greek chorus columnist, "is still hanging around the set of the star whose separation he is said to have caused?"

An intoxicated Max invades Lonnie and Mary's bedroom.

In keeping with the downbeat tonal shift the film has taken, the subsequent studio scene that Mary is seen filming is a somber one. She walks down an empty city street at night. Rain machines generate a storm. She stops before an iron fence and slumps forlornly to the pavement. The replacement director calls, "cut." As the news column reported, an unemployed, not so perfectly dressed, Max waits off-set to hand her a cup of hot coffee. Adding to the gloom is Saxe's continuing refusal to reinstate Max and a telegram from Lonnie indicating that his divorce from Mary has been finalized. "I am no longer Mr. Mary Evans," he adds pointedly. When Saxe tries to comfort her, she reveals that she is pregnant and due to have her child in just a few months. Slow fade-out.

A close-up magazine insert signals that a year has passed and that the press is upset with Mary for not letting her young son be photographed. "Is America's pal becoming 'high hat'?" the headline asks. Assisted by Bonita, a butler, and a nanny for her cherubic blond son, Jackie, she lives now in a large airy mansion—the kind of ornate *mise-en-scène* that Cukor is so good at. There is a grand piano, mirrors, large vases of flowers, and lots of space between the furnishings. It's Easter and, with Max absent for over three months, there is a possibility of rebirth and renewal. Mary and her son are gathering Easter eggs while Saxey looks on as a surrogate grandfather. Even Lonnie hints at reconciliation by sending a pleasant note and a pet rabbit for Jackie. But the tranquility is short-lived; an attorney calls to say that Max is in jail and, despite Saxe's warning that the public will mistake loyal friendship for sordid romance, Mary leaves to bail him out. In striking contrast to the brightness and openness of her home, Cukor uses the jail's shadows and confinement to foretell Max's final downfall.

The cell is dark and crowded. With rumpled clothing and several days' worth of beard, Max looks heavy and dirty next to Mary in her tight white evening gown and fur wrap. He averts his eyes as they stand close together in the jail's tight waiting area.

Back home, Mary puts Max to bed in a dimly lit guest bedroom. She is gentle and solicitous with him. "Now how do you feel, darling?" she asks after she and the butler have eased him under the covers. "You mustn't be unhappy over a man who doesn't exist anymore," he advises her. He is straightforward and honest about his demise. "I'm burned out... and dead inside," he continues. Neither blaming nor disparaging the studios, he admits that he alone has chosen to drink and is solely re-

The ever-loyal Mary bails Max out of the drunk tank.

sponsible for his alcoholism. He alone has depleted his talent; Hollywood has not siphoned it from him. "I'm washed up in pictures… it's all gone in here," he concludes, pointing to his heart.

As Mary turns to leave the room, Max briefly calls her back. "I just wanted to hear you speak again that's all," he says. It's a classic line, a variation of which will appear in every one of the *A Star Is Born* films. Laced with longing and regret, it carries an overtone of doom in its measured assessment of a future that does not exist.

After she departs, Max gets out of bed and pours himself a drink in an adjoining sitting room. The interior is webbed with shadows that have lingered since the jail scene. Picking up a cigarette, he looks in a desk drawer for matches but finds a gun instead. Still in search of a match, he pauses at a mirror and looks closely at the wrinkled and puffy face staring back at him from the darkness. Below the mirror is a framed photo of Max, handsome and debonair at the height of his success. The contrast too much to bear, he turns the frame over, returns to the desk and retrieves the gun from the drawer.

Max's suicide is occasion for another memorable Vorkapich montage. A close-up of Max's haggard face is superimposed with the undulating concentric waves of a pinwheel and shots of him sipping champagne in a tuxedo. Slant angled images of the jail cell bars are layered in, and a buzzing noise, which Cukor biographer Emanuel Levy describes as "achieved by attaching a string inside a cigar box and spinning it around" (page 61), rises steadily in volume. Max's eyes shift to screen right, followed by a close-up of his feet in slippers that are also moving to the right of the frame. In close-up, his hand reaches into the desk drawer, pulls out the gun, and presses it to his chest. The whirring noise, like an angry fly trapped in a bottle, reaches a crescendo until broken by the sound of a fired bullet. A low angle full frame image of his body falls forward in slow motion; several shots of his past life are rapidly superimposed up until the moment he crashes to the floor.

In an adjoining room, Mary hears the gunshot and bursts inside—actress discovering corpse in the exact frozen moment of shock that Max had rehearsed so carefully for her very first scene in a movie. The irony is quintessential Cukor, real life and stage life overlapping in a shared performance. The print world goes crazy with the subsequent scandal, reminiscent of the sensational coverage of the shooting death of director William Desmond Taylor in 1922. The first headline is shown to us as it is inked and printed: "Director Max Carey Dies of Wounds in Star's Home." The fact that only one shot was fired suggests more distortions and hysteria to come.

In an ironic reference to her first film role, Mary discovers Max's lifeless body.

The next Vorkapich montage shows Mary's fall from public grace and reverses the structural elements used earlier to chart the birth of her stardom. Four separate images are superimposed. In close-up, her head bows downward. A full-figure shot of her in an evening gown recedes from the foreground to the background. Above her "shrinking" head, a multi-pointed star similarly decreases in size. Newspaper pages flutter like dead leaves over the full frame. Additional headlines appear and follow each other in quick succession: "Police Quiz Mary Evans in Death of Max Carey"; "Mary Evans Collapses on Stand at Inquest"; "Film Star Faints at Grave of Former Director-Friend." A final newspaper insert announcing that various women's clubs have banned Mary's pictures is splattered with mud that is thrown from an off-screen source meant to represent the smear campaign in general.

A throng of reporters is gathered outside Mary's mansion. "How long do you think this story is gonna hug the front page?" asks one of them. "Long enough to wash her up in pictures," answers a colleague. Two aggressive newspapermen climb through a balcony, disappear inside, and then rush off to file some hot "tip" they have received (maybe from the same unknown inside source feeding information to the "You Ask Me!" writer). A skeletal nasty-looking female columnist taunts Mary by shouting "Hey you, waitress, when did you become so high hat?" and then adding "She's afraid to talk to a decent woman."

Inside the house, Mary hears everything and is unaffected by Saxe's attempts at consolation. She strides angrily to the window, and the tracking camera rushes behind her. Explaining that the public can't understand a relationship like the one between Max and Mary, Saxe also admits, "You belong to the public—they make you and they break you." Once again the film has saved its strongest concern for the volatility of fans, for their tendency to be manipulated by opinion makers. Mary feels it, too. When Max tells her that Mary Evans may be forgiven in a few months, she responds, "In a few months Mary Evans will be forgotten."

The moment Saxe succeeds in convincing Mary to call the reporters together and tell them her side of the story, the butler appears with a message from outside that asks, "Is it true Lonnie Borden is on his way here to get possession of his son?" She panics and decides she must take Jackie to Europe; her fear pushes the narrative into an abrupt resolution.

A newspaper story titled "Mary Evans Living Quietly in France" fades in to a scene of Mary puttering in the garden of her chateau. Some re-emergent comic relief has Bonita ("This new French language sho´ is gettin´ me down") mistake the cook's intentions and Bennett once again display her skill in speaking French. A hysterical report by a nun that Jackie has been kidnapped is immediately defused when Lonnie strolls into the garden carrying his son. Then, in about two minutes of screen time, several story lines quickly are concluded. First, Lonnie delivers a note from Saxe that reads, "Dear Mary—just bought a new story. It will make a great comeback for you." Next, he explains that he was never coming to Los Angeles to claim Jackie but just to offer his help to her. Finally, he confesses that he has never stopped loving her and asks her to marry him again. Like Max repeating the yodel motif, he says, "Let's have dinner" and promises a 30-piece orchestra and orchids. "Suppose I said no?" she teases. "Well, you know what happened the last time," he responds. Final fade-out as the two of them embrace.

So what exactly was the price of Mary's Hollywood success? Apparently not all that much. Tragic and untimely as it was, Max's death was his own doing. He hated its phoniness but never blamed Hollywood for his alcoholism or his eroded talent. While the ride lasted, Hollywood provided him with a very comfortable life. Mary endures bad publicity and tarnished popularity

Mary and son are reunited with Lonnie in the final scene.

but in the end regains both her work and her millionaire husband. The brief sojourn in France probably strengthens her future foreign box office potential, as well. The career she struggled so hard to obtain never disappoints in its artistic and material rewards. Moviemaking is seen continuously as a creative endeavor inspiring lively camaraderie among its talented, specialized practitioners. It is not the studio but rather the gossip industry that is targeted for criticism. Saxe is motivated by profit, but he is not ruthless. The film takes a brief early swipe at Hollywood for its undue influence on public taste and consumerism but never develops the point much further. If there is any message here, it is that unprincipled reporters and overheated fans should back off and treat movie people as professionals.

Public reaction to *What Price Hollywood?* was positive. "Given a lavish publicity campaign," writes Emanuel Levy, "the film opened in New York at the Mayfair Theater and soon became one of the year's top-grossing films" (page 62). In his book-length conversation with Gavin Lambert titled *On Cukor*, the director himself remembers the film as "a big success at the time" (page 37). There was much speculation about whether it was a film 'a clef and, if so, who the characters' real-life counterparts might possibly be. Max was generally assumed to represent Marshall Neilan, an actor-writer-producer-director, whose major success in silent and early sound films was later eclipsed by his alcoholism. The executive at one time of his own production company, Neilan directed *The Lotus Eater* (1921), *Minnie* (1923), *Dorothy Vernon of Haddon Hall* (1924), *The Vagabond Lover* (1929), *This is the Life* (1935), and over twenty other pictures. His last directing assignment was in 1937.

"Max Carey," writes David Thomson, "is based on Marshall Neilan, a director ruined by drink. Yet he cannot be separated from the dark presence of the actor Lowell Sherman, himself a director and a drunk and a man who died in 1934 at the age of forty-nine… Carey is also a version of John Barrymore or Myron Selznick—men too intelligent and unyielding to ignore the insanity of Hollywood" (page 136). As mentioned earlier, Saxe is Samuel Goldwyn by way of Harry Cohn.

For producer David Selznick, *What Price Hollywood?* provided an opportunity to explore his fascination with everything related to making movies. "Like the audience at that time," recalls Cukor, "Selznick had a very romantic view of Hollywood, a real love of it" (Lambert, page 32). The bustling sets, the lively story conferences, the glamorous premieres—these are all the kinds of details Selznick treasured. The scorn for invasive reporters and gossip columnists is also part of Selznick's view of the place. He understood both the splendor and the sleaze. Cukor explains that "Largely through David's influence, we didn't kid about the basic idea of Hollywood. Most of the other Hollywood pictures make it a kind of crazy, kooky place, but to David it was absolutely real, he believed in it. I think that's why *What Price Hollywood?* was one of the few successful pictures about the place, in the face of a tradition that they never succeed" (page 32).

What Price Hollywood? is also memorable for its expression of themes and ideas that George Cukor elaborated throughout his career. The interest in performance and the tension between real life and acting is central to *What Price Hollywood?* It is there, as well, in Cukor's *The Royal Family of Broadway* (1930), *Sylvia Scarlett* (1935), *A Double Life* (1948), *The Actress* (1953), *A Star Is Born* (1954), *Les Girls* (1957), *Heller in Pink Tights* (1960), and *Let's Make Love* (1960). Of special significance to Cukor was how an actor or more often an actress crafts a performance, how experience and inspiration coincide to yield a hyper-reality. Andrew Sarris notes in his *The American Cinema* that "the director's theme is imagination, with the focus on the imaginer rather than on the thing imagined" (page 89). Questions of spectatorship, perception, illusion, mirrored observation, and duplication that surface in Mary Evan's work before the cameras will be developed even more completely in *A Star Is Born* (1954).

Cukor's deep personal interest in acting (as compared, for example, with Hitchcock's casual disregard for it) partially explains his ability to draw such remarkable performances from his casts. Bennett is a case in point. "Selznick originally envisioned Clara Bow as the female lead—the story needed an exciting actress to lift up its melodramatic aspects—but Bow's career was fading, and Selznick could not dissuade her from retiring," reports Levy. "Instead Constance Bennett was offered the role, and the script was rewritten to fit her particular talents: sophistication, glamour, and wit" (page 60).

Going on to direct her in two other films (*Rockabye* and *Our Betters*) within the next year, Cukor worked hard to balance Bennett's tendency toward stridency with her quieter, more relaxed naturalism. Bennett found Cukor's direction especially generous and helpful. "He is a rare thing, an unselfish director. He doesn't make a show of what he's giving the actor," Bennett has stated. "He doesn't specialize in so called, 'directorial touches' to emphasize his own activity. He keeps himself in the background... Naturally you'll work like a slave, because you realize you are safer in his hands than in your own" (page 62). The collaboration worked and as Patrick McGilligan writes in *George Cukor: A Double Life*, "Bennett was never as natural and compelling as she was under Cukor's direction here" (page 81).

The problem with *What Price Hollywood?* is not the performances—Lowell Sherman and Gregory Ratoff are equally believable and compelling. The problem is in the story and the uninspired love affair between Mary and Lonnie. When the film focuses on the studio, it soars; when it details the courtship and marriage, it falters. The truly interesting romance is the one between Max and Mary that neither ever acknowledges. "The narrative is incoherent," Levy correctly observes, "shifting to a silly romance between Bennett and her polo-playing husband that ultimately weakens the film. Cukor fought to keep the story focused on the relationship between the star and the director, but Selznick overruled him" (page 61). The distracting love affair is a weakness that will be remedied in *A Star Is Born* by blending the alcoholic mentor and the romantic lead into the same tragic character.

3

A Star Is Born
(1937)

The most direct line of connection between *What Price Hollywood?* and *A Star Is Born* runs through David O. Selznick. Despite the success of *What Price Hollywood?*, Selznick felt there was still more to say about Hollywood. He also knew that Cukor had been right about the Lonnie Borden character. The new story idea was for an older alcoholic actor to "discover" and fall in love with a rising young actress. In a letter quoted in *Memo from David O. Selznick*, editor Rudy Behlmer's collection of the producer's famously detailed correspondence, Selznick writes, "*A Star Is Born* was really a concept of my own... I believed that the whole world was interested in Hollywood and that the trouble with most films about Hollywood was that they gave a false picture, that they burlesqued it, or they over sentimentalized it, but that they were not true reflections of what happened in Hollywood. And my notion was to tell this in terms of a rising star in order to have the Cinderella element, with her path crossing that of a falling star, to get the tragedy of the ex-star, and we created this more or less as we went along" (page 98).

Notice the "concept of my own" and the "my notion." Selznick always claimed that the original story idea, based roughly on real life personalities and enriched with insights into Hollywood society, was mostly his. Irene Mayer Selznick, Louis B. Mayer's daughter and David Selznick's first wife, remembers it the same way. In her autobiography, she writes that Selznick "...had a pound of ideas he had dreamt up... I was sick of the phony films about Hollywood and longed to see one with some reality. He tried with *What Price Hollywood?* and promised me someday he'd make a proper one. It turned out to be *A Star Is Born*" (page 171). The film's director, William

Wellman, always maintained, however, that he and writer Robert Carson came up with the original idea. In fact, Wellman and Carson submitted a story outline to Selznick (who had departed RKO and was now making his own independent pictures) that was titled *It Happened in Hollywood* and that included most of the Esther Blodgett/Norman Maine narrative elements that would constitute *A Star Is Born*. It is not clear whether they were writing under Selznick's supervision and whether he had given them the basic formula. As Wellman continued to push for story credit and a bonus, Selznick continued to resist. In a memo to Daniel O'Shea, Selznick's assistant and Secretary of Selznick International Corporation, the producer instructed, "I wish you would give immediate study to whether or not Wellman is entitled to a bonus on the story of *A Star Is Born*... *Star is Born* is much more my story than Wellman's or Carson's. I refused to take credit on it simply as a matter of policy... Wellman contributed a great deal, but then any director does that on any story. The actual original idea, the story line, and the vast majority of the story ideas of the scenes themselves are my own... If, however, I am wrong in my recollection of our contract, and it states that Wellman is entitled to a bonus on *Star is Born*, as it is his story, I would not for a moment quibble on whose story it is, and we should by all means pay him" (Behlmer, pages 108-09).

Ultimately Wellman got the bonus and the story credit along with Carson. Short story writer Dorothy Parker and her husband, Alan Campbell, were hired at $1,750 a week to also work on the script, creating dialogue, and revising scenes. Although uncredited, Budd Schulberg and Ring Lardner, Jr. contributed story ideas, as well. Selznick solicited all of his friends for insider details and claimed that "... ninety-five percent of the dialogue in that picture was actually straight out of life and was straight 'reportage,' so to speak" (Behlmer, page 98).

The issue of the writing credit surfaced again when, on March 10, 1938, at the Biltmore Hotel, Wellman and Carson received the Academy Award for Writing (Original Story). David Thomson suggests that Wellman actually may have acknowledged Selznick's true authorship with his acceptance comments. "This remains a mystery," says Thomson, "for when Wellman and Carson received the Oscar... Wellman made a public statement that the Oscar really belonged to David—to this day, the Selznick family possesses the statuette" (page 217).

For all his attention-getting, Wellman had not been Selznick's first choice as director. Having already made six pictures with George Cukor, Selznick wanted him also to direct *A Star Is Born*, especially since he was so familiar with the subject matter and could effectively coach the female lead in her big dramatic moments. Besides, Selznick and Cukor were also friends who even resembled each other physically. According to Thomson, "Not only was Cukor David's favorite director and his best. George was also a chum in high spirits, teasing, the bantering exchange of memos, and a shared attitude as to the desirability of grace and talent rising above the squalor of the picture business" (page 134). But Cukor decided to pass, making *Holiday* for Columbia and concentrating on preproduction for *Gone with the Wind* (another film Selznick had offered him and which he actually began shooting before being replaced by Victor Fleming). As his biographer Patrick McGilligan put it, "Cukor fought against assignment to the first production of *A Star Is Born*, saying he didn't want to do another Hollywood picture so soon after and so similar to *What Price Hollywood?*" (page 139).

William A. Wellman seems a curious choice to substitute for Cukor on a tragic romance set in Hollywood. Best known up to that point for *Wings* (1927), *The Public Enemy* (1931), and *Wild Boys of the Road* (1933), he would go on to direct *Beau Geste* (1939), *Ox-Bow Incident* (1943), *Story of G.I. Joe* (1945), and *Across the Wide Missouri* (1950). His strength, such

William Wellman (standing) directs Fredric March (far left) and Janet Gaynor in a scene from *A Star is Born*.

as it was, lay in Westerns, adventures, and war films. Irene Selznick was not a big fan: "We had nothing in common: he was a terror, a shoot-up-the-town fellow, trying to be a great big masculine I-don't-know-what. David had a real weakness for him. I didn't share it. I never had an interesting conversation with him" (Thomson, page 217). Despite any obvious affinity for the subject matter, Wellman went on to do a competent job and received a Best Director Oscar nomination.

For the part of fading alcoholic screen star Norman Maine, Selznick wanted to cast John Barrymore, whose own heavy drinking was well-known throughout Hollywood. By 1937, most of Barrymore's great screen successes—*Beau Brummel* (1924), *Don Juan* (1926), *Grand Hotel* (1932), *A Bill of Divorcement* (1932), *Dinner at Eight* (1933), *Twentieth Century* (1934), and *Romeo and Juliet* (1936)—were behind him. His real-life similarity to Norman Maine would have made for freighted viewing, but at this point in his career Barrymore (who was Lowell Sherman's brother-in-law) balked at memorizing dialogue. McGilligan asserts that "... partly on Cukor's advice, Selznick would cast Barrymore—and fire him—as the lead in the William Wellman version of *A Star Is Born*. By then, Barrymore's lifestyle had taken its toll, and at times the fading star was reduced to reading his dialogue from cue cards" (page 107). In Barrymore's place, Selznick cast his talent agent brother Myron's client Fredric March, who had won an Academy Award for Best Actor in 1931 for *Dr. Jekyll and Mr. Hyde* and had also scored big with *Design for Living* (1933), *The Barretts of Wimpole Street* (1934), *Anna Karenina* (1935), *and Anthony Adverse* (1936).

For the Esther Blodgett role, Selznick selected Irene's best friend and bridesmaid Janet Gaynor. Beginning her career in silent film, Gaynor was the first person to win the Academy Award for Best Actress. Under Academy rules that took multiple roles into consideration, she was honored for *Seventh Heaven* (1927), *Sunrise* (1927), and *Street Angel* (1928). During the next decade, she transitioned successfully to sound and starred in *Adorable* (1933), *State Fair* (1933), and *The Farmer Takes a Wife* (1935), among others. Selznick's leading man and lady, then, were highly regarded stars, and his second film about Hollywood promised to be a quality production. Max Steiner was also along again for the score; even though he had taken up residence at Warner Bros., his contract there specifically allowed him to continue working for Selznick as well.

The Selznick name is splashed all over *A Star Is Born*. Before anything else, the first image we see is a title reading "Selznick International Pictures Incorporated" followed by the camera tilting down on the studio's columned, Colonial style front office building. Max Steiner's score quotes "California Here I Come." Next comes an extreme long shot of the Hollywood basin and hills at night, the same inviting calling card that opens *What Price Hollywood?* Scrolling up onto this image is "Selznick International Presents" along with the credits for Gaynor, March, supporting players, and crew. The final acknowledgment is not for the director but for "Produced by David O. Selznick." Wellman may have gotten his story bonus but Selznick literally got the last word.

In a touch of Brechtian distancing that reminds us we are viewing artifice not reality, the title page of the script itself is pictured on screen. It reads "Screen Play 'A Star Is Born'" and a hand reaches in to stamp "FINAL SHOOTING SCRIPT" across it. In exact industry format and further foregrounding of moviemaking conventions, the first page of text appears:

> *A Star Is Born*
> Scene 1
> Fade In:
> MOONLIGHT. LONG SHOT EXPANSE OF SNOW.
>
> In the foreground a wolf silhouetted in the moonlight.
> In the background the isolated farmhouse of the Blodgetts.
> As we hear the melancholy howling of the wolf, we
>
> DISSOLVE TO:

A transition from exactly that establishing shot takes us inside the farmhouse. Esther and her little brother are arriving home from the movies. Unlike *What Price Hollywood?* and the other two *A Star Is Born* films, the action here does not begin in Hollywood. Esther is as obsessed with show business as her counterparts, but she dreams in isolation, in a rural setting that many moviegoers could identify with. It will become especially important for the film's theme that we see Esther's origins and her journey westward.

Waiting in the living room are Esther's father (J.C. Nugent) and her Aunt Mattie. Dad is looking at slides on an old-fashioned stereoscope, his own way of dreaming and traveling elsewhere. With her steel-gray hair tied in a bun and her high-collared dress wrapped in a shawl, Mattie scuttles around like Auntie Em's demonic double (actress Clara Blandick, in fact, does play Aunt to both Dorothy and Esther). "Well, home from the movies at last," scowls Mattie as her niece and nephew enter. Mattie is almost hysterically negative about Esther's love of movies and her desire to be an actress. "I caught her talking to a horse with a Swedish accent," she reveals and later warns Esther, "You better be getting yourself a good husband and stop mooning about Hollywood."

Esther even has to take teasing from her much younger brother, who mocks her admiration for actor Norman Maine (whose movie they have just seen) by claiming that he "never does anything except kiss a lot of girls." Sure of her tastes and her judgment, Esther responds, "Norman Maine's one of the best actors in pictures." Having characters talk about Maine before we see him builds interest the way Shakespeare does with his tragic heroes and makes the eventual Esther/Norman encounter seem more fated.

Esther's father is of little support to her in the face of Mattie's negativity. He lamely remarks, "Now, sis, we're only young once," but never defends his daughter's interests. Her real ally is her feisty grandmother (May Robson) who strides in from the kitchen and tells Mattie (presumably her daughter) that no one has asked for her opinions.

Aunt Mattie (Clara Blandick) lectures Esther (Janet Gaynor) as Esther's father (J.C. Nugent) and grandmother (May Robson) look on.

This is a ragged family unit, one that has been touched by loss. Esther's mother apparently has died, her grandfather is gone, and her aunt is unmarried. The women have all been hard hit, a family history which darkens her own prospects for finding marital happiness.

Grandma, however, remains upbeat and defiant. Seventy-nine years old in 1937, May Robson specialized in strong matriarchal parts. She was the Lane sisters' Aunt Etta in *Four Daughters* (1938), Ana Neagle's Granny O'Dare in *Irene* (1940), Jean Harlow's grandmother in *Reckless* (1935), and, perhaps most memorably, Katharine Hepburn's irascible Aunt Elizabeth in *Bringing Up Baby* (1938). Here she plays Grandmother Lettie as an indomitable frontier woman who passes on her sense of adventure to Esther.

When Aunt Mattie betrays Esther by announcing, "You know what she wants to do? She wants to go to Hollywood," Grandma looks stricken at first but then proudly well-satisfied. After Esther angrily asks her aunt, "What's wrong with wanting to get out and make something of myself? What do you do that's so much better?" and runs to her room, Lettie follows behind to console and advise. "There's a difference," she tells her, "between dreaming and doing." As a young pioneer, Lettie came west with her husband "to make a new country" and she encourages Esther to summon the same determination. "When I wanted something better I came across those plains in a prairie schooner with your grandfather," she declares. Esther sees the similarity in her own quest and finally accepts her grandmother's offer to finance the trip with money that had been saved for a funeral but won't be needed now since Lettie feels she isn't "ever going to die." The connection between building a career in the movies and building a homestead is made explicit when Grandmother Lettie says, "You know, Esther, there'll always be a wilderness to conquer. Maybe Hollywood's your wilderness now."

Describing southern California in her essay, "Some Dreamers of the Golden Dream," Joan Didion writes, "The future always looks good in the golden land because no one remembers the past. Here is where the hot wind blows and the old ways do not seem relevant. Here is the last stop for all those who come from somewhere else, for all those who drifted away from the cold and the past and the old ways. Here is where they are trying to find a new life style, trying to find it in the only places they know to look: the movies and the newspapers" (page 4).

Lettie herself has pursued that new territory, the last stop, the edge of the continent. "Here's your prairie schooner," she says as she watches the train that will take Esther westward to her own golden dream. The

Lettie facilitates Esther's transformative journey westward.

pioneer references elevate Esther's Hollywood job search to a manifestation of American individualism and a test of character. Earlier, back at the farmhouse, Lettie recounted how her husband was shot and killed and how she "buried him out there on those plains and went right on" to her destination. "For every dream of yours that may come true," she told Esther, "you'll pay the price in heartbreak." The ominous notion that Esther, so much like her grandmother, also may find a dream and lose a love rides along with her on the train to California.

Lettie waves good-bye and retreats into the dark, cold night. Esther arrives in the bright, warm sunshine of Hollywood. A long shot of what looks like Cahuenga Boulevard cutting through to the San Fernando Valley slowly pans to the right across landscaped green hills. Laid over the image is a title, "Hollywood!... the Beckoning El Dorado... Metropolis of Make Believe in the California Hills." A legendary lost city of gold, "El Dorado" extends the frontier metaphor and equates movie success with material gain.

To anchor us even more firmly in the "beckoning" ambiance of Hollywood, a medium long shot pans to the left along the edge of a swimming pool where a film crew has assembled for an outdoor location. Esther is just one of many hopefuls influenced to make a pilgrimage to the promised land, a demographic fact rendered apparent by three quick shots of a bus, train, and plane rushing forward from the background to fill the frame like an Eisenstein battleship. Instead of a Russian chorus, we again hear "California Here I Come."

The camera then tilts down off the side of Grauman's Chinese Theatre to reveal Esther exploring the courtyard just as Kim Novak will do in *The Legend of Lylah Clare*. Stopping at the cement hand and foot prints of Jean Harlow, Harold Lloyd, Joe E. Brown, Shirley Temple, and Eddie Cantor, she ultimately finds Norman Maine's spot. Certain that no one is looking, she steps over the ropes and slides into his prints to link herself with him for the second time since the film began.

Norman's signature and inscribed "Good Luck" message slowly dissolve into a somewhat more prosaic piece of text—an advertisement for cheap housing. "$6 weekly," the ad promises. "Large rooms, running water. No Cowboys. Convenient to all studios. Oleander Arms, 1312 Marion St. nr. Hollywood Blvd." Another dissolve as Esther enters the Oleander Arms to meet its manager, Pop Randall (Edgar Kennedy).

There's always a Pop, Mom, Birdie, or a Gramps running a boardinghouse for actors, whether it is in Hollywood or New York (cf. *Stage Door*, also 1937). Pop definitely has been to the rodeo, and at first sees Esther as

Looking east down Hollywood Boulevard as Esther arrives in the bustling Promised Land.

just another of the hopeful hundreds who have passed through the Oleander Arms. When she asks if the studios are really close by, he says all "…except British Gaumont," and when she checks for phone messages a few weeks after moving in, he replies, "Jesse Lasky and Samuel Goldwyn must be writing letters."

Along with the cynicism and caustic wit, Pop also has the not unexpected heart of gold. He may ask Esther for her $6 in advance, but after she has fallen a month behind in rent he simply tears up the bill and goes back to marking his horse racing bets. Taking over the older, wiser protector role from Grandmother Lettie, Pop introduces Esther to Danny McGuire, a fellow tenant and assistant director, who will become her closest Hollywood friend.

It is in the boarding house, with the conversations between Esther and Danny, where we realize that the Technicolor, which seemed muted and muddy back at the Blodgett farm, has not gotten any better. It will remain unsatisfactory for the entire film. Limited in range, the palette is lifelessly dull, like the colors on picture postcards of the 1920s and 1930s. Strangely enough, that correlation between the film's images and the postcard images re-enforces our collectively erroneous "memory" of the period, that is, our false assumption of what reality looked like then. Still in its infancy, three-strip Technicolor had only been used for the first time in a feature film in 1935's *Becky Sharp* (RKO/Pioneer, directed by Rouben Mamoulian) and not for another two years would there be a Technicolor film to blaze with bright incandescent colors (*The Wizard of Oz*, 1939, MGM, directed by Victor Fleming and several other uncredited directors including George Cukor). An additional side effect of this early use of Technicolor was that it required large heavy camera equipment—thus, the static feel to many of the set-ups, especially those in the boardinghouse involving Esther, Pop, and Danny. Wellman's camera was never that fluid to begin with and here it is constrained even further. Master shot logic predominates; camera placement is straight-on, level, and often perpendicular to the action.

For her first trip beyond Oleander Arms, Esther pays a visit to Central Casting Corporation. Informed in a brief Paramount form letter that Central handles all the studio's extra work, she reconciles herself to starting small and building experience. But even her reduced expectations are shattered when the female office manager tells her, "We haven't put anyone on our books for over two years." Taking her into a massive room filled with switchboard operators, the manager explains that each of the

At the Oleander Arms, Esther is befriended by Danny McGuire (Andy Devine) and the seated manager Pop Randall (Edgar Kennedy).

blinking lights represents an applicant who won't be accepted. The visual metaphor is powerful—thousands of faint blips that will never ignite into stars. "You know what your chances are," asks the manager, "one in 100,000." Shaken but not defeated, Esther replies, "But maybe I'm that one." And it's the randomness of fame, really, that is an essential part of the film's message because, as we will see, Gaynor's Esther Blodgett is not any more innately talented than is Bennett's Mary Evans.

Esther again leaves the boardinghouse to have a drink with Danny after they get off to a bad start, and he apologizes by taking her to a nearby bar. Danny is played by Andy Devine in one of his non-cowboy roles but with the same grumpy and "gargly" teddy bear affability that defines his Western sidekicks like Cookie (to Roy Rogers) and Jingles (to Wild Bill Hickok). Danny's decency will counterbalance the callousness that Esther encounters later with studio insider Matt Libby. The bar scene also introduces the heavy drinking motif but tempered here to match her innocence; both she and Danny are drinking glasses of milk mixed with rum. As Esther gets tipsy, she slaps him on the back and almost gets knocked off her stool when he does the same. Promising him that he is going to direct all her pictures, she announces that if the studio balks at her request, she just won't sign her contract. If they have a couple more rum milkshakes, he answers, they can open their own studio. As in the early scenes of *What Price Hollywood?*, getting buzzed is played for physical comedy.

The next time Esther and Danny come together outside the Oleander Arms it is to celebrate his new job as assistant director on a war picture. She is uncharacteristically depressed over her own lack of success but rallies for his benefit. They are attending a concert of Beethoven and Chopin at the Hollywood Bowl. Just before the music begins, Norman (in the film's third reference to him) stumbles into the box seating with glamorous Anita Regis (Elizabeth Jenns). He is introduced to us for the first time just as Max Carey is in *What Price Hollywood?*—publicly drunk in a famous Hollywood setting. Hearing the audience applaud, Norman rises to acknowledge the recognition but is pulled back by his date. "Sit down, you dope," whispers Regis, "that's for the orchestra leader." He crashes into his seat and then gets into a fight with photographers pestering him for a picture. "I'll shove that Brownie Number Two of yours down your throat," he shouts as he smashes one of the cameras.

Fascinated and attracted despite the spectacle, Esther asks Danny if Norman is always like this while the now restrained actor, who has fallen off his folding chair for a second time, turns around and pretends to seriously shush her. Although fleeting and barely discernible, there is a spark in the exchanged glances that advances the connection slowly and, so far, unilaterally developing between the two but that stops short of a fully completed meet-cute. It is a unique variation on a classic convention and still a promise, certainly, of more to come.

Our deferred narrative gratification is realized finally at a fancy Hollywood party. Danny has gotten Esther a job serving food at director Casey Burke's house. Reluctant initially to work as a waitress, she reconsiders when Danny reminds her that there will be plenty of Hollywood big shots in attendance to impress. On the night of the party, she stalks the living room in a black and white maid's uniform that Danny borrowed from the wardrobe department. Like Mary Evans, she has a hokey Garbo imitation and she uses it to demonstrate her acting talent. "Vould you like a leetle hors d'oeuvres?" she asks two guests who have been disparaging Norman's latest picture. "Zey are verry niice." When she elicits only shocked stares, she moves on to other guests and to Katherine Hepburn ("Lovely hors d'oeuvres, rally they are") and Mae West ("Pardon me big boy, would you like a little hors d'oeuvres, they say they're the best in town"). One of the partygoers recognizes the Mae West impersonation but still doesn't offer her a contract on the spot.

Ironically, after all the build-up, the face to face introduction between Norman and Esther comes quietly. Subdued and in her own voice, she offers him some caviar and he is struck immediately with her simple charm. Pretending to need help selecting the right appetizer, he chats her up until the haughty and jealous Anita Regis drags him back to the party. Later, as Esther is putting dishes away in the kitchen, Norman reappears and offers to help. "Won't they miss you?" she asks. "No, they'll just look under the table," he answers, "and when they see I'm not there, they'll just forget the whole matter." Immediately at ease and comfortable with one another, they speak intimately, now and then tentatively gazing in each other's eyes.

When Esther reveals that she saw Norman at the Hollywood Bowl, he asks if she was disappointed. She says yes and he drops a plate, embarrassed at how he must have appeared to her. The comic payoff to their meeting occurs here in the kitchen. Once again, Anita Regis angrily interrupts the conversation, this time smashing a platter over Norman's head before exiting. With his amazing recuperative powers, he shakes away the blow and asks Esther to help him off the floor. Telling her the "wolves" will be after them, he asks her to escape with him. "I can't, the dishes aren't

Esther finally meets Norman Maine (Fredric March) at a private Hollywood party where she is working as a server.

finished," she protests. "Oh, yes, they are," he says, shoving a whole pile onto the floor. He grabs her hand and they flee through the back door.

Two other plot objectives, in addition to the coming together of Esther and Norman, are accomplished during the party sequence. First, additional characters are introduced. One of Casey Burke's most important guests is his boss, studio chief Oliver Niles (Adolphe Menjou). All things considered, Oliver is a mostly positive executive, more Carl Laemmle than Harry Cohn. Confident and only occasionally choleric, he is a benevolent despot. As in most of his roles, Menjou is well-dressed, charming and debonair.

Working in films from 1916 to 1960, Menjou was well-known for his sophistication and his wardrobe (when asked in *Sunset Boulevard*, if he borrowed his vicuña overcoat from Menjou, Joe Gillis replies, "Close, but no cigar.") A conservative pro-McCarthy Republican in real-life, Menjou was especially convincing with authority figures, playing Major General Broulard in *Paths of Glory* (1957) and producers in both of Katharine Hepburn's pictures about young Broadway actresses, *Morning Glory* (1933) and *Stage Door*. His Oliver Niles believes that he can assert control over events, even over Norman's heavy drinking, which director Burke tells him has spoiled their latest film together. "His work is beginning to interfere with his drinking," Burke sarcastically reports.

Just as Oliver claims that he will be able to control Norman like he can all actors, he gets a phone call from Matt Libby, head of the studio's publicity department. The last major character to be presented, Libby (Lionel Stander) will be dramatic foil to Oliver and to Norman, making both men look noble by contrast. Libby, who dislikes Norman intensely, reveals that the actor was apprehended driving an ambulance down Wilshire Boulevard. "He explained he was a tree surgeon on a maternity case," says Libby. Oliver is worried about the bad publicity, but Libby assures him he was able to keep the story out of the papers. "Prince Charming," Libby calls Norman, seething with a resentment that he is carefully waiting to unleash.

With his gravelly voice and blunt features, Lionel Stander specialized in tough guy roles like Cornelius Cobb in *Mr. Deeds Goes to Town* (1936), Curly in *The Last Gangster* (1937), and Sergeant Butch in *Guadalcanal Diary* (1943). As far to the left politically as Menjou was to the right, Stander gave defiant, "uncooperative" testimony before the House Un-American Activities Committee (HUAC) that resulted in an industry blacklisting not finally lifted until the mid-1960s. Stander then went on to achieve

Adolphe Menjou plays studio boss Oliver Niles (left), and Lionel Stander (far right) is his publicity chief Matt Libby.

public recognition and popularity in his seventies playing Max, the butler and loyal assistant to amateur sleuths Robert Wagner and Stefanie Powers, in the ABC television series *Hart to Hart* (1979-1984).

The other narrative goal of the party scenes is to elaborate on Norman's alcoholism. In addition to the warnings from Burke and Libby, Oliver witnesses plenty of evidence himself. Just after Libby guarantees that Norman has been restrained for the evening, Oliver turns to his side and sees Norman, famous for his marathon drinking stamina, come bounding down the stairs in immaculate evening clothes. Oliver watches disapprovingly as Norman has the bartender pour him a full tumbler of scotch. "The word is pronounced 'when,'" advises Oliver. "Bad dialogue, Oliver," answers Norman. Friends and colleagues for many years, the two men speak affectionately yet frankly. Oliver tells Norman that his performances are suffering, that he is not remembering his lines. Cameramen, he warns, are "struggling to hide your hangovers." Listening intently, Norman promises to do better, but nothing is resolved. During the conversation, Norman has been playing a game on Casey Burke's pinball machine. Taking one of the coin slugs used to operate the machine, he shows it to Oliver and says "here's my epitaph." The coin reads "good for amusement only."

After they make their broken dishware escape from the party, Norman drives Esther back to the Oleander Arms. The camera tracks in for a medium close two-shot as they sit in the front seat. He invites her back to his place to discuss her interest in making movies, but she politely declines. "Has anyone ever told you that you're lovely?" he asks. As if in response, the camera holds for about thirty seconds on an over the shoulder close-up of her face, softly lit and slightly veiled by a shadow that drops across her right cheek. The length of the take seems to be making the case for her career—she deserves to become a star because she is photogenic. As she departs, he quickly calls after her. "Hey, you mind if I take just one more look?" he asks in a variation of the signature line from *What Price Hollywood?* that will later take on the same poignant overtone of vanishing happiness for Norman that it held for Max Carey.

At home in bed, Norman orchestrates Esther's entry into pictures. He phones Oliver and asks him to arrange a screen test for her. It is apparently a call that Oliver has received before. Still half asleep, Oliver wants to know what is so special this time, and the best Norman can offer is that Esther has "sincerity and honesty." He says it twice, in fact, unintentional evidence of both his clouded preoccupation and her limited dramatic range. Once Oliver agrees to the test, Norman jumps out of bed still fully dressed in his tuxedo and clutching a bottle of champagne to search for Esther's number in an out-of focus, upside-down phone book. Everything—Oliver's drowsy responses, Norman's intoxicated muttering and bumbling, Esther's surprise at receiving a 3 a.m. phone call—is imagined as comedy. The telephone conversation is shot from Esther's point of view only. We see her incredulity, confusion, and exhilaration but nothing of him. It is an unfortunate decision. On the one hand, we avoid hearing unnecessary details of where the test will occur and what it will involve, but on the other we miss seeing more of Norman's nurturing, unselfish side, revelations that could have given greater dimension to his character.

Esther's screen test is introduced with detailed realism. An Oliver Niles Productions call sheet dated Tuesday, February 4, announces that test number 12,432 will be shot on Stage 14 by director Casey Burke. Principals Norman Maine and Esther Blodgett will be wanted on the exterior garden set at 9 a.m. with Esther reporting to make-up at 7 a.m. and Norman at 8 a.m. Wardrobe will be a boulevard coat and silk hat for Norman and a "dress as fitted" for Esther.

The camera irises in and cuts to a clapboard repeating the test number, director, and actress names, and the designation of "Haley" as cameraman. Esther stands on a set swarming with technicians. Lights and filters are adjusted; "Pull down on that 150," calls an unseen voice. A wardrobe assistant adjusts Esther's floor-length gown and a make-up man scrutinizes her face. The set is sprayed with an atomizer, the camera length measured, the microphone swung in to position. "All ready, Mr. Burke" echoes throughout the stage. Summoned from his off-set trailer, Norman gives the frightened Esther a pep talk. "They all had to go through this," he tells her, "Harlow, Lombard, Myrna Loy." She is ready. The clapboard signals action. And then—nothing. No close-up, no dialogue, no screen test. An anticlimactic dissolve reveals Esther Victoria Blodgett signing an Oliver Niles contract. We never see her performing or the director providing feedback. Most disappointingly, we miss the opportunity to see Esther and Norman on camera together, responding to each other's vocal inflections, gestures, and expressions.

The decision to exclude the screen test is one of the film's major failings. Without it, there is no real demonstration of Esther's unborn "star" power. For a country girl with no training, no local theater experience, and no recognized talent other than the ability to do mannered imitations of movie stars, her ascent is hard to understand. There was a similar problem in *What Price Hollywood?*, but at least there we had Mary Evans practicing her scene, responding to Max's advice, and ultimately delivering a polished performance. Here we have nothing other than Oliver telling her during the contract signing that he has a hunch the public will like her. As David Thomson argues, "We do not believe she has extraordinary screen presence or that her stardom is earned" (page 236). Consequently, the film is more about the randomness of fame and about Norman's faith in her ability to surmount that randomness. Our interest resides primarily in Norman.

In case we missed the foreshadowing provided by Grandma Lettie, Oliver also tells Esther that success entails a cost. "Nothing you really want is ever given away free," he says, invoking the commercial imagery of the *What Price Hollywood?* title. "You have to pay for it and usually with your heart." She seems to see her future shaped by that counsel and states that she has heard it once already. Before he passes her along to "our demon press agent Libby" with his "heart of gold, only harder," Oliver also gives her a piece of acting advice: "Learn to close your mouth and keep it closed—even in your love scenes."

Esther's session with Libby is one of the critical swipes the film takes at Hollywood, not at the movies themselves but at the hype used to sell them. For a business that deals in illusion, truth is a slippery concept and is often manufactured to facilitate profit. After the sliding doors to Libby's adjoining office (the geographic proximity to Oliver indicating his importance) close, a matching wipe opens on Libby seated at his typewriter and interviewing Esther for her studio biography. Disappointed that she is not Russian, he asks her where she was born. "Fillmore, North Dakota," she replies. "Ah no," says Libby and instead types, "A trapper's hut high up in the Rockies," a slight difference of just a few hundred miles. "What did your father do?" he continues. She indicates that "he's a farmer" but Libby is still not satisfied. "Nah, social registrarite father, fed up with the 400, sought wilderness for consolation" is how Libby transcribes it. Libby's greatest unhappiness, however, is reserved for Esther's real name. He chokes out "Blodgett" like it is some repulsive taste stuck in his mouth.

Oliver, when Libby rushes back into his office with the bad news, agrees that Esther's name must be changed immediately. From "Victoria" Olivier comes up with "Vicki" and after rhyme riffing on "Sester, Bester, Fester" he gets around finally to "Lester" as a plausible sounding last name. "Vicki Lester—say, I like it," encourages Oliver's secretary and, thus, a new screen personality is christened.

The sycophantic cottage industry of Hollywood "reporters" is quick to come on board. A gushy radio announcer played by Franklin Pangborn at his flamboyant best swoons over "a Cinderella of the West—her name is Vicki Lester." She is "divoon," he reports, "her voice is a symphony" and "her very walk is enough to drive men wild."

Cut to the newly minted, less than divine, Vicki Lester practicing how to walk properly on screen. "Get the lead out of your feet," snarls her coach as she traipses over stage steps with a book balanced on her head. "Lift them up." The exaggerated premise immediately undercut by the dull reality works like a piece of visual comedy and is in keeping with the silent film-like gags used elsewhere in the film, for example the broken dishes or the low hanging boardinghouse hallway light which everyone ducks to avoid and which veteran comic Edgar Kennedy, reacting with his patented slow burn, finally smashes into during Norman's late night phone call.

Several more "gags" continue to erode Esther's alleged perfection. Instead of the "symphonic" voice, we see and hear Esther reciting the "quality of mercy is not strained" speech from Act Four of *The Merchant of Venice* to the obvious displeasure of her voice teacher. "Through the mouth, my child, through the mouth," he instructs her. Disturbed by the nasal quality of her speech, he advises, "The nose is for smelling roses." A point which

Studio make-up artists go to work in an attempt to "transform" Esther.

leads to a close-up of Esther's face as she sits before a mirror. Two make-up artists are scrutinizing her. "Does she have to look surprised all the time?" asks one. "Pretty small mouth, isn't it?" frets the other. They go to work first on her eyes, repositioning and arching the brows. Trying for the "Crawford smear," they apply a heavy coat of red lipstick to widen the mouth. Next they sculpt the contours of the cheeks to make her look more like Dietrich. After each experiment the men look at Esther unhappily and fix her with accusatory stares. "We're on the wrong track," concludes one of them. "She still looks surprised." The idea that stars, female ones in particular, can be manufactured has some unintentional credibility here since we still have not seen any indication of Esther's unique talent or charisma.

Esther is having an equally tough time perfecting the single line she has been given in her first film for Oliver Niles Productions. Sitting in the studio commissary, she repeats "Acme Trucking Company. No, Mr. Smith is not in" as a bored, sassy, and heavily accented version of the switchboard operator she will briefly play. There are multiple levels of performance; Esther impersonating Vicki who is in turn impersonating the various operators.

In what could almost be an additional meet-cute (this one between Norman and Vicki), Norman struggles in for his usual morning pick-me-up. Mixing a raw egg in a glass with Worcestershire sauce and salt, he looks around confusedly trying to identify the annoying "Acme" echoes until he finally discovers Esther. "I'd like to speak to Mr. Smith, please," he jokes, sliding in next to her. What follows seems more or less inevitable given all the random breaks Esther has received already. Norman explains how his own new picture is on hold while they search for the right leading lady. "This one has to be different," he says, "cute, sweet, intelligent," before stopping in mid-sentence when he realizes that such a person, of course, is sitting next to him. Norman and Esther rush to Oliver's office, where Norman pitches him on casting Vicki Lester as his co-star. In an appeal to Oliver's profit margin, Norman argues, "If she clicks, you have a star overnight." Oliver likes the odds, and when he quickly agrees, Esther's subsequent faint is emphasized by a slow fade to black.

Out of that darkness, which is now the blank screen of a theater, comes an audience announcement: "You are about to see the Preview of a picture that has not been finally edited. Your opinion will be appreciated. Please mail comment cards." Having seen neither the shooting nor the rough editing of said picture, we are finally getting our delayed glimpse of Norman and Esther on screen together. We also watch the two of them watch themselves. "Oliver Niles presents Norman Maine in 'The Enchanted Hour'" is the first credit, followed by "Introducing Vicki Lester." As an audience member, Norman holds Esther's hand and crosses her fingers. As costumed and bewigged actors, Norman and Vicki rush through a terrace doorway and embrace. "Do you think we were noticed?" she asks. "By no one," he answers, "they're much too busy playing at croquet." In a medium close two-shot, Norman says "I've loved you all my life," and Vicki gently demurs, "But we only met two days ago." To swelling music and a tightened embrace, Norman delivers the *coup d'amour*, "That's when my life began." It's like a parody of a romantic movie, overblown and artificial. A turgid costume drama seems like the wrong vehicle for displaying Vicki's fresh believability and Norman and Vicki's on-screen chemistry, but Selznick harbored a fondness for such pictures and, deep into the apparently endless preproduction of *Gone with the Wind*, he had scenery-laden period pieces very much on his mind.

Filing out of the theater, preview audience members are ecstatic about Vicki and bored with Norman. "I think she was much better than he was," says one. "It's Vicki Lester's picture," concludes another. A reviewer tells Libby that Vicki is "a Knockout." When Libby asks the reviewer and a colleague if they also liked Norman, the colleague answers, "Was he in it?"

Esther (lower right corner) rehearses a line in the studio commissary.

Sneaking out of the side door, Norman and Esther join other studio insiders for a celebration party at Café Trocadero (the upscale, black-tie supper club that was opened at 8610 Sunset Boulevard in 1934 by *The Hollywood Reporter* owner William Wilkerson). They look out from the strip onto what would be the lights of West Hollywood and mid-Wilshire. Norman tells Esther that it all belongs to her now and that "it's a carpet spread for you," reminding us again how much of the film's language and imagery deal

Norman and Esther at the premiere of her first film.

with value and ownership. Over the strains of "Dancing in the Dark" on the soundtrack, Norman pronounces that "a star is born" and hopes that stardom will make Esther happy. Asked by Esther about his own feelings, Norman sees happiness but wishes "it wasn't too late." Combined with the negative reactions of the preview-goers, Norman's comments close the Trocadero scene on a somber sense of foreboding, matched by another slow fade-out.

In synch with the rhythms of Norman's manic-depressive personality, the action next switches to a wild boxing match at the Hollywood American Legion Stadium (located at El Centro and Selma, the Post 43 facility hosted popular weekly fights, often attended by movie celebrities and covered by gossip columnists). Chewing their gum ever more energetically as the boxers get more aggressive, Norman and Esther react to every punch. In between shouts of advice, Norman asks Esther to marry him. "Suppose we get married," he suddenly blurts out, and when she initially refuses because he drinks and spends too much, Norman adds "Suppose I quit drinking" and "Suppose I save my money."

With the same speed he used to engineer the screen test, Norman shows up with Esther in Oliver's office to announce their plains. The dialogue and the action involving the wedding will be repeated almost exactly in Moss Hart's script for the 1954 Cukor version. "We're going to be married," reveals Norman. Responding to Oliver's silence, he continues, "I guess I didn't read that line right," a reference to the overlap between performance and reality that will have even more resonance in Cukor's picture. After Norman repeats the news to still no reaction, Vicki asks, "What's the matter?" Oliver, answers Norman, is "trying to decide if it's good for the studio." The couple intend to elope but as soon as they leave the office, Libby brainstorms elaborate public events. "That's a charming match," he comments dismissively, "a nice girl like Vicki and public nuisance number one." To maximize positive publicity, he suggests a wedding at the beach. There could be "bridesmaids in bathing suits" and "20,000 Santa Monica School children spelling out the word 'love.'" Or "why not City Hall?" he proposes. "Like the Lindbergh reception in New York only bigger."

Instead, we cut to two drunks behind bars as the camera tracks out to reveal a justice of the peace marrying Esther and Norman in a rural county courthouse with Danny as best man and witness. "Do you, Alfred Hinkel, take this woman....?" intones the judge in a tightly composed four-shot featuring the main players in the foreground and the prisoners looking on from the background. Despite the humor and joy of the occa-

Norman proposes at the American Legion fights.

sion, there are details that will seem ill-omened in retrospect. The incarcerated barflies foreshadow Norman's own subsequent time in the drunk tank, and Esther's serious expression during the "for better or for worse" pledge portends the challenges she will endure when Norman falls off the wagon. For now the scene concludes comically as the drunks applaud and Danny shouts "Quiet!" like he's giving orders back on a studio set.

"Anyway, we got away from Libby," laughs Esther, as she and Norman leave the courthouse. On cue, Libby appears and confronts them outside. "If you'll be kind enough to glance between my shoulder blades, Mr. and Mrs. Hinkel," he fumes in another example of the script's caustically witty dialogue, "you'll find there a knife buried to the hilt. On the handle are your initials." Determined to still score a publicity plant, he rushes inside and interrupts the judge's trial to call the *Tribune* with a scoop on the elopement.

A slow fade-in discloses a newspaper photo of Norman and Esther and a large headline that reads "Vicki Loves in Trailer." An additional fade opens on a long shot of a green sedan and a green Slipstream trailer tooling across a mountain landscape. What follows is like slapstick from another movie, like some physical comedy that Lucy and Desi might borrow later for *The Long, Long Trailer*. Whistling to the accompaniment of a jaunty nondiegetic tune on the soundtrack, Norman steers the car while Esther tries to fry a steak in the cramped Slipstream. With each bump in the road, she careens against the walls. It is her honeymoon, however, and she happily sings, "Give me a horse, a horse, a great big buckaroo and let me wahoo, wahoo" in what is supposed to be a western cowgirl accent. Circling up the mountain, Norman plows into a patch of mud abruptly halting the car and throwing Esther to the floor. "I don't want to sound immodest," says Norman as he opens the trailer door, "but I think I stripped the gear."

Fredric March, already a veteran of Lubitsch's *Design for Living* and about to make *Nothing Sacred* that same year, could pull off innuendo and repartee with the right co-stars, actresses such as Carole Lombard or even Miriam Hopkins, but Janet Gaynor, who had made some light musical comedies, was not quite up to the task. While Esther dusts off her steak, Norman squeezes into a closet-sized enclosure to take a shower and discovers he doesn't even have room to raise his arms over his head. Just as he releases a torrent of cold water, an old man in a beat-up truck passes by and Norman rushes outside in his monogrammed bathrobe to get a tow out of the mud. The whole incongruous sequence ends on another seemingly comic note that contains somewhat darker overtones. In order

A passing motorist fails to recognize Norman during the comic honeymoon trip.

to convince the reluctant old man to help, Norman finally admits who he is, but the man just introduces himself in reply and drives away. "So you're Norman Maine," teases Esther in a joke that will sound less funny as Norman's popularity and fan base rapidly disappear.

This cautionary gloom is reinforced immediately by a newspaper insert titled "Cinema Sidelights by Artie Carver." The first in a series of printed Hollywood artifacts used as they were in *What Price Hollywood?* to advance the narrative, the column asks, "What famous male star has stopped gargling the grog and is now taking a non-alcoholic honeymoon? But why do friends think his bride came about six performances too late as far as the public is concerned?" Echoing Norman's own speculation at the Trocadero about whether happiness has come "too late," the notion of missed opportunity moves the film irrevocably from comedy to melancholy and furthers the inevitability of Norman's decline.

In confirmation, the gossip column dissolves to a two shot of Libby standing next to Oliver's desk and explaining that he can't get "a decent mention of Maine" in any of his usual outlets. The problem, he continues, is that "the critics don't like him, the exhibitors don't like him, the public don't like him, and I don't like him." Frustrated as well as justified, he wonders, "Who likes him?"

The answer, of course, is Esther, seen in the very next shot strolling arm in arm with Norman across the lawn of a splendid mansion he has bought for her as a surprise wedding gift, the acquisition of property signifying (as it always does in Hollywood films) the completion of their romantic union. The lush natural setting, Eden-like in its beauty, suggests Norman's almost desperate attempt at new beginnings and rebirth. He hopes that the estate will be a sanctuary where "the studio never intrudes," but almost as soon as he has set that idyllic goal, Libby appears with a celebrity photographer to generate publicity. "Let's get some pictures," he commands, positioning Norman and Esther beside the swimming pool for a series of informal portraits. In anticipation of the future caption, Libby announces, "Their honeymoon begins anew."

When Oliver unexpectedly joins the group poolside, Norman breaks off the photo shoot and responds, "Their honeymoon ceases abruptly," leaving the photographer only too happy to concentrate on Esther. Conversing privately with Oliver and sensing his reluctance to discuss business, Norman pointedly asks, "Do you think I'm slipping?" "The tense is wrong," answers Oliver. "You're not slipping. You've slipped."

The characterization of studio executive Oliver Niles is a diplomatic dance here, especially in the context of producer Selznick's own sensitivities and self-image. A clear-headed and aggressive businessman, Oliver is loyal to his friend but also unwilling to mismanage a hot new property. Esther, he reveals, will star "in a picture of her own with that young Pemberton. He's coming along nicely" and Norman will be given another chance on a solo vehicle. Aware of the demotion, Norman puts his best face on the news and says, "We'll make a try at it, let's hope it's not too late," one more reference to the eroding passage of time.

The consequences play out in several emblematic shots that function metonymically to show Norman's sliding career arc. It is the kind of meaning-driven ellipsis that classic Hollywood cinema does so efficiently. To begin, a studio worker covers Norman's name with Vicki's on a billboard advertising *The Enchanted Hour*. Looking through an Oliver Niles publicity book, a theater exhibitor turns to a photo of Vicki Lester and remarks, "I'll take plenty of these." When he gets to a portrait of Norman described as "the Screen's Most Finished Actor," he sneers, "I'll say he's finished. He keeps them away in droves."

A dissolve to the studio Fan Mail Department reveals a clerk flipping a single letter onto Norman's nearly empty shelf and then dumping buckets onto Vicki's overflowing pile of envelopes. Finally, we track in on a newspaper headline declaring "Norman Maine Contract with Niles Cancelled." The text of the article reads, "Theatre men who were short-sighted enough to buy the Norman Maine pictures on this year's Oliver Niles Schedule will be glad to learn that they will be released from this burden on them and their audiences. Niles has finally bought off the Maine contract for an unknown figure… Orchids to Niles!"

Two points stand out in the treatment of Norman's downward spiral. First, Esther's soaring popularity is presented as a kind of rivalry with Norman, a zero sum quest for success in which one person must always be crushed. Norman's steadfast loyalty to Esther and support for her career therefore attest even more convincingly to his generosity. Second, the Schadenfreude over Norman's decline seems particularly vindictive and unwarranted. His jostling of a photographer at the Hollywood Bowl is minor compared to the boorishness James Mason will unleash backstage at the Shrine Auditorium in Cukor's version of *A Star Is Born*. Norman is a witty and cranky drunk but not a violent one. The delight in his demise is a hypocritical reaction from characters like Libby and the gossip columnists who already have been set up to take the brunt of the film's anti-Hollywood criticisms.

Following the newspaper insert, there is a fade to waves lapping the shore and a ground-level shot of Norman putting golf balls in the living room of his Malibu beach house. He is out of work and restless. "No, I'm not the butler," says Norman, eagerly answering a phone call that he had hoped might have been for him. It is the "Cinema Sidelights" columnist Artie Carver, who enquires about the contract cancellation and then asks Norman to use his influence in arranging an interview with Vicki. The conversation provides further evidence of Norman's integrity and graciousness amid the sleaze represented by Carver. Pushed for a settlement figure, Norman explains that he did not demand a buy-out ("We just called it quits."), and Artie Carver replies that he will make up his own number anyway. It is the same kind of distortion that characterized the reporting in *What Price Hollywood?*

Esther hurries home still dressed in a Puritan costume from the day's shooting, and Norman focuses his affectionate attention on her. Rather than going out, he has prepared milk and sandwiches so that he can "have you to myself" and she can relax from her long hours at the studio. In two separate instances, mirrors are used to emphasize the multiple identities that impact their ever fluid relationship. As Esther removes her lace hat and combs out her hair, Norman wheels a cart of food into the mirror's background. Movie star Esther is reminded of the reversed roles, her play-acting and Norman's new reality. Later, Norman embraces Esther in a full-length mirror, whispering "Don't look now but I think that guy on your left is in love with you." He scrutinizes the reflection carefully, aware of Esther's innocent freshness and his own faded, once photogenic, appearance.

An additional, more jarring, humiliation comes soon after. Answering the doorbell, he encounters a deliveryman with a package for Vicki Lester and he offers to sign for it. "Who are you?" asks the man, unaware that he is speaking to Norman Maine. "I'm her husband," responds Norman after a painful beat. "Oh sure, sign here, Mr. Lester." Defeated and reduced to personal assistant, Norman returns to Esther with the package and with several messages he has taken during the afternoon:

1. The Shrine Auditorium has her scheduled for a benefit.
2. The Academy needs to know if she would like a table reserved for her.
3. Artie Carver wants his interview.

Ominously, Norman forgoes his food and decides, "I think I'll fix me a little drink."

The next sequence, the Academy Awards banquet, is handled with a reverence that once again sanctifies the "art" of making movies. A fade-in accompanied by brassy fanfare displays an invitation which reads "Academy of Motion Picture Arts and Sciences Eighth Annual Award of Merit Banquet in the Biltmore Bowl, Biltmore Hotel, Los Angeles." A thumb partially obscures the date; only the letters "Ma…" are visible. Wellman's establishing shot is appropriately ornate: Potted palms line the bottom of the frame, chandeliers across the top and a layer of glimmering, formally set tables through the middle. The rhetoric is equally ostentatious.

While the camera slowly tracks out from five Oscar statuettes displayed on the dais, the tuxedoed master of ceremonies solemnly pronounces, "And now we arrive at the climax…the highest award within our power to bestow." Esther, nervously deferential, watches the proceedings from a stage-center table with Oliver Niles. "She has already had the world's acclaim, but this is the tribute of her fellow workers," raves the speaker. Referring to the actress "who created the unforgettable Anna in *Dream without End*," he finally identifies Miss Vicki Lester as the winner of the Best Actress of the Year award.

Norman, delivering Esther's package, reacts badly to his fading popularity.

Esther takes the stage and, in medium close-up, confesses that she is so overwhelmed that all she can do is express a simple thank-you to everyone present. This is Esther Blodgett's apotheosis, her admission to the ranks of professionals like the attendees, the scriptwriters, Wellman, and Selznick, who all understand the seriousness and the value of making movies. She is awed to be in such company. Then, at the moment of triumph, Norman, whose gravest sin many not be his alcoholism but rather his failure to be impressed by Hollywood, arrives to disrupt the celebration. Drunk and underdressed, he stumbles down the steps and commandeers Esther's acceptance speech. "I want to be the first one to congratulate you on that valuable piece of bric-a-brac... now I want to make a speech," he shouts, daring to actually mock the golden talisman itself. The sense of public embarrassment is dream-like, acutely painful to watch—so effective that it will be repeated in both the 1954 and the 1976 versions of *A Star Is Born*. "I want a statue for the worst performance of the year," continues Norman. A quick cut to Anita Regis shows her smugly enjoying the humiliation of her ex-boyfriend. As Esther leaves the stage to intercept Norman, he swings his arm around wildly and accidentally smacks her on the side of the face. Mortified, he is led back to the table. Music starts, Anita Regis stops by to say "how proud" Esther must be, and Norman pleads in anguish, "Somebody give me a drink."

Fredric March later will portray another serious drinker in Al Stephenson from *The Best Years of Our Lives* (1946, RKO/MGM, directed by William Wyler). In both roles, he is genuine and free of cliché—or, as Frank Nugent bluntly wrote in his original review for *The New York Times*, "Fredric March's waning Norman Maine is not an outrageous ham" (Quirk, page 149). Under the inebriation, there are regret and disgust with his own behavior. March gets the details right: the controlled body movements, the shifts in mood, and the empty eyes. In *The New Biographical*

Esther receives her Oscar just before the ceremony is disrupted by a drunken Norman.

Dictionary of Film, David Thomson perceptively calls it "a performance of great daring... the most glamorous thing March ever did" (page 562). So complex and tragic is his Norman Maine that in big emotional scenes like the Academy Awards presentation, where Gaynor should be capturing all the attention, we cannot help but stare transfixed at March instead. Even with the post-awards dissolve to Esther removing unconscious Norman's shoes and placing them on the floor next to her symbolically overturned Oscar, we are interested in his pain as much as hers.

Esther's worries follow her back to the studio. When Oliver visits her dressing room, he notices that she has been crying. Costumed as an eighteenth century French aristocrat in blue gown and blond wig, Esther admits that concern over Norman is affecting her concentration. With a touch of defensiveness, Oliver responds, "Letting Norman leave the studio was the hardest thing I ever did." (Ironically, Adela Rogers St. Johns quotes Louis B. Mayer as later saying something remarkably similar about Judy Garland: "The bitterest moment of my life was when I had to let her go" (page 46). It is this dismissal from MGM that led Judy and husband Sid Luft to a production deal with Warner Bros. that resulted in the 1954 *A Star Is Born*.) The mood, as reflected by a steady rain coincidentally streaming down the windows of Esther's bungalow, is mournful. In this pre-rehab era, Esther confides that Norman "has gone to a sanitarium... he really wants to stop drinking." With more loyalty than studio bosses ever really showed their troubled stars, Oliver decides to visit the sanitarium and offer Norman a job in front of the cameras again, ending the scene on a hint of optimism.

The sanitarium is actually an old Los Angeles Victorian (in another of the film's reversals, Norman now finds himself living in a place very much like Esther's former residence at the Oleander Arms). Accompanied by a personal caretaker whom he has nicknamed "Cuddles," Norman joins Oliver in the parlor of the ironically misnomered Liberty Hall. He moves slowly and unsteadily, but with his customary charm, he tries to make Oliver feel comfortable. "They even have iron bars on the windows to keep out the draft," he jokes. The drabness of the setting is heightened by Wellman's pedestrian blocking. Norman and Oliver sit on either end of a sofa in a flat master two-shot; their conversation is covered in alternating medium close-ups linked by eyeline matches.

When Oliver offers Norman a part in an upcoming movie, he brightens noticeably and asks, "Who plays opposite me?" Taking a supporting role might have been acceptable (plenty of former matinée idols, such

Norman and his attendant meet with Oliver in the sanitarium.

as Ramon Navarro, Gilbert Roland, Richard Barthelmess, and even John Barrymore transitioned successfully to character acting), but Oliver specifies, "It's not exactly the lead, young Pemberton is doing that." The thought of performing alongside the kid groomed as his replacement is too much for Norman's pride. He tells Oliver he has several pending deals with other studios, and Oliver graciously pretends to believe him.

The exteriors of the Santa Anita Racetrack scene that follows were shot on location and the interiors were done in the studio. Nick Carraway's judgment that Gatsby is "worth the whole damn bunch put together" applies equally well in this scene to Norman and the Hollywood vultures who turn on him.

As he enters the clubhouse lounge, Norman greets three acquaintances and they barely acknowledge his presence. Behind his back, one of them sneers, "How I hate to run into these has-beens, gives me the creeps." Norman sits at the bar, orders a ginger ale, and soon notices that PR man Libby has taken a seat nearby. Libby is particularly vindictive. "Why it's Mr. America of yesteryear," he taunts by way of greeting. Norman tries to laugh off the hostility and asks, "What do they do with the actors when you're away?" Unsoftened, Libby snipes back that "they cut 'em in slices and fry 'em with eggs." In an effort to connect, Norman confides that it is "pretty lonesome with Esther away working all day," but Libby is like Iago spewing his hatred for the flawed but significantly nobler Othello. "I wouldn't squawk about that if I were you," he jeers. "It's nice to have somebody in the family making a living." When a provoked Norman says, "I don't want to forget we're friends," Libby unleashes years of repressed resentment: "Friends my eye. I got you out of jams because it was my job. I don't like you and I never have liked you. Nothing made me happier than to see those pranks of yours land you on your celebrated face." Pushed further by the sponging off Esther accusations, Norman takes a swing at Libby and gets knocked to the floor. It is an incident that Norman would have finessed in the past, but Libby has the juice now. As policemen intervene to restrain Norman, Libby indicates that he is harmless and should be left alone. "He can't fight any better than he can act," says Libby disdainfully.

Wellman handles the follow-up shot deftly. The camera tracks slowly backward from a crowd of people, and as they separate, we see Norman stand, alone and embarrassed, in the middle of the emptying frame. He walks to the bar and darkly demands, "Give me a scotch double. Leave the bottle here." Fade to black.

The consequences play out in a series of ironic reversals. In the Malibu beach house, Esther and Oliver discuss Norman's latest bender. "He's been gone four days without a word. Four days!" frets Esther. A brightly decorated Christmas tree glitters behind them, its promise of seasonal festivity negated by the worry over Norman. Summoned to night court, Esther and Oliver find that Norman has been placed in the drunk tank, alongside the same kinds of men who once witnessed their marriage. Norman is not released because of his celebrity but because Esther promises the judge she will be responsible for him. Previously uninterested in Norman, the newspaper photographers swarm him as he and Esther leave the court, and the headlines emphasize the connection to Esther—"Norman Maine Released to Custody of Vicki Lester After Drunk Conviction" and "Night Court Drama as Star Pleads for Husband's Freedom." Finally, Norman decides that the only way he can salvage Esther's life is by taking his own.

The suicide issue caused some trouble for Selznick with theater exhibitors. In a letter to his General Sales and Distribution Manager related to an objection from 20th Century Fox West Coast Theatres executive Spyrous Skouras, Selznick wrote, "Concerning the tragic ending, this is the sort of comment about pictures that dates back twenty years, and that I didn't think anybody seriously advanced today. I will be satisfied with a long line of pictures that do as well as *Anna Karenina*, in which Garbo

Esther, accompanied by Oliver, secures Norman's release from jail.

threw herself under a railroad train; or *A Tale of Two Cities*, in which Mr. Colman had his head chopped off; and if anybody wants further examples, I will sit down and list about fifty sensational successes with tragic endings" (Behlmer, page 107). Despite the bravado, Selznick saw to it that Norman's suicide was conveyed through suggestion and synecdoche.

Esther and Oliver stand outside the bedroom where Norman is supposedly sleeping. "It's awful to be with someone you love," says Esther, "and know it can't get any better." A cut to Norman reveals him lying in bed and listening to the conversation. He is in total darkness except for a shaft of light that falls across his left eye and emphasizes the pain that gathers there. "I can't do any more pictures," concludes Esther. "I'm going away for good with Norman." Blaming herself, she tells Oliver, "Maybe if I hadn't been away from him so much, last night and what went before, it wouldn't have happened." Both Oliver and Norman are troubled by her reasoning. "It's your life you're giving up," argues Oliver. "Maybe I can give Norman back his," she answers.

Resigned to Esther's decision, Oliver leaves the house and somewhat ostentatiously delivers the valediction, "Goodbye, Vicki Lester, you were a grand girl. Good luck, Mrs. Norman Maine." The discussion of being and identity has an immediate effect on Norman and will give added significance to the film's last scene and last line of dialogue.

Alone in the living room, Esther glances at the revered Oscar, symbolic for her and for the film of all that is worthwhile in Hollywood, and bursts into tears. Entering the scene, Norman watches Esther and steels himself for the upbeat part he now must play. "I'm just coming out of jitters and you're going into them," he jokes. Announcing that he intends to become physically fit and asking Esther to make breakfast, he prepares for a swim in the ocean. "I'm going wading out in our front yard," he continues to banter.

Once again, March is brilliantly understated in his ability to convey Norman's regret and exhaustion. The imagery, which might have seemed obvious and saccharine if matched with someone else's acting, also works. As Norman hugs Esther, an over the shoulder shot reveals the devastated sorrow that he has concealed from her with his joking. Norman's subsequent point-of-view shot shows a faded orange sun slowly setting into the Pacific (one of the few times the film's colors seem effective). Norman walks toward the camera, and then a reverse cut positioned behind his back has him confronting a sunset both literal and figurative. The iconic, wrenching farewell—"Hey, do you mind if I take just one more look?"—comes right before he closes the glass terrace door and exits screen left.

Selznick originally envisioned Norman's actual suicide to be accompanied by dramatic special effects similar to the flashback montage in *What Price Hollywood?* Writing to Selznick International Vice-President and *King Kong* director Merian C. Cooper, Selznick suggested, "My own feeling is that we should get a conclusion on a higher note. I feel we should get in scenes of his past, accompanied by an increasing tempo in the film, the music, and sound effects; that these scenes of his past triumphs will have to be exceedingly brief and perhaps shot for the purpose; that they should be followed by such high spots of the story... so that we clarify what is troubling him... confining ourselves perhaps to such things as the marriage scene, the trailer, the slap on the face at the Academy, and the overhearing scene. I feel we may be able to get a great effect out of the roar of the ocean, plus perhaps some trick effects such as the buzzing... when Lowell Sherman shot himself..." (Behlmer, page 110).

Fortunately, none of these ideas were included in the final film. Instead, the drowning is handled with the evocative parts-for-whole selectivity often used in classic Hollywood cinema to treat suicide and sacrifice. Viewed from the knees down, Norman kicks off his sandals and drops his brown robe onto the sand. As he leaves the frame, waves wash over the robe, dragging it out into the ocean. In a long shot, Norman enters the water and begins to swim out toward the horizon. A cut returns to the robe which now swirls around in the current and slips beneath the surface. In solemn retreat and closure, the camera tracks backward and fades to black.

As polished a moment as in any glossy melodrama, the scene's gravitas is quickly dispelled. The ever-present newspaper headlines announce "Norman Maine's Body Found off Malibu: Ex-Star Perishes in Tragic Accident" and "Wife Vicki Lester Overcome by Grief."

Then, in a nasty little coda, Libby stands at a bar and berates Norman. "First drink of water he had in twenty years and then he had to get it by accident," he tells a guffawing bartender. "Pardon me, how do you wire congratulations to the Pacific Ocean," he adds to even bigger laughs. Ironically, Libby has become exactly what he always accused Norman of being—a loud, mean-spirited drunk.

The funeral itself deteriorates into something out of *The Day of the Locust*. It looks and feels like the wedding scene in *What Price Hollywood?* Veiled and dressed in black, Esther appears at the top of a staircase leading from the church. Oliver holds her right arm, and Danny holds the left one. As they descend, the crowd (photographed to fill the frame) breaks loose and rushes Esther. "Come on, Vicki, let's see your face," shouts one of the most overzealous fans. Esther and her escorts are jammed into the center of the melee. "Don't cry, dearie, he wasn't so much," croaks an old harpy just before she lifts the veil from Esther's face. Amid the pandemonium, Esther shrinks backward and screams, providing the possibility for a sordid gossip column headline.

The photograph that follows, however, is a picture of Norman peeling potatoes in the honeymoon trailer. The mood is somber again as Esther looks through various mementos and supervises the moving men packing up her house. In a reprise of Norman's good-bye, she picks up the photo and says, "Do you mind if I take just one more look?" The dark lighting and the covered furniture make it seem as if Esther is in a wax museum or a morgue.

Re-enter Grandma Lettie. "Put down those trunks," she commands, bursting through the front door of Esther's house. May Robson's appearance seems startling at first, but recall the "I buried him out there on those plains and went right on" speech and it soon becomes apparent why she has been brought back into the narrative. When Esther confides that she plans to return to the farm, Lettie asks, "What are you running away from, little girl?" Esther's life in Hollywood, claims Lettie, has given her "more fame, more success, and even more personal happiness" than she possibly could have expected. In a tightly framed two shot that emphasizes the link between the women, Lettie says, "I was proud of you. I was proud to be the grandmother of Vicki Lester."

For Lettie, it is a question of perseverance and courage, and she argues the point on both a philosophical and personal level. "Tragedy is a test of courage," she proposes. "If you can meet it bravely, it will leave you bigger than it found you." Playing on Esther's obligation to Norman, Lettie further confides, "I never knew Norman Maine. He wrote me a very

Grandma Lettie reappears to jolt Esther out of her depression and to enjoy the glamour of Hollywood.

sweet letter when you were married saying how much I meant to you and I know how much you must have meant to him." Wives go on, she knows from experience, they push the frontier forward, they finish the job. "I can't believe he'd be happy knowing his great love for you has made you a quitter." Lettie is elevating her granddaughter's career to something patriotic and praiseworthy. Esther's filmmaking is like Lettie's pioneering; both endeavors confirm the American spirit.

When Esther decides to stay and resume her film career, she legitimates everything that David O. Selznick always believed was special, meaningful, and even redemptive about his world. Like most insider films that pretend to be critiques of Hollywood, *A Star Is Born*, at its core, believes in the grandeur of making movies and in the exceptionalism of the people who create them.

It is appropriate, then, that the film closes with Esther lavishly premiering her new picture at Grauman's Chinese Theatre, Hollywood's stylistically challenged shrine to itself. With her name literally up in lights and emblazoned across the courtyard, she arrives in the requisite black limousine accompanied by Granny, Danny and Oliver. A bombastic master of ceremonies announces, "The entire motion picture industry has come to pay tribute to the girl who has won the heart of Hollywood, to the girl who has won the heart of the world." The event is treated with great pomp and circumstance, "entire motion picture industry" being the phrase always used to make the studios seem vital and significant.

Asked to greet the radio audience on an "international hook-up," Grandma Lettie remarks, "Maybe some of you listening in dream of coming to Hollywood and maybe some of you get pretty discouraged. Well, when you do, just think about me. It took me over seventy, er, sixty years to get here but here I am and here I mean to stay." Forget that it is Esther and not Grandma who has the successful movie career, Lettie has become the voice of Hollywood boosterism, an advocate for the hope and opportunity it offers a nation still emerging from the Depression. On her way to the microphone, Esther sees Norman's inscription in the cement and momentarily freezes. "Hello, everybody," she says almost defiantly, "this is Mrs. Norman Maine." It is a big moment, a classic line, a dramatic pay-off honoring Norman that Selznick had been contemplating for some time.

In a note to Wellman, he wrote, "I have been thinking about my new idea for the end, and I believe that we can retain Gaynor's entire approach up the aisle in front of the Chinese, simply retaking the reaction to the footprints, more or less as it is; with her then pulling herself together; the announcer asking her if she will say a few words… Gaynor saying she will, advancing with all the pride in the world, throwing her head back, with tears in her eyes, and saying 'This is Mrs. Norman Maine speaking'…" (Behlmer, page 109). This time, if his account is to be believed, Selznick had the right intuition.

Bookended by the same conceit with which it opened, the film dissolves from Esther in white fur and emerald necklace to the last page of the script itself:

ESTHER AT MICROPHONE
Esther
Hello everybody… This is Mrs. Norman Maine.

The ovation is tremendous. CAMERA MOVES IN TO BIG CLOSEUP OF ESTHER. Tears are starting down her cheeks. She looks out past all this crowd, this confusion, to some distant point of her own. The music swells up.

FADE OUT.

THE END

While Esther's triumph resonates with viewers, the script is offered up as an even more valuable Hollywood artifact, one of those precious texts that, when properly manipulated by studio professionals, can yield stories that entertain and just possibly inspire millions of people. Making sure one last time that appropriate credit be acknowledged, Selznick includes a final tag card that reads "A Selznick International Picture."

Selznick's second Hollywood paean disguised as critique was well-received. "The film was very warmly reviewed," reports David Thomson in his Selznick biography, "and it did immediate business. It had cost $1.159 million, and it would gross about $2 million. By the summer of 1939, it was reckoned to have shown a profit of $181,000…" (page 235).

Howard Barnes gave the picture a rave review in the *New York Herald Tribune*: "The photoplay has its fabulous aspects, but through it runs a core of honesty that makes it the most remarkable account of picture

Esther Blodgett/Vicki Lester proudly introduces herself as Mrs. Norman Maine.

making that has yet reached the stage or screen. The authors have achieved narrative substance and fidelity of detail… William Wellman has directed the script superbly, employing Technicolor without affectation and bridging a variety of moods triumphantly. With Fredric March, Janet Gaynor, and the supporting players handling their roles with restrained intensity, the work becomes an exciting document of the world's biggest show business, and an exciting entertainment" (Quirk, page 149).

Kate Cameron, writing for the *New York Daily News*, was equally enthusiastic and claimed the film: "…gives Miss Gaynor an opportunity to display her considerable talents as a comedienne, and as an emotional actress, too…" and features Fredric March in "…one of the best performances of his career as the glamorous, irresponsible, impulsive and generous screen star Norman Maine" (page 149).

Selznick's father-in-law Louis B. Mayer particularly admired the film, boasting, "If there is anybody in this business who can take Irving Thalberg's place, David Selznick is the one. Did you see what he did with *A Star Is Born?* He took that story… and made a tremendous picture out of it" (Thomson, page 238).

A Star Is Born was nominated for six Academy Awards, including Best Screenplay Adaptation, Best Original Story, Best Direction, Best Picture, and Gaynor and March for Best Actress and Best Actor. The only win, as mentioned before, went to Carson and Wellman for original story, over which the issue of credit so obsessed Selznick. Nominated four years in a row as best picture producer (*Viva Villa!, David Copperfield, A Tale of Two Cities*), Selznick finally won the coveted honor and nearly ran the table in 1939 with *Gone with the Wind.*

As there had been with *What Price Hollywood?*, there was much speculation over possible real-life counterparts to the characters in *A Star Is Born.* Barbara Stanwyck biographer Axel Madsen believes the original story treatment closely paralleled Stanwyck's marriage to alcoholic stage comic Frank Fay. He writes that "Wellman and Carson submitted a detailed story line that Selznick found so close to the Fay-Stanwyck marriage that he asked attorneys specializing in invasion-of-privacy litigation to go over it. The lawyers came back with a twenty-page brief, listing similarities in incidents and situations between the script and Frank and Barbara Fay. Wellman and Carson decided one way to distance their plot line from the Fays was to make the husband a dejected and humorless person. Selznick, who was never content with letting writers develop a script on their own, ordered another rewrite. In the new version, the husband was more comic in tone, that is, more like Fay" (page 75). Perhaps because Stanwyck and Fay were involved in acrimonious divorce and custody hearings of their own, no legal proceedings ever came of the perceived similarities.

Other observers felt the Esther Blodgett-Norman Main relationship mirrored silent film star Colleen Moore's marriage to publicity man John McCormick. David Thomson wryly points out that none of the proposed suicide references—John Bowers or Paul Bern—make any logical sense. "That sort of altruistic gesture has no model in life," he declares. "Picture people would never fall for the claptrap of making that sort of sacrifice for someone else" (page 238).

As the accolades accumulated, Selznick seemed satisfied with his revamped Hollywood fairy tale. Certainly he had fixed the confusing love triangle of *What Price Hollywood?* by making his leading man both husband and mentor. What he had not established, however, was the credibility of Esther's rise to stardom and Norman's immediate belief in her talent. It would take George Cukor, James Mason, and Judy Garland to solve that problem.

4

A Star Is Born
(1954)

Much about the 1954 version of *A Star Is Born* was regrettable for the players involved: the three-hour masterpiece that was taken out of director George Cukor's control and butchered down to just over 150 minutes; the much deserved Best Actress Oscar for Judy Garland that was given instead to Grace Kelly's tepid performance in *The Country Girl*; and the box office bonanza for Warner Bros. and Garland's and husband Sid Luft's Transcona Enterprises that never materialized.

Despite the pain of what might have been, there is still much to celebrate in this stunning iteration of *A Star Is Born*. In his first musical and first color film, Cukor took the new CinemaScope frame size and shaped it into visually beautiful and thematically rich compositions. Garland revealed hitherto unknown gifts as a dramatic actress and provided insight into her unrivaled power as a stage performer. James Mason showed American audiences the moodiness, strength, and vulnerability that already had made him a star in England. Moss Hart penned a witty, sophisticated screenplay brimming with keen observations of Hollywood routine and ritual. And Harold Arlen and Ira Gershwin composed a vibrant musical score that included a blockbuster ballad destined to become as closely associated with Garland as "Over the Rainbow."

As Sid Luft remembers it, he thought of the whole project one day in 1951 when he read that low-budget producer Edward Alperson had the remake rights to Selznick's *A Star Is Born*. Retooled as a musical, it would make a perfect vehicle for Garland, who coincidentally enough had done a 1940s broadcast version of *A Star Is Born* with Walter Pidgeon and

Adolphe Menjou on CBS's *Lux Radio Theatre*. Despite some initial reluctance to sell the property and to cast Garland in the Esther Blodgett role, Alperson ultimately entered into a deal with Luft.

According to Ronald Haver in his definitive *A Star Is Born: The Making of the 1954 Movie and its 1983 Restoration*, the two producers "formed a corporation called Transcona, after a town in Manitoba where Luft used to fly. Transcona was designed as a holding corporation, its assets being the rights to *A Star Is Born*: Alperson held 20 percent of the corporation; Garland as star and Luft as producer held 75 percent; and the remaining 5 percent went to Luft's millionaire friend and racing partner, Ted Law" (page 25). If it could now get financed and made, the movie would be Garland's screen comeback.

At just thirty years old, America's sweetheart, the star of *The Wizard of Oz,* (1939), *Meet Me in St. Louis* (1944), and *Easter Parade* (1948), was considered washed up in the picture business. Fired in 1950 by MGM for alleged erratic behavior, delays, and absences on *Summer Stock* (1950) and for her inability to complete either *Royal Wedding* (1951) or *Annie Get Your Gun* (1950), Garland was without a studio contract for the first time since she had signed with MGM in 1935.

During the interlude, she had completed a hugely successful concert tour of Great Britain and an acclaimed, record-breaking nineteen-week engagement at the Palace Theater in New York City. It was this massive and highly-publicized new popularity as a concert singer that tempted Jack Warner to think about making a film deal with the Lufts. By the 1950s, Warner Bros., like the other four "major studios," had seen its hegemony weaken through the rise of television and a monopoly-busting federal court order to divest itself of the theater component of its production/distribution/exhibition operation. More than ever before, Warner Bros. was open to arrangements with independent producers to finance and distribute valuable properties that could expand studio profits. Garland's enormous success at downtown Los Angeles's Philharmonic Auditorium in April, 1952, sealed Warner Bros.' interest.

As explained by Ronald Haver, a general agreement was reached by which Warner Bros. would finance and distribute three films from Transcona Enterprises with an option every six months on six additional films. Garland would star in the first one, the musical version of *A Star Is Born*, as well as two of the future projects. It took several months for a final contract to be hammered out—a dense, eighteen-page document detailing budgets, contingencies, options, rights, and responsibilities.

According to Haver, the other two pictures in the first round of production would be *Snow Covered Wagons*, a Donner party adventure budgeted at $500,000, and *Man O'War*, a biography of the famous racehorse, at $650,000. *A Star Is Born* would be financed at $1,500,000 (a figure that would grow quickly to at least four times that amount) and Garland would be paid $100,000 to perform. Once agreed-upon expenses had been covered, Warner Bros. and Transcona would split the profits 50/50.

Ronald Haver quotes contract details providing that if Transcona was "...required to expend more than the budgeted cost of a photoplay to complete it, then Warners will advance the additional financing. If Transcona spends more than 10% in excess of the budgeted cost, then Warner Bros. forthwith has the option to elect whether it shall assume control of production of the photoplay involved" and "when any photoplay has been previewed, 'sneak,' press, or public on two (2) different occasions, Warner Bros. has the right, in its sole discretion, to re-cut or re-edit with a view to giving it the highest box-office appeal to the general public" (page 35-36).

That right to final edit, to cut the film in any manner and to any length that Warner Bros. deemed appropriate, would have a disastrous effect on *A Star Is Born*'s fortunes. Another clause specified that Transcona had complete ownership rights and was legally qualified to grant the rights to Warner Bros. without "...any claims, etc. against any of said photoplays which can interfere with Warners' rights" (page 36). A seemingly insignificant detail except for the fact that *A Star Is Born* godfather, David O. Selznick, had reacquired exhibition rights to the original film in thirteen foreign countries and that, therefore, Alperson didn't really own all the rights and that any producer making a new version could not show it in those countries without Selznick's approval. This would also complicate things later for Jack Warner and Sid Luft.

With Warner Bros. formally on board, the crucial next step was to secure a writer for the script and a composer for the music, and since this was to be Garland's grand return to film, they had to be the best. Studio executive, producer, and star all wanted Moss Hart to write the screenplay. A major force on Broadway, Hart already had written a series of hit plays with George S. Kaufman, including *Once in a Lifetime* (1930), *Merrily We Roll Along* (1934), *I'd Rather Be Right* (1937), *The American Way* (1939), *The Man Who Came to Dinner* (1939), *George Washington Slept Here* (1940), and the Pulitzer Prize-winning *You Can't Take it With You* (1936). On his own, he had written the book for the musicals *Face the Music* (1932), *As Thousands Cheer* (1933), *The Great Waltz* (1934),

At the happily optimistic start of production, Judy Garland links arms with husband Sid Luft (left) and studio boss Jack Warner. Director George Cukor stands next to Warner.

Jubilee (1935), and *Lady in the Dark* (1941), and had both written and directed *Winged Victory* (1943), *Christopher Blake* (1946), *Light up the Sky* (1948), and *The Climate of Eden* (1952). Married to actress and early television game show personality Kitty Carlisle, he would later go on to direct the Broadway mega-hits *My Fair Lady* (1956) and *Camelot* (1960). For Hollywood, he had scripted *Broadway Melody of 1936*, *Gentleman's Agreement* (1947), and *Hans Christian Andersen* (1952) among others. Only forty-eight years old in 1952, he was a show business Wunderkind grown effortlessly into an all-purpose, go-to veteran.

"Moss liked Garland," writes Hart biographer Steven Bach. "He admired her in pictures like *The Wizard of Oz* and *Meet Me in St. Louis* and had known her since 1945, when she and his old friend Vincente Minnelli honeymooned for three months in New York… He was intrigued, he said, by Garland's 'curious instinct' as an actress that had 'nothing to do with technique' but resembled 'a great musician plucking the strings of a harp'" (page 312).

Garland and Luft drove down to Palm Springs to visit the winter vacationing Moss Hart and convinced him to write the screenplay. Agent Irving Lazar (nicknamed "Swifty" by Humphrey Bogart for the speed with which he negotiated deals) arranged the contract with Warner Bros.; Hart would be paid $101,000, "...a symbolic $1,000 more than Garland would be paid for playing Esther" (page 313).

Like Hart, composer Harold Arlen was a top choice to collaborate on *A Star Is Born*. A friend of Garland's, he had written the music for *The Wizard of Oz* (lyrics by E.Y. Harburg), "Down with Love" and "Last Night When We Were Young" (lyrics by Harburg), "Stormy Weather," "Get Happy" and "I Gotta Right to Sing the Blues" (lyrics by Ted Koehler), "Blues in the Night," "My Shining Hour," "That Old Black Magic," and "St. Louis Woman" and "Ac-Cent-Tchu-Ate the Positive" (lyrics by Johnny Mercer). He also wrote hundreds of other songs, including the Garland concert standards "Come Rain or Come Shine" (Mercer), "When the Sun Comes Out" (Koehler), "Happiness is a Thing Called Joe" (Harburg), and "Any Place I Hang My Hat is Home" (Mercer). He composed for Cotton Club revues, Broadway shows, and Hollywood musicals, winning an Academy Award for "Over the Rainbow." He and Harburg would later write the score for *Gay Purr-ee*, the 1962 animated musical starring the voice of Garland, and "I Could Go on Singing," the theme song for her similarly titled final film in 1963. Garland loved his brassy emotional ballads and felt they would be just the right thing for the high dramatic moments of *A Star Is Born*. With his work completed on *The Farmer Takes a Wife* at 20th Century Fox, Arlen was available and eager to sign on with Garland.

It seems fitting that Ira Gershwin would be recruited to write the lyrics. Having worked with both Hart (*Lady in the Dark*) and Arlen (*Life Begins at 8:40)*, Gershwin was well-connected in Hollywood and another of Garland's favorite social acquaintances. Nor could it have hurt that Gershwin, Hart, and Arlen were all represented by the same agent—the ubiquitous Irving Lazar. Beginning with *Lady, Be Good* in 1924, Ira and his brother George wrote a string of important Broadway musicals including *Tip-Toes* (1925), *Oh, Kay!* (1926), *Strike Up the Band* (1927), *Funny Face* (1927), *Rosalie* (1928), *Girl Crazy* (1930), *Of Thee I Sing* (1931), and *Porgy and Bess* (1935). The credits "lyrics by Ira Gershwin" and "music by George Gershwin" appeared on the covers of such classics of the American songbook as "But Not for Me," "I Got Rhythm," "They Can't Take That Away from Me," "Embraceable You," "Nice Work if You Can Get It," "S Wonderful," and "Someone to Watch Over Me." Lured to Hollywood, they most notably wrote the scores for two 1937 Fred Astaire films, *Shall We Dance* and *Damsel in Distress*.

Although he scaled back when George died unexpectedly at age thirty-eight of a brain tumor, Ira continued to write for Hollywood and Broadway, teaming with composers such as Jerome Kern (*Cover Girl*, 1944) and Kurt Weill (*Where Do We Go From Here?*, 1945, and *Lady in the Dark*, 1941). Dissatisfied by his stint writing songs with Burton Lane for Stanley Donen's unsuccessful 1953 MGM musical *Give a Girl a Break*, Gershwin was looking for more of an artistic challenge and agreed quickly to collaborate with his old friend Harold Arlen.

The contract between Warner Bros. and Transcona was very specific about who would be brought in to direct the new *A Star Is Born* project. According to Haver, attached to the agreement was a list of six acceptable directors: John Ford, Daniel Mann, Henry Koster, Charles Vidor, Michael Curtiz, and George Cukor.

Clearly this was not Ford's kind of material, and Mann, known mostly as a director of television dramas, had yet to make a feature film in Hollywood. Vidor, who had worked often with Rita Hayworth, and Koster, a veteran of Betty Grable pictures at 20th Century Fox, both had experience with musicals and color films. So did Curtiz, who had directed the hugely successful *Yankee Doodle Dandy* (1942) and had been a valued Warner Bros. house director for many years.

But Garland wanted Cukor, who had background in neither. What he did have, however, was that reputation for bringing out the best in his actresses and for mounting glossy, polished productions. "I wanted George," commented Garland in an interview from the time, "The picture had to be the greatest... it couldn't be merely very good. I had too much at stake... I had to prove things" (Haver, page 37).

Cukor had worked with all of the big MGM dramatic stars that Garland envied; now he finally would be directing her, as well. Despite her reputation for unreliability, he also wanted to work with her. "I gave a birthday party for Ethel Barrymore—it was her seventieth—and Judy came and sang 'Happy Birthday' to her," Cukor told an interviewer. "She did it with such feeling and emotion that I thought Ethel would dissolve in tears. Anyone who could sing like that, I thought, had the emotional ability to be a great dramatic actress. That was the first time I got the idea I wanted to direct Judy" (Haver, page 39).

Many of Cukor's important films had been written by Garson Kanin and/or his wife Ruth Gordon, such as *A Double Life* (1947), *Adam's Rib* (1949), *Born Yesterday* (1950), *Pat and Mike* (1953), and *The Actress* (1953). At the height of that seven-year run, Cukor recently had coached *Born Yes-*

For her comeback movie, Judy Garland was adamant about having George Cukor direct her.

terday's Judy Holliday to a Best Actress Oscar over Bette Davis in *All About Eve* and Gloria Swanson in *Sunset Boulevard*. He believed that Garland had the same kind of raw, untapped acting talent. Besides, he had intimate knowledge of the subject matter and was ready now to have another crack at it. In a deal with Warner Bros., MGM (with whom Cukor was still under contract) "asked for and received $6,250 weekly against Cukor's $4,000 salary for loan-out of the director's services" (McGilligan, page 218).

Cukor was determined to make creative use of color. Coming somewhat late to the medium, he had been impressed with John Huston's Toulouse-Lautrec inspired palette in *Moulin Rouge* (1952) and was interested in a similar sense of artistic experimentation and innovation.

For assistance in achieving the desired effects, he convinced Luft and Warner Bros. to hire George Hoyningen-Huene as color consultant. A former *Vogue* photographer and close Cukor friend, Hoyningen-Huene had studied with Cubist painter André Lhote, completed several travel books, and directed documentaries on influential figures in history and culture. He would help Cukor arrange the color, mass, and empty space of his elongated frame in ways that suggest the shifting emotional dynamics between his characters. With *A Star Is Born*, writes Patrick McGilligan, Hoyningen-Huene "became a kind of painter for movies (Cukor called him an editor of color), mixing strange and dark colors to infuse scenes with emotion and vitality. Huene had an exhaustive collection of art books, and would bring them in to show the cameramen or department heads his models for color or lighting. The photographer had extreme ideas for the use of shadows and backgrounds, smoke and gauze, flash and shine" (page 224).

Equally essential to his creative visual team, or as Cukor called them, his "art boys," was Gene Allen. A former child actor and blueprint assistant in the Warner Bros. art department, he had just rejoined the studio as a sketch artist and was recruited by Lem Ayers, the Broadway stage designer, who had been hired by Luft as art director, to attend the preproduction meetings. Ayers was having trouble providing the level of visual detail Cukor wanted, and so Allen took over responsibility for the scenic drawings and storyboards, addressing camera positions, cuts, angles, composition, lighting, color, and costumes. Pleased with his skill and suggestions, Cukor delegated more and more responsibility to Allen, eventually giving him a screen credit for "production design." Allen communicated Cukor's and Hoyningen-Huene's vision to the technical departments and served as go-between when any issues surfaced.

Before shooting began, Lem Ayers became sick and was replaced by Malcolm Bert, whom Allen respected greatly and supported in the same professional manner. Intensely loyal to Cukor (who employed him as chief assistant for all of his subsequent films), Allen stayed on during Cukor's postproduction absence and tried, albeit unsuccessfully, to protect the director's work from the studio interference and ruthless re-editing that damaged it irrevocably.

The careful deliberation used to secure Cukor's services was also evident in the casting of the Norman Maine role. Everyone had Cary Grant high on the list of possibilities. Luft escorted him on multiple occasions to the horse races at Hollywood Park and lobbied heavily. George Cukor convinced him to read the script aloud at Cukor's home in the Hollywood Hills and called the performance "absolutely magnificent, dramatic, and vulnerable beyond anything I'd ever seen him do" (Haver, page 67).

Luft claimed the hang-up was that Jack Warner refused to meet Grant's demand for $300,000 against 10% of the gross, while Cukor believed that Grant was reluctant to open himself up so fully and emotionally on the screen. Perhaps Grant, about to turn fifty and challenged by career fluctuations that saw hits such as *I Was a Male War Bride* (1949) followed by less successful pictures such as *Crisis* (1950), feared that audiences would see unintended real-life parallels in a story about an ageing matinee idol on the skids. Whatever the reason, Cary Grant passed on the part, leaving the Lufts, Warner Bros., and Cukor to turn to other possibilities.

Laurence Olivier already had declined. Richard Burton and Tyrone Power were under contract to 20th Century Fox. Burton was unavailable, and Tyrone Power carried too high a price tag. Luft suggested Humphrey Bogart and Frank Sinatra, but apparently Jack Warner vetoed both suggestions.

Stewart Granger, the London-born actor who had achieved major successes in *King Solomon's Mines* (1950) and *The Prisoner of Zenda* (1952) for MGM, also was invited to read the part and actually rehearsed several different times with both Cukor and Garland. The experience was not a positive one for Granger, who claimed that Cukor continually interrupted him with trivial, insignificant corrections and suggestions. "In the end I couldn't take it," Cukor biographer Emanuel Levy quotes Granger as saying, "so I got a bit drunk one night, called George up, and said, 'I'm coming down to see you.' I drove to his house and said, 'George, sit down and shut up. Don't wag your finger at me, and I will tell you how to play this fucking scene.' I played the scene, and he said, 'Why didn't you do that before?' 'Because you wouldn't give me a chance. You can take the script and stick it up your ass.' And I walked out" (page 222). In addition to Granger, other actors reportedly considered at one time or another were James Stewart, Gregory Peck, Robert Taylor, Ray Milland, Glenn Ford, and Montgomery Clift.

Eventually the part of Norman Maine was offered to James Mason. In one of those fortuitous alignments of availability and suitability, he ended up being the best possible choice. Having reached British stardom in films such as *The Seventh Veil* (1945) and *Odd Man Out* (1947), Mason had impressed American audiences as General Erwin Rommel in *The Desert Fox* (1951) and as the double agent valet in *Five Fingers* (1952), both for 20th Century Fox, and was looking for his first major leading man part in Hollywood. *A Star Is Born* seemed to offer the opportunity, and he eagerly accepted.

Mason expertly captures Norman's mercurial temperament—the boorishness and threat of violence alternating almost simultaneously with the graciousness and sensitivity to others. Ann Todd, his co-star in *The Seventh Veil*, observed, "There was something electric and at the same time very dangerous about James, which had nothing at all to do with conventional screen stardom in postwar years. He was one of the few people who could really frighten me, and yet at the same time he was the most gentle and courteous of men" (Morley, page 3).

Despite the prolonged shooting schedule and frequent delays (many of which were caused by his leading lady), Mason liked Garland very much and enjoyed working with her. As he later remembered, "To get something as unique as Judy's talent, some patience and sacrifices were needed... Judy was by no means a temperamental star. 'Temperamental star' is usually a euphemism for selfish and bad-tempered, and a temperamental star of this sort can be a real time waster. I know. I have worked with some... But this was not Judy" (Haver, page 186).

To the *London Times*, Mason admitted "an admiration, a sort of love, for Judy who was marvelous to work with" (Morley, page 105). With some Garland biographers claiming an affair between them, the two co-stars remained friends long after filming ended (Mason delivered the eulogy at Garland's New York City funeral in 1969).

Rounding out the cast were Charles Bickford as studio boss Oliver Niles, Jack Carson as publicity department head Matt Libby, and Tommy Noonan as best friend Danny McGuire, changed from an assistant director to a piano-player in the same orchestra for which Esther sings. Often described as "gruff voiced" and "craggy," Charles Bickford played Greta

Seen here shoving Matt Libby (Jack Carson) into a mirror, James Mason clearly understood Norman Maine's darker side.

Garbo's sailor lover in *Anna Christie* (1930) and then quickly moved to the character parts he preferred, earning Oscar nominations as Best Supporting Actor in *The Song of Bernadette* (1943), *The Farmer's Daughter* (1947), and *Johnny Belinda* (1948). Like Menjou, he plays Oliver Niles as a benevolent executive who looks after his family of employees and tends to their emotional needs.

A Warner Bros. contract player since 1941, Jack Carson was adept at scheming second fiddle roles like Wally Fay in *Mildred Pierce* (1945) and later Gooper Pollitt in *Cat on a Hot Tin Roof* (1958), and was hired from a short roster that also included Howard Duff, Pat O'Brien, and Murvyn Vye. His Matt Libby is less repellent than Stander's but seethes with the same bullying resentment. "A big man, fast with his tongue, sure of himself, expert at his work" (Haver, page 56), Moss Hart described the character, and Carson's size and swagger fit the requirements.

For Esther's loyal friend and confidant Danny, Cukor chose newcomer Tommy Noonan, who had played Marilyn Monroe's rich and nerdy boyfriend Gus Esmond in *Gentlemen Prefer Blondes* (1953) and partnered until 1962 in a nightclub comedy act with Peter Marshall, the once and future host of the television celebrity game show *The Hollywood Squares*. Although Noonan was relatively inexperienced, Cukor felt confident enough in his dramatic abilities to go ahead and give him the big emotional scene with a grief-stricken Esther at the end of the movie.

While director, composers, and writer sweated content and style, Jack Warner obsessed over the format of the film. Like every other studio head in the early 1950s, he was caught up by the various technical innovations that promised to compete with television by altering the size and shape of the movie screen. In 1952, *Bwana Devil*, a truly bad adventure yarn about railroad workers and lion attacks in Kenya directed by Arch Oboler and starring Robert Stack, raked in big profits by advertising its use of "Natural Vision," a crude 3-D technique that used dual cameras and projectors to convey the impression of depth. By donning special cardboard glasses, audiences could see lions and warriors leap out from the screen at them.

Almost concurrently, *This is Cinerama* was drawing box office lines in New York by offering crowds a huge, curvilinear picture created by three separate cameras and projectors running in synchronization. Anxious that Warner Bros. be at the forefront of the new technology just as the studio had been with the advent of sound, Jack Warner made a deal with the Natural Vision Corporation and announced that *A Star Is Born* would utilize the new process. His reasoning was that if a minor little

Warner Bros. horror film such as *House of Wax*, featuring Vincent Price at the beginning of his macabre period and directed by second tier veteran Andre de Toth, could be a box office sensation (a $5.5 million gross against a $1 million investment), just think what Natural Vision could do for a top quality production like *A Star Is Born*.

Clearly, Natural Vision, 3-D, and Cinerama were gimmicks that could prove short-lived. Searching for a more practical and lasting widescreen phenomenon to trump television, 20th Century Fox, under president Spyros Skouras, purchased the option on an anamorphic lens developed in the 1920s by Henri Chrétien that squeezed an image to half its size and widened it in a projector to a width to height aspect ratio of 2.35:1 (roughly two and half times the width of what was then the normal screen size). Calling the process CinemaScope, the studio paid Bausch and Lomb to redesign both the photography and the projection lenses to correct the distortion and graininess of Chrétien's originals.

To broaden industry usage and convince theater owners to invest $25,000 per screen in converting to the new projection system, the studio offered to license CinemaScope to other studios at a cost of $25,000 a picture. Jack Warner, hesitant to pay any fees to Fox, entered into a deal with a Chicago optical company for rights to an anamorphic lens that did not violate the Chrétien patent. Calling his version Warner Super Scope (later shortened to WarnerScope), Warner next contracted with a German manufacturer to improve the inferior lenses (which more severely distorted clarity and color) and quickly revealed to reporters that *A Star Is Born* now would be shot in the untried Warner big-screen process.

Cukor, in particular, was not thrilled with the idea of shooting in Warner Super Scope but went ahead with the studio's plan. When tests (especially those shot at night) revealed how dim and fuzzy the images continued to appear even with the new German lenses, Warner reconsidered and told Cukor the film would be shot on a somewhat wider, but non WarnerScope-size format and in Technicolor. Momentarily reversing himself and returning stubbornly to the Warner Super Scope edict a couple of weeks later, Warner then abandoned his pet technology one more time and the issue seemed to be settled once and for all. Filming began on a few key scenes.

Meanwhile, 20th Century Fox had released *The Robe*, its first feature-length film shot in CinemaScope. A slow-moving costume drama based on Lloyd C. Douglas's novel about a Roman centurion involved in Christ's crucifixion, the movie was directed by Henry Koster and starred Richard

Burton, Jean Simmons, and Victor Mature. Accompanied by mostly positive reviews, it had racked up a $3 million gross in its first two weeks of limited release. Jack Warner's older brothers and financial nemeses Albert and Harry were impressed and entered into negotiations with Fox to license the process. Pressured by his brothers and convinced by the superior quality of Fox demonstration footage, Jack reshuffled his cards once again and made what turned out to be the definitive closing decision on format: *A Star Is Born* would be shot in CinemaScope and Eastmancolor, which was cheaper than Technicolor and could be branded as Warner-Color. The Eastman negative would be printed on Technicolor positive exhibition prints. The soundtrack would be four-track magnetic stereo.

The conversion to CinemaScope meant that the scenes already filmed had to be filmed all over again, including Esther's appearance as an extra on the train set, her late night consideration of Norman's offer, her early morning wait for his call, her on-location carhop waitress job, Norman's sanitarium conversation with Oliver, and "The Man That Got Away" number. The retakes added about $300,000 to the escalating budget. The additional costs had nothing to do with Garland, but she would be held responsible by reporters and studio executives for the film's overall excesses.

Along with the fluctuations in format came changes in cinematographers. Harry Stradling, who had worked in France and Germany in addition to Hollywood, started out behind the camera. Nominated for fourteen Academy Awards, he had won the Best Cinematography (black-and-white) Oscar in 1945 for *The Picture of Dorian Gray* and would take home the Best Cinematography (color) award in 1964 for George Cukor's

One of the unused versions of "The Man That Got Away."

My Fair Lady. As an experienced veteran of Technicolor musicals, such as *Easter Parade* (1948), *Words and Music* (1948), *The Pirate* (1948), and *In the Good Old Summertime* (1949)—all four with Garland—Stradling was a safe and logical choice.

With the start of production continually postponed, however, Stradling had to move on to another assignment and was replaced by Winton Hoch. Equally adept at Technicolor, Hoch had already won three Academy Awards for Best Cinematography (color) before coming to Cukor's musical: *Joan of Arc* (1948) directed by Victor Fleming and *She Wore a Yellow Ribbon* (1949) and *The Quiet Man* (1952) directed by John Ford. A Caltech graduate in chemistry and a former research technician at Technicolor, Hoch was a traditionalist regarding procedure and precedent, and he clashed with Cukor on several occasions over lighting and camera movement. Just before the switch to CinemaScope, Hoch was released over what might be termed "irreconcilable differences."

Milton Krasner was brought in to photograph the retakes. On loan from 20th Century Fox where he was the resident expert on CinemaScope, Krasner worked on over 160 films during a career that stretched from 1933 to 1970. Between 1954 and 1955 alone, he shot nine different CinemaScope pictures for the studio, including *Garden of Evil*, *Désirée*, *Demetrius and the Gladiators* (a sequel to *The Robe*), *The Seven Year Itch*, and *Three Coins in the Fountain*, for which he won an Academy Award for Best Cinematography (color). Obviously much in demand at 20th Century Fox, Krasner could only give Warners a few days.

He was followed by Sam Leavitt, who went on to finish the film and received the sole credit for cinematography. Stradling's former camera operator, Leavitt was fearless in the face of CinemaScope, lighting the sets quickly and willing to try intricate camera movements and long takes. He and Cukor got along very well; Leavitt, says Ronald Haver, was "unpretentious, loved his work and was eager to please his director" (page 128).

Well-prepared by his experience on *A Star Is Born*, Leavitt later served as director of photography for Otto Preminger, who famously liked to move the camera into and around busy, long-take scenes filled with people, props, and action. Among their collaborations were *Carmen Jones* (1954), *The Man with the Golden Arm* (1955), *Anatomy of a Murder* (1959), *Exodus* (1960), and *Advise and Consent* (1962). Leavitt also worked twice for Stanley Kramer, in 1958 on *The Defiant Ones*, for which he won the Oscar for Best Cinematograpy (black-and-white), and in 1967 on *Guess Who's Coming to Dinner*.

In one final postproduction push that will be discussed in more detail later, a fifth cameraman, Harold Rossen, was brought in to shoot the extremely long "Born in a Trunk" musical number that was added to the first half of the film.

Decisions involving sound, choreography, and costumes came somewhat more easily. Ray Heindorf, the head of Warner Bros.' music department, was selected as musical director. Over the course of a forty-plus-year career, most of which was spent at Warner Bros., Heindorf was nominated for eighteen Oscars and won three of them, Best Scoring of a Musical for *Yankee Doodle Dandy* (1942), *This is the Army* (1943), and *The Music Man* (1962). A meticulous and experienced craftsman, Heindorf created complex arrangements that added just the right emotional overtones to Cukor's atmospheric visuals. Lloyd "Skip" Martin assisted with the orchestral arrangements. He was a big band saxophonist/arranger for Count Basie, Benny Goodman, and Glenn Miller, and an MGM studio orchestrator on *The Barkleys of Broadway* (1949), *Summer Stock* (1950), *Singin' in the Rain* (1952) and many other films. His talent and experience were as prodigious as Heindorf's, and together the two musicians shaped the Arlen/Gershwin compositions to best complement Garland's range, phrasing, and intonation.

When vocal coach Hugh Martin left the production after a heated dispute with Garland over the best way to sing "The Man That Got Away" (she insisted on doing it full force and brassy, which turned out to be the right call), Jack Cathcart was brought in to handle the vocal arrangements. Married to Garland's sister Suzy, he had known Garland since she was part of the Gumm Sisters vaudeville act, and he had conducted the orchestra for some of her concert and television appearances. A versatile technician who would later become musical director at the Riviera Hotel in Las Vegas, he also meshed easily with Garland's performing style.

Perhaps the artist with the shortest film resumé to join the musical team was choreographer Richard Barstow. Performance director for the Ringling Brothers and Barnum and Bailey Circus and choreographer on some early television variety shows, he had staged dances for the Broadway shows *Sally* (1948) and *New Faces of 1952*, designed the circus production numbers for Cecil B. DeMille's *The Greatest Show on Earth* (1952), and created the choreography for the 1953 June Haver-Dan Dailey musical, *The Girl Next Door*, including the innovative film noir parody, "Nowhere Guy." Despite his scarcity of major film credits, Garland liked and trusted him. He was a former vaudeville performer like she was and had overcome a childhood foot deformity to become a professional dancer.

Barstow would return many years later to stage Garland's 1967 "At Home at the Palace" shows. He knew how to showcase her considerable dancing talents. Like Rita Hayworth, Leslie Caron, and Cyd Charisse, Garland had danced with both Gene Kelly and Fred Astaire and was regarded by both men as an excellent partner. "Judy's not primarily a dancer," Astaire commented on their work together in *Easter Parade*. "But she's the best of her type; an amazing girl. She could do things—anything—without rehearsing and come off perfectly. She could learn faster, do everything better than most people. It was one of the greatest thrills to work with her" (Fricke, pages 102-03).

Referring to his experience with Garland on *For Me and My Gal* (1942), Kelly was similarly effusive in his praise: "I was amazed at her skill; she knew every mark and every move. All I could do for her was help with the dancing. She wasn't a dancer, but she could pick up a step instantly. She was a very relaxed, marvelous person… the most talented performer we've ever had" (Fricke, page 70).

Relying on these same basic instincts and natural talents, Barstow designed production numbers where Garland tap dances, cane taps, high kicks, romps around a living room, and keeps up with several different chorus lines. In addition to making her look good in all the dance sequences, he also provided a degree of stylistic continuity by both choreographing and directing the "Born in a Trunk" number after Cukor had concluded his work on the film.

Irene Sharaff designed the multiple costumes for "Born in a Trunk" and received a screen credit along with Mary Ann Nyberg and Jean Louis. When Luft and Garland convinced Jack Warner to add the elaborate MGM style "narrative" production number, they convinced him to hire Sharaff, a Broadway and MGM legend, to dress it. By 1953, forty-three-year-old Sharaff had already won her first Oscar for Best Costume Design (color) with *An American in Paris* (1951) and her first Tony for Best Costume Designer (*The King and I*, 1952). She had designed costumes for over forty different films and would go on to complete twenty more, winning four additional Best Costume Design Academy Awards for the movie version of *The King and I* (1956), *West Side Story* (1961), *Cleopatra* (1963), and *Who's Afraid of Virginia Woolf?* (1966).

Sharaff moved easily between history, fantasy, and high fashion in her designs with a penchant for flowing lines, sharp silhouettes, and the striking use of red, orange, and pink fabrics. For "Born in a Trunk," she created minstrel costumes, Southern finery, formal wear, and several special gowns for Garland.

Most of the other scenes were done by Mary Ann Nyberg, a young designer, who had just delivered big for MGM with the wardrobes for *Lili* (1953) and *The Band Wagon* (1953) and who, like Sam Leavitt, would next move on to work with Otto Preminger on *Carmen Jones* (1954) and *The Man With the Golden Arm* (1955). About the same age as Garland, Nyberg worked closely with the actress and endeavored to make her look glamorous for her comeback.

"Mary Ann Nyberg's experience of this film seems typical enough," wrote Christopher Finch in *Rainbow*. "Never having worked with Judy before, she went into the project with some trepidation and a good deal of excitement. At first, she thought Judy one of the most delightful and charming people she had ever met. The star put their relationship on a chummy girl-to-girl basis, and this happy state of affairs continued for several months" (page 196).

Dressing Garland to appear chic could be a challenge. Haver quotes MGM designer Walter Plunkett as remembering, "She was heavy, she had no waistline, and her hips started under the bustline" (page 109). Nyberg compensated by cinching the waist and lengthening the train; Garland was so pleased with several of the results that she borrowed them for her own personal use.

"If she liked the dress," says Finch, "she would go to Jack Warner and tell him that she simply had to borrow it for such-and-such a party or premiere, arguing that it would be a valuable promotion for the picture if she was seen wearing these things" (page 194). Finch further recounts one episode where Judy so damaged an extremely expensive French lace dress that it had to be destroyed and remade and another in which she faked angry dissatisfaction with a white gown for the Academy Award scene so that she could keep it for herself. (Most famously, in the late 1960s, Garland also would lift the sequin paisley pantsuit from her aborted *Valley of the Dolls* Helen Lawson role and the mink coat from her Blackglama "What Becomes a Legend Most?" photo shoot.)

With the continually lengthening production schedule came tensions over various details, including the costumes. Concluding his account of the Garland/Nyberg relationship, Finch explains, "As Judy became exhausted, however—and she drove herself mercilessly—her mood shifted and the tantrums and bitchiness began. At first there were occasional outbursts, then they became regular occurrences. The atmosphere changed" (page 196). The final rupture happened after either Garland's fury over an ill-fitting dress or Nyberg's refusal to run a personal errand for her on her day off. Whatever the cause, Mary Ann Nyberg was out.

Jean Louis was called in to finish the assignment. As head designer at Columbia from 1944 to 1960, he made gowns for Rita Hayworth (including the famous strapless back satin one in *Gilda*), Irene Dunne, Claudette Colbert, Judy Holliday, Marlene Dietrich, Deborah Kerr, Gloria Grahame, Joan Crawford, Kim Novak, Lana Turner, and others. (In 1962, Marilyn Monroe would turn to him for the notorious nude-colored, beaded gown she wore to sing "Happy Birthday" to President Kennedy at Madison Square Garden.)

What his leading ladies appreciated even more than the fourteen Academy Award nominations was how elegant he made them look in his sleek, form-fitting designs. He was able to do something similar for Garland; she wears a tight navy blue jacket and skirt, split up the side, to emphasize her shapely legs in the Shrine Auditorium number and another dark blue, high-collared, three-quarter sleeved dress to look dramatically slim against the blue and red background of "The Man That Got Away" set. Garland, Luft, and Cukor all were pleased with the results.

On August 13, 1953, after various postponements and delays, studio work officially began on Production #386. The script and the score were ready, but dancers were still being rehearsed, sets constructed, and locations scouted. Personnel were continuously shifting, and no decision had been made about which Arlen/Gershwin songs would be used and what song would climax the first half of the picture. Even more ominously, no agreement had been reached with Selznick on foreign distribution rights.

Yet, like a fully loaded Titanic steaming out of Cherbourg, the production sailed on. Tales of its ill-fated progress have the scent of uncertain legend. Stressed and exhausted, Garland was taking pills to sleep and pills to get going in the morning, and on days when she consequently was unable to work, shooting had to be scheduled around her. Sid Luft was often away from the studio, attending the races or raising money, and production supervision could be lax. When he was on the lot, he sometimes issued orders concerning script or sets that angered Cukor.

After shooting had begun, Jack Warner, as previously discussed, made the switch to CinemaScope and all the scenes that were completed had to be redone. Cukor and his "art boys" worked for hours on painterly details that in some cases never could be properly realized and were scrapped. Days lengthened, the budget expanded, and tempers shortened. Eager to begin his European vacation, Cukor left before filming ended and fifteen minutes of the final film were directed by Richard Barstow.

When shooting finally wrapped on July 28, 1954, several points soon were clear. First, with a final budget exceeding $5 million, *A Star Is Born* became the most expensive picture Warner Bros. had ever produced up to that time (some observers estimate a more likely final cost of $10 or even $20 million). Second, if preview and opening week audiences were to be believed, the movie was a major hit justifying all the hard work, heartache, and expense. And finally, despite the ecstatic reception and glowing critical reviews, Harry Warner and Warner Bros. distribution executive Benjamin Kalmenson were worried about its three-hour length.

A Star Is Born begins spectacularly with a celebrity-filled charity benefit at the Shrine Auditorium in Los Angeles. Among the most effective openings ever conceived for a musical, the sequence immediately accomplishes several important objectives. Buzzing with energy and activity, it conveys the infatuation with show business that will animate the entire film. It introduces all of the major characters, their personalities, and the relationships between them.

Among those connections is the initial attraction between troubled star Norman Maine and up-and-coming band singer Esther Blodgett. Esther's self-identification as a performer, a meme that will shape even her most personal behavior, is established at once through music, dialogue, and movement.

On the prowl behind the scenes as entertainers prepare for their entrances, Cukor's camera reveals the first of many stunning CinemaScope compositions that pack the widened frame with visual detail and artistic references. Using the elongated space to stage multiple planes of actions, Cukor also sets up a key thematic framework—the literal and psychological fragmentation of lives simultaneously lived onstage in full public view and offstage without artifice.

The film's first image is the by-now familiar panorama looking out across a glittering Los Angeles basin at night. Made even more stunning by the ascendant opening measures of an overture featuring "The Man That Got Away" and played by the 60-piece Warner Bros. orchestra, the shot is overlaid with the Warner Bros. logo and then the bold, red block letter credits of the cast and crew.

As the titles fade, multiple searchlight rays sweep across the night sky from the right edge of the screen, announcing not only the general attraction that is Hollywood but also the star-studded benefit gala that is specifically important to the narrative. In a shock cut that would be typical for an Orson Welles but unusual for the more unobtrusive Cukor, a bank of klieg lights high above the street suddenly arcs to light and flashes directly into the camera lens. Another overhead tilts down onto a busy street as limousines line up for arrival. An off-screen emcee salutes the Motion Picture Relief Fund, his enthusiastic voice echoing over the activity. A red neon light advertising a drugstore lines the right edge of a frame with a very gauzy and dark blue background. A low angle shot showing a searchlight playing along the top edge of the Shrine Auditorium is followed by a long shot of the entrance, where bright red flags and banners flutter in a blue haze.

Cukor's careful orchestration of red and blue, the sequence's predominant color scheme that will soon take on symbolic overtones, has begun subtly with seemingly peripheral details. Another angle on the entrance, shot from behind a television camera scaffold, quickly gives way to a second shot of the traffic-jammed street, where a red trolley car from the then-existent Pacific Electric line rings its bell and proceeds down the track. Clearly visible on the opposite side of the street is the Cinegrill, located then as now in the Roosevelt Hotel just across Hollywood Boulevard from Grauman's Chinese Theatre, a geographic fact which indicates the liberty Cukor is taking with city topography. To best capture the excitement of an opening night, he is combining actual footage that he and a Warner Bros. camera crew took of *The Robe's* premiere three months before at Grauman's with the staged action photographed at the Shrine, situated on Jefferson Boulevard several miles to the south and east of Hollywood.

Various angles of the crowd and Shrine entrance are intercut with shots of cars approaching the red carpet. The brief hand-held shots, coupled with Cukor's rapid editing and the "real" coverage from Grauman's, give the scene an almost documentary-like feel. "The rhythm of the montage," writes James Bernardoni in *George Cukor: A Critical Study and Filmography*, "conveys excitement; the variety of shots suggest disorder; the dramatic lighting and elegant costumes of the arriving gods and goddesses of Hollywood suggest glamour. This is the frantic periphery of the world of show business, a world which will be examined closely in the film, giving *A Star Is Born* a compelling sub-text that amounts to a small documentary within the larger fictional narrative" (page 67).

Seated in one of the approaching cars are studio executive Oliver Niles and starlet Lola Lavery (Lucy Marlow), the first of the main characters to be introduced. They exit the limo and walk past the camera before granting the requisite celebrity interview. "Norman Maine is the great attraction at the Shrine Auditorium here tonight," intones the announcer, who also suggests a romantic link between Norman and Lola. After she delivers a few breathily innocuous words, Lola preens for an older female reporter—"She's wearing a black sheath and a white fox and the diamonds in the hair—did you ever—it's darling." There are reaction shots of cheering fans in red jackets, red berets, red sweaters, red coats. Cukor plays the moment for satire, like the premiere scene in *Singin' in the Rain*, and introduces the crowd and the media sycophants as major characters who, as in *A Star Is Born*'s two predecessors, will grow increasingly negative and unstable. The fatuousness of the exchange could be any contemporary Oscar Red Carpet interview; the only thing missing is the specificity of the designer and the jeweler. "Did you ever see anyone so unspoiled and down to earth? She's a darling girl," gushes the reporter as Oliver and Lola finally exit toward the auditorium.

From inside the lobby, a reverse medium shot picks up publicity head Matt Libby greeting Oliver and immediately informing him, "Norman's not here. I've looked all over town, the usual places. Not a sign of him." It's significant information, economically delivered, that adds "unreliable" and "careless" to the emcee's description of Norman as a wildly popular star and that provides a rationale for Libby's festering resentment of Norman. As the camera tracks with them, Oliver and Lola exit frame right, continuing on in the next shot toward their box seats above the stage.

Cukor next brings us into the audience to share a pre-curtain sense of expectation. A long shot from the side of the orchestra looks up toward the mezzanine. A series of quick shots shows attendees, several of the women dressed in red gowns, taking their seats. Slowly, with the reverence Cukor always expresses in his films for a performance about to begin, the camera tilts up from a photographers' well to the auditorium chandelier, which dims gradually and turns dark blue. Cut to one of the first of Cukor's remarkable CinemaScope compositions, an extreme angled long shot with the audience in darkness on the left half of the frame and a Wild West Show at full throttle on the right.

It's a spectacle to make former circus director Richard Barstow feel right at home. Cowboys are riding horses back and forth across the rear of the stage, acrobats are tumbling in the center, and chorus girls dressed as Indian maidens are advancing toward the front. Most of the costumes, like the acrobats' body suits and the cowboy gear, are bright red. The stage is bathed in light and backed with a brilliant crimson curtain. Almost like the tonal match cuts used by Ozu and Antonioni in their color films, Cukor has used the splashes of red to skillfully transition from the observing to the observed. Back in the audience, Libby enters the rear of Oliver's box (which is illuminated by a dim red house light) and makes his way to Oliver's side. A clear, angled view of the stage indicates that additional performers in red gowns, fluorescent pink headdresses, and red shirts have joined the show. "He's here," Libby tells Oliver, "he's drunk." As if this has happened often, Oliver asks "How bad?" and Libby replies, "Very. What do you want me to do?" Calculating potential public relations damage, Oliver decides, "Get him off. Don't let him go on, Libby." An extreme long shot of just the stage itself fills the screen with shouting cowboys and whooping Indians and bridges to a similar swirl of activity backstage.

Establishing shots show dancers stretching, actors adjusting costumes, and crew members moving props and wardrobe. This is the creative bustle of staging a play or shooting a film that Cukor loves so deeply and conveys so knowledgeably. The energy is intense but more purposeful and less frantic than the surging crowd chaos outside the Shrine. The shots backstage are held longer and the camera movements are slower. Cued like we are for Norman's appearance, several ballet dancers look off frame right toward a sudden commotion.

In a long shot from their point of view, we see Norman dressed elegantly in white tie and tails staggering into performers and interfering with their preparations. He is intoxicated. More than that, he seems to be a familiar ("Norman Maine, probably drunk" says an off-screen voice), messy and ill-tempered lush. His initial impression on us is negative; his behavior invites derisive curiosity as evidenced by a low angle shot of several half-dressed entertainers bending over an upper stage level to get a better look at him. The costumes, curtains and even the floor backstage are bright red—an overwhelming explosion of "hot" color that symbolizes Norman's toxic disruption of the performance. The camera pans along with Norman as he makes his way toward the main stage. He grabs the cap of a busker dressed in a silver "button coat," attempts to dance onto the stage as part of the Indian princess chorus line, and jumps on the back of a horse about to perform. In each case he is restrained by stagehands before the audience can see him; deep focus shots from the stage left wing capture Norman struggling in the semi-dark foreground and the show continuing on unaffected in the background.

Libby appears backstage and confers with an exasperated stage manager played by Sam Colt. In medium shots with action swirling behind them, they decide that the Glenn Williams Orchestra will go on in place

A Star Is Born (1954) • 133

Norman Maine creates chaos at the Shrine. Backstage reality threatens to impinge on the ordered illusion of a performance.

of Norman. Cukor demonstrates his thorough command of the complex blocking and camera movement backstage in, for example, even the seemingly simple transition from this conversation to the introduction of orchestra singer Esther Blodgett and piano player Danny McGuire. As Libby walks out of his scene to the left, Glenn Williams hurriedly crosses from there to screen right. With a panning cut on movement, he enters a new frame (again left to right) instructing the orchestra to be ready and passing in front of Esther and Danny, on whom the camera lingers after Williams exits. Esther straightens a stocking and Danny checks his music score.

Looking up, Danny notices the disturbance and remarks, "Get a load of Norman Maine, will you?" The loop of characters has been completed and Norman has now been visually linked to Danny and Esther. Centered in the frame, they both gaze to the left; Esther wears a fitted tuxedo top with a single large red carnation in the lapel, a black tie, and the slitted Jean Louis skirt. Danny wears a light blue double-breasted jacket and a black bow tie. The reaction shot from their point of view shows Norman continuing to cavort with the cast members. "Mr. Maine is feeling no pain," laughs Esther. Less annoyed and more amused by Norman's antics than everyone else, Esther watches him with a lingering fascination. The economy with which Cukor literally has brought his characters on stage and established several of the relationships between them has been exceptional.

With focus shifted back to the crisis, Libby intercepts Norman and tries to steer him to a makeshift dressing room where reporters are waiting to interview and photograph him. "Mr. Libby," says Norman to one of the buskers, "looks after me like a fond mother with a good sense of double entry bookkeeping." The humorous introduction is very similar to the one Norman later will use for his sanitarium attendant, the "looking after me" reference in both cases suggesting Norman's own image of himself as a child in need of supervision.

The camera tracks slowly to the left with Norman and Libby until Norman stops suddenly and pushes Libby away. "Take your hands off me," he snarls. Then, just as unpredictably, he asks for a drink and agrees to photos equal in number to however much liquor Libby brings him. "You're not a bad fellow, Libby," he says, appeased for the moment. "Why do you disgust me? Why do I hate you so?" Supercilious and violent to a degree way more extreme than anything Fredric March projected, Mason is taking big risks here as an actor, unafraid to make his Norman Maine a complicated, initially unlikable character with considerable viewer animosity to have to overcome later in the picture. In answer to Norman's insulting question, Libby says, "I wouldn't know about that Norman" and maneuvers him away from the stage while one of the buskers unobtrusively slides Norman out of the button coat he has somehow appropriated.

Preparations resume. Dancers in red dresses descend from the top of the frame as they hurry down a spiral staircase. Behind them, in the same shot, several different planes of action fill the screen—performers rushing in opposite directions, scenery moved into position, costume accessories adjusted, another spiral staircase in the far background discharging more entertainers. It is a dynamic deep focus celebration of theater, the same knowing tribute to show people that Cukor will pay in the backstage shots of *Les Girls*, his other 1950s masterwork. A photographer on the side of the frame prompts a subtle match cut to a close-up of multiple cameras popping flashbulbs at Norman and at the viewer. Norman's interview is ending as Cukor tracks forward and to the right to follow his dismissal of the reporters. Norman stands in front of several make-up mirrors, and various fragmented reflections of himself are visible on the glass surfaces. Cukor uses mirror imagery here and throughout the film to reference the various roles and identities that both Norman and Esther will struggle to integrate and keep whole. When Libby tries to prolong the session, Norman erupts again, shouting "Are you trying to stop me?" and shoving Libby into one of the mirrors. Amid breaking glass, Libby falls out of frame right and Norman staggers back toward the stage, smashing cameras and tearing down the makeshift curtains that enclosed the make-up area. It is the first of several occasions where someone will pull away a curtain to reveal a new reality or a different perception of a character. The repeated gesture signifies a narrative that also peels layers to get at the truth of personal and professional relationships.

From the Norman Maine-inspired chaos backstage, we escape into the silent audience for an overhead looking down at the proscenium. An overture begins, the red curtain opens and a cut to a medium shot reveals the Glenn Williams Orchestra rolling out toward the front rows on a moveable stage. In a quick reaction shot, Lola Lavery checks her red program (Haver reports that the program was tested four different times to get the precise color intended) to see why Norman has been bumped.

A side angle of the orchestra and another audience reaction shot are followed by a full frontal long shot of the stage. Esther and two chorus boys stand up from the frame left edge of the orchestra and begin performing "Gotta Have Me Go with You." The choreography is simple but effective. Singing in unison, they dance in and around each other, punctuating the lyrics with arm thrusts and leg slides. Cukor uses a tracking long take, the technique Fred Astaire argued should always be used to best showcase a dance, to cover the performance. Esther's movement increasingly takes her toward stage left, where back in the wings Norman is pushing aside people on his way to the spotlights. Parallel cutting between the two tracking cameras, the one covering Esther and the one following Norman, place the two characters on trajectories that seem destined to intersect. Tableau-like, several ballerinas in pink costumes are stretching before a gauzy light blue curtain, a composition directly influenced by Degas's ballet paintings, *The Dancers* and *The Dancing Class* in particular. Suddenly, the curtain is shredded and Norman bursts through from behind, pulling an overwhelming blaze of red along with him. The color and curtain imagery overlap here to reflect the mood swings and shifting facades inherent in Norman's behavior.

More unsteadily than ever, Norman moves to the very edge of the stage. Various reaction shots signal the impending disaster. Danny looks up from his piano and shoots a troubled glance frame right, frightened faces pull back a curtain (again) to watch Norman's progress, Esther nervously looks to the side. An angled shot from the wings contrasts Esther dancing out front in the light to Norman looming beyond her in the darkness, the audience blissfully unaware of the difference in the two realities. Medium close-ups alternate back and forth between a concerned Esther and a blurry Norman.

Finally Esther, in a foreshadowing of how she will also interrupt her career for Norman in the future, leaves the dance number and moves to the right of the frame. There is a cut to the shadows, where Norman struggles with Esther, physically thrusting her (as he accidentally will do again later in the Academy Award scene) aside. Unable to intervene, the chorus boys and Danny watch in distress. A long shot returns to full stage just as the darkness of screen right is illuminated by an ill-timed spotlight that discloses Esther standing behind Norman and holding onto his waist. While Esther improvises, Cukor adroitly manipulates the pacing to create a suspended pause. The music slows, the singers lower their voices, the audience shifts uncomfortably, and Libby holds his breath. In a long shot from about mid orchestra, Esther fakes a dance in which she rhythmically snaps Norman's arm forward on the beat. Emblematic of her future sacrifices for Norman, Esther literally props him up on stage. As she at-

Esther saves Norman from public embarrassment by incorporating him into the act.

tempts to dance him into the wings, Norman, who has recovered from his fog and is now enjoying himself, pulls her back on to do a quick minstrel shuffle and a hand-clasping, finger-wagging, boogie woogie finale. Libby breathes again, Oliver is relieved, and the audience is delighted. Norman embraces Esther in medium close-up and leads her out for a bow. To the sound of sustained applause, a slow dissolve transitions to backstage after the benefit has ended.

Throughout the Shrine Auditorium show, light and dark figure importantly in the *mise-en-scène*. Cukor often masks part of his widescreen compositions in shadow, drawing comparisons between what is happening there and what is taking place in the illuminated areas. James Bernardoni sees a clash between Esther's aspirations and Norman's nihilism in this element of Cukor's style. "This movement between light and dark," he writes, "is one of the film's important motifs: at various points in the course of the film, Esther is faced with a choice between her career, which is associated (although, as we shall see, the association is not always a straightforward one) with light; and Norman, who is associated with darkness" (page 69). Certainly there are multiple instances, here at the Shrine and later at the after-hours nightclub, where Norman watches Esther from the shadows and then emerges to either interfere (Shrine) or assist (nightclub), but the light-dark contrast seems to be part of a larger dichotomy based on issues of control and perception.

In the full stage long shots where Esther leaves the spotlight to intercept Norman or in the wing angles where Norman stands just beyond the curtain poised to invade Esther's lighted performance space, the point is the simultaneity of the actions. Cukor is showing us a character, usually Esther, suspended between the observed, ordered work before an audience or in front of a camera and the concealed, disordered struggle with personal afflictions that occurs out of public sight. For Cukor, the drama lies in the pressure of living both realities at the same time.

With the show over, the Glenn Williams Orchestra packs up and prepares for its real job—playing at the Ambassador Hotel's Cocoanut Grove. Crossing from frame left, Danny draws aside the curtain of another improvised dressing room and introduces us to the everyday version of Esther wearing street clothes. She is positioned in front of a mirror adjusting her make-up. Still within the same take, Danny takes her hand, and the camera tracks to the right as they hurry around a partition and Esther crouches down to apply lipstick before another mirror that has been leaned against the wall. "I thought he was going to come staggering back on… it's a wonder to me that Mr. Norman Maine is still in pictures," she says to Danny.

A male figure, seen from the knees down, walks in behind the mirrored image of Esther. "It is indeed," replies the unmistakably sensual West Yorkshire voice of James Mason. The blocking here is freighted with meaning. For their first private encounter, Norman and Esther regard each other as fragmented reflections in a looking glass. The sharp angles and truncated lines of vision make communication difficult. Neither character has a complete or precise view of the other. To begin a relationship within an environment where the manufacture and reproduction of images confound self-awareness is to ignore the prescience of one more early warning. Esther stands and Norman walks to the right, looking directly at each other now without a mirrored intermediary. "I ask myself that each morning when I shave," continues Norman. "I ask, 'mirror, mirror on the wall, who's the greatest star of them all?' And do you know what the mirror answers?" Together, Norman and Esther both laughingly respond, "Norman Maine." Norman's self-deprecation and humor begin to counter some of the distaste caused by his bad behavior earlier.

In a three-shot long take, Esther, a possible focus of male conflict, stands between Norman on the left of the frame and Danny on the right. When Norman asks to know his rescuer, Esther gives her real name and Norman chuckles, "You must have been born with that; you couldn't have made it up." Taking Esther's lipstick, Norman turns to the wall behind them and the camera reframes to center itself on the brick surface. He draws a large heart and writes the initials "E.B." and "N.M." in the middle. "To mark the occasion," he explains, "when Esther Blodgett saved Norman Maine from making even more of a fool of himself than usual."

The acknowledgment of his boorishness warms Norman to us ever so slightly more, but not to Danny. When Norman invites them to "take supper" with him, Danny reaches for Esther, says "come on" and turns toward the exit. Close to a rekindled eruption, Norman lashes out and grabs Danny, patting and "testing" his chest just as he did earlier with Libby. In a fairly cogent assessment of alcohol's effect on him, he argues "Don't you try and stop me. I know myself extremely well. I'm just near the fighting stage at the moment. If I don't get my way I begin to break up people and things." Quick once again to defuse the situation, Esther explains the Cocoanut Grove commitment and promises they will get together in the future, once she has laid in a big supply of lipstick. After Esther deflects

Norman's attention to the arrival backstage of Oliver, Libby and Lola, she and Danny make their escape. Lingering for a moment at the stage door, she looks back fondly at Norman. She is wearing a light blue coat and the wall behind her is a reddish pink, the soft colors proving new visual cues to the reduced sense of tension. "You know, drunk or not," she tells Danny, "he's nice. Awful nice." And so the romance begins.

Although not boasting the most sophisticated lyrics Ira Gershwin ever wrote, the "Gotta Have Me Go with You" number sung by Esther tells the story of a budding courtship and, like all the songs in *A Star Is Born*, helps to advance the narrative. The opening lyrics, delivered as Esther and her two partners proceed to center stage, are "What a spot this / Not so hot this / Hey there shy one / Come by my one / Please don't rush off / Want no brush-off."

As lead singer, Esther is the one pushing romance, just as she is later when Norman expresses a reluctance to go beyond simply helping with her career. Interspersed with the iambic dimeter is a chorus that elaborates the come-one: "You wanna have bells that'll ring / You wanna have songs that'll sing / You want your sky a baby blue / You gotta have me go with you."

Norman borrows Esther's lipstick to write their initials on the wall. Danny McGuire (Tommy Noonan) is on the right.

During Norman's interference the second chorus slows down and then Esther incorporates Norman into the act with: "Why the hold out? / Have you sold out? / Time you woke up / Time you spoke up."

The closing words cement the union, showcase Norman and Esther's handshake dance finale, and portend a real future relationship between the two: "You wanna live high on a dime / You wanna have two hearts in rhyme / You gotta have me go with you / All the time."

It is Garland's ability to manipulate a lyric that transforms what would otherwise be a fairly pedestrian production number into something exciting and even suspenseful to watch.

Moss Hart gets right at the Norman-Esther relationship, as well. Scrapping the Grandma Lettie character and the farm family background, Hart concentrates from the beginning on the glittery excitement of Hollywood. His Esther is not a rural dreamer when we first meet her but an accomplished show business professional already rising through the ranks. "With a single stroke Moss eliminated North Dakota and the grandmother, the bus ride [sic] to Hollywood, and most of the more wide-eyed clichés of 1937," writes Steven Bach. "He placed the first song right at the beginning, opening his screenplay (brilliantly shot by Cukor) with Klieg lights raking the sky, limousines discharging precious cargo, and players large and small bumping into each other backstage in the chaos of a benefit at the Shrine Auditorium… Getting rid of North Dakota made Esther the product of no one and nowhere but show business. The role was for and *about* Judy, no longer an ingénue, but a grown-up weighted down by garish personal baggage the world knew too much about" (page 314).

Unlike Janet Gaynor's Esther, Garland's Esther does not first idolize Norman Maine from afar but sees him initially in the most unflattering of close quarters as a deeply troubled and flawed human being. She has no illusions about Hollywood or about Norman Maine.

The Shrine Auditorium sequence launches *A Star Is Born* with an assured mastery of all its component elements. The collaborators, at the top of their games, mesh seamlessly. Script, direction, acting, music, choreography, set design, and cinematography—each succeeds and holds our attention. Running for fifteen minutes and often with real time and screen time coinciding, the Shrine opening has an almost Aristotelian perfection to it. Like Visconti's formal ball in *The Leopard* or Fellini's harem bath fantasy in *8 ½*, it is one of cinema's great protracted, single-event social sequences.

Esther and Danny's getaway dissolves to Norman's bedroom. The camera opens on a close-up of Norman's formal white shirt spread on the floor and tracks slightly to the right as the butler stoops to pick it up along with Norman's pants. Accompanied by a slight camera tilt, the butler looks up toward the bed where Norman is passed out asleep and whispers, "When he goes off like that, he's good for the night, Mr. Libby." The continuing tilt now shows Libby at the head of the bed, frame left, looking down at Norman. Haver reports that the detail "of the actor's tuxedo shirt on the floor, its arms outstretched as if it were floating in the dark" was especially important to Cukor because he intended it as "a subtle bit of symbolism... to try to hint at Maine's fate" (page 161).

The camera tracks in on Libby, who stares disapprovingly at Norman while the butler assures him, "He'll smile in his sleep in a minute like a child." Unimpressed, Libby remarks, "Like a child with a blow torch," capping off another of the film's references to Norman as a spoiled child requiring care. The furnishings in Norman's room, a dark red and black Chinese screen behind the bed and light blue draperies, reference the color scheme of the Shrine sequence and convey a further cooling of the tensions that were on display there. This is one of Cukor's long takes and as Libby walks around the bed and toward the door, the camera tracks left along with him. "Now you understand, 6:00 a.m. sharp, have him dressed and ready," Libby tells the butler before also tossing him Norman's car keys for safe keeping. Libby and the butler exit, the lights are turned out and the off-screen voice of the butler provides an important narrative marker: "He'll sure be surprised when he finds himself on location in the morning."

Visually prominent as Libby circles Norman's bed are the rustling drapes. Wind billowing the curtains of an open window is a leitmotif used often in the film. On one level, it simply animates the *mise-en-scène*, allowing an artificial studio set to appear organically alive. "I don't like doing exteriors on an interior set," Cukor explained in one of his interviews with Gavin Lambert, "but if you keep the air going you can keep the scene alive" (page 40). Beyond the mimetic, however, there is a representational dimension, as well. The wind is emblematic of a restlessness that drives Norman to search for peace and Esther to seek professional success.

Appropriately, Norman's sleep is fitful. The camera tracks in slowly on the bed and the blowing curtains while the underscoring features a soft string arrangement of "Gotta Have Me Go with You." Suddenly, Norman sits bolt upright and the music gets louder. Turning on his beside lamp, he marks time with his finger in an attempt to remember the song and the girl he wanted to take to dinner.

In the first draft of the script, Moss Hart handled this exposition by having Norman talk to himself in a spoken aside, but Heindorf's orchestration works much more effectively. "As he tries to clear his head and think," notes Haver, "the brass jogs his memory by playing the first eight bars of the song, which is then repeated in a minor key by the strings and percussion as the scene segues into the Cocoanut Grove ballroom" (page 199). Norman throws back the bedcovers, and Cukor dissolves to a long shot of the Ambassador Hotel's Wilshire Boulevard entrance and an illuminated sign announcing the Cocoanut Grove appearance of the Glenn Williams Orchestra.

The Grove ballroom scene is another stylistic *tour de force* for Cukor. The camera tracks continuously in a single long take that follows Norman through the nightclub. There are no cuts during the dialogue-intensive three-minute shot, a directorial choice that required careful blocking of actors, props, and camera. Norman descends the steps and walks into a studio set built to resemble the real Cocoanut Grove; the camera dollies laterally alongside him. He skirts the edge of the room, passing in front of a series of palm trees, which intermittently form a visual buffer between him and the camera.

In the middle of the room, people sit at tables or dance, and in the far right background, a band plays underneath a tented canopy. When Norman pauses before a cluster of three intersecting palms, Bruno the maître d' (played by Frank Puglia) enters from screen right to greet him. "There's a little dark girl—sings with the Glenn Williams Orchestra," explains Norman, who has now moved around to the camera side of the trees, by way of inquiry. "The Glenn Williams Orchestra finishes at 1:30 and then the rhumba band takes over," responds Bruno. "They finished about an hour ago."

Turning toward frame left and inspecting the room, Norman casually minimizes his search and states, "The whole thing seems rather silly." He pulls a cigarette from a gold pocket case and Bruno lights it for him. "The bands that play here, the musicians, they go to a little place on Sunset after they finish here," adds Bruno, still trying to be helpful. "Maybe she's there. They're crazy people, Mr. Maine. They blow their heads off here all night and then instead of going to bed they blow their heads off there for themselves for nothing."

During Bruno's speech, Norman has continued his surveillance of the room and its patrons. "Would you like a table, sir?" asks Bruno. Humorously and without the attendant malice of his Shrine comments, Norman replies, "Not unless you wish to rhumba with me, Bruno," the use of "wish" rather than "want" reflecting Norman's as well as Mason's refinement. Norman now circles around to the front of the trees again and begins to prowl the ballroom; Bruno and the camera move with him. Heading screen right, Norman asks, "Is there anyone here I know?" Reduced now to classy flesh peddler and pimp, Bruno points to a table and suggests, "There's a new little girl from Paramount." Both men pass in front of her table, staring hard at the young woman and her older male escort. From a hiding place within another clump of trees, Bruno and Norman consider the options. "She's very pretty, Mr. Maine," tempts Bruno. Peering through the latticed palm trunks, Norman hesitates and remarks, "She's with someone, isn't she?" Aware of all his customers' backstories, Bruno confides, "Only her agent, he'd be glad to leave." It is as if the men are on a sexual safari through the Cocoanut Grove jungle, Bruno playing native guide to Norman's bwana and recommending when to pounce. "Too young," Norman finally decides, "I had a very young week last week."

The camera tracks forward into and around the trees as the hunt again advances screen right. "Anyone else?" asks Norman. "Miss Sheldon," offers Bruno. They gaze out at the dance floor from another tree blind and track the new prey as it rhumbas by them. "No, she hit me over the head with a bottle," demurs Norman. "I remember. It happened right here," recalls Bruno somewhat resignedly, "but I thought everything was all right now." Moving on, Norman explains, "No, they only hit me once." At the far end of the ballroom, Norman stops short and points, "That little girl in the green dress." The camera reframes on a composition showing Bruno on the left edge of the screen, Norman next to him, a palm tree in the middle, and then a table with two boys facing each other and a young woman posed across the top. "No, Mr. Maine," warns Bruno. "Pasadena. Leave it alone." Norman nods, acknowledging the folly of engaging with the reckless offspring of well-connected old money. Unable to deliver any big game, Bruno excuses himself and exits frame right. As Norman turns to the left and retraces his steps through the nightclub, the camera reverse tracks with him. Finally, he reaches the steps and the shot ends, dissolving to the little place on Sunset Boulevard mentioned by Bruno.

Not exactly essential to the narrative, the Cocoanut Grove scene was costly, adding to the always escalating budget, and complicated to film.

Haver details some of the technical challenges: Puglia and Mason "rehearsed the scene while Leavitt and his crew lit the set, which took almost an hour, because the palm trees kept getting in the way of the actors and the camera. Another half hour was spent moving some of the trees, then relighting the set, placing the bit people, rehearsing them in their action, and getting the dancers to stay within camera range as the camera movements were set and the blocking for Mason and Puglia was worked out... The rhumba band had been recruited from the local Zenda ballroom and was playing live music instead of prerecorded as was the usual custom. This led to further complications, as the music tended to drown out the dialogue, so some time was spent getting the band to play down to an acceptable level. By the time more trees had been added, and all had been repainted, the ninety-five extras carefully placed and rehearsed, then more lighting and camera adjustments made and a break taken for lunch, it was three p.m. before Cukor and Leavitt took the first shot" (page 144).

Despite the expense and the trouble, the uninterrupted tracking shot is a pleasure to watch and an insight into additional aspects of Norman's character—his loneliness, his troubled history with women, his weariness, and his impulsiveness. Visually, the deep focus, reframing, and movement are all things that Cukor had been warned not to try with CinemaScope. In an interview with Gene Phillips, the director recalled, "The day I began shooting *A Star Is Born*, the technical people told me that I must forget everything I knew about composing shots, because the new wide screen lens lacked the depth of focus of the ordinary camera lens I was familiar with; and that therefore I must line up the actors right in front of the camera at all times, because anyone placed even a short distance away from the camera would automatically go out of focus. I shot that way for exactly one day; and then I said, 'To hell with it! I can't abandon everything I have ever known about making movies just because of some damned new process.' After that I went ahead and composed each shot precisely the way I always had, and everything worked out alright" (page 172).

Both Ronald Haver and James Bernardoni see a critical swipe at Hollywood in the Cocoanut Grove scene. Social interaction, they argue, is merely the trading of sexual favors in a marketplace controlled by successful male celebrities. Once beyond the sexist, cringe-worthy references to the "little dark girl" and the "new little girl from Paramount," however, there is a humor to the Cocoanut Grove interlude that, when considered along with the stylistically beautiful staging, tends to undercut the harshness of the anti-Hollywood criticism. Indeed, the camerawork brings to mind some of the wilder ideological film criticism of the late 1960s, which affirmed that the tracking shot by its very nature could never be politically incisive since it tended to deepen and mystify the decadent, late capitalistic world it was exploring.

The dissolve to Sunset opens on an exterior of the musicians' after-hours bar. Crew memories and critical commentary refer to the place as the Downbeat Club, but the entrance sign reads "Bleu Bleu." The entrance itself reflects the colors, albeit muted, of the Shrine: a gauzy blue facade on the left, a padded door in the center, and a dim red light and poster boards on the right.

The mellow lighting is reinforced by the hushed opening orchestral notes of "The Man That Got Away." As Norman walks toward the entrance, the camera tracks in behind him. He slowly opens the door giving us a sustained look at cleared tables and empty space. A cut on movement completes Norman's entry from inside, and in medium long shot he steps closer to the bar's small stage area. The carefully arranged composition we see next is from his point of view. In the left foreground, chairs are piled on top of the empty patron tables; behind them is a wooden bar bathed in soft red light. Esther and Danny sit at a piano in the center and close to them are a drummer, a trombonist, and a trumpet player. Framed in a red-lighted doorway on the far right are a bass player and a clarinetist.

Cut back to Norman, who walks forward and quietly takes a seat. A waiter with a tray crosses in front of Norman from the left, and the camera pans and then tracks with him as he walks up among the band members. "Take it, honey. Come on," says Danny, and Esther follows the cue.

The musical number was shot on four different occasions, with various camera formats, blocking, and costumes for Garland each time. A standard widescreen version and a CinemaScope version were done as trials, and the CinemaScope effort emerged as the clear preference. An "improved" CinemaScope rendition was then filmed with less garish lighting, set design adjustments, and blocking in which Esther sang while she moved around the band serving coffee. Later, toward the end of the production, that version was scrapped, and a new staging in which Garland wore a slimmer-fitting Jean Louis dress and delivered just the song and no coffee was completed and selected for the final cut. The time and money were well spent. Garland's "The Man That Got Away" is one of the most brilliant singing performances ever captured in a musical.

After Danny's prompt, Esther stands, walks forward on the stage, and then pivots to face the piano, her back briefly turned to the camera.

Norman watches in wonder as Esther performs.

A cut to a medium shot of Norman shows him watching her intently. The camera returns to Esther and will stay with her in another uninterrupted long take for the entire number. While Esther hums over the orchestral beginning, she waves her hand to beckon the trombonist into frame left, and the trombone's blues-like introduction swells on the soundtrack. Esther sings the first four bars in a low tone that establishes the song's melancholy: "The night is bitter. / The stars have lost their glitter. / The wind grows colder, / And suddenly you're older."

The trombone recedes from the edge of the frame and Esther remains in a two-shot with Danny (which Tommy Noonan almost spoils with his incessant, open-mouthed gum chewing). From the waist up and back against the piano, Esther continues in subdued phrasing to lament, "And all because of the man that got away." The left side of the screen is dominated by the hazy red lighting of the bar, and the right side is an equally hazy blue; cigarette smoke drifts across the stage. With "No more his eager call / The writing's on the wall / The dreams you dreamed have all / Gone astray," Esther strides forward, and the camera tracks out, collecting first the drummer and then a saxophonist on the right corner of the frame.

Simultaneously, the percussion and the bass become more intense and the horns more pronounced. Esther walks left now, picking up the trombone and trumpet players and returning to the piano. With the rising brassiness that Garland better than vocal coach Hugh Martin instinctively knew was the right approach, Esther builds up the drama of the next lyrics, each word crisp, clipped, and booming: "The man that won you / Has gone off and undone you. / The great beginning / Has seen the final inning. / Don't know what happened."

In the first of the song's climaxes ("It's all a crazy game!"), Esther thrusts her arm up and out of the top of the frame and then, during the descent ("No more that all-time thrill/For you've been through the mill"), rapidly sweeps the hair off her forehead in a second trademark Garland gesture.

Like a color guard presentation, the horns and trombone point up at her from the left as Esther does a quick hand dismissal on "Good riddance, good-bye / Every trick of his you're onto" and slides an arm around Danny. For the next emotional high point, Esther rushes forward, slipping out of focus for just a fraction of a second, to sing "But fools will be fools / And where's he gone to?" in a reframed medium close-up. Both arms are dramatically stretched out of the top of the frame.

Swiveling around and looking at each of the band members, she elevates the crescendo on: "The road gets rougher. / It's lonelier and tough-

Judy Garland builds the drama of "The Man That Got Away" with signature emotions and gestures.

er. / With hope you burn up. / Tomorrow he may turn up." Off-screen strings, woodwinds, and brass augment the arrangement. The camera tracks swiftly forward to emphasize Esther as she steps down from the stage and belts: "There's just no letup the live-long night and day."

Entering the frame are the bass player and some additional, previously unseen band members, as well as two women and a man watching from the shadows of screen right. Esther is center frame and the camera tracks in for the overwhelming all-stops-out climax: "Ever since this world began / There is nothing sadder than / A one-man woman looking for / The man that got away."

Garland is full-voiced with a splayed-finger hand grasping the air, and the entire Warner Bros. orchestra is pounding out the final stark phrases. Then, on an extended diminuendo and circled with horns and trombones on the sides and even across the front of her, Esther repeats the final phrase, sits down at a table, brushes her forehead again, and quietly ends the song with a satisfied little laugh.

Appropriately, there is a cut to Norman, who is overwhelmed by the performance. Just like that, Hart and Cukor have solved one of the most glaring weaknesses that plagued both of *A Star Is Born*'s predecessors.

We experience along with Norman the incredible talent destined to make Esther a star. We understand why Norman immediately recognizes her potential. With Constance Bennett and Janet Gaynor, we hesitatingly take the script's word for it. With Garland, we enthusiastically believe it.

"The Man That Got Away" offers insight into what made Garland such a legendary entertainer. While her final film, *I Could Go on Singing* (1963, United Artists, directed by Ronald Neame), particularly the "By Myself" and "Hello Bluebird" numbers, best captures her allure as a concert performer and her alchemy with a hand microphone, *A Star Is Born*'s Downbeat Club number also helps to illustrate why she was a great singer's singer. Like Frank Sinatra and José José, she was able to perfectly enunciate and read a lyric, telling its story and acting its drama. She could, therefore, be incredibly personal and intimate with an audience. Like Ethel Merman and Shirley Bassey, Garland could also belt a song at full force and volume, punctuating the words with emotional intensity.

Assistant director Earl Bellamy referred to this power in his recollection of the grueling multiple takes that Cukor required of her for "The Man That Got Away": "We had the playback machine there with the recording of the song; and, you know, most singers just mouth to the play-

Cukor's extended single take is packed with visual detail.

back. Not Judy. When she sang to a playback, you couldn't hear anything. That playback was turned on to its peak, but you could hear Judy above it. She was unbelievable when she sang to a playback. She wanted me to start it full blast and then she started singing and she topped it… she went to her dressing room, and we waited about fifteen minutes, and she came back fine and did the whole thing again. Each time she was as tremendous as she ever was" (Haver, page 130).

On stage, in concert, Garland reached the upper balcony as effectively as the front rows, without the aid of audio compression technology, such as Dolby, or large-screen television, such as Jumbotron. Striding onto and commanding a stage like a five foot Olympian, microphone cord slung over a shoulder and hand perched on hip or jabbing into the spotlight, she could convey, in writer John Fricke's words, "the heartrending pathos of human existence" as well as "the determination to rise above and carry on…" (page 8). To have been lucky enough to have seen Judy Garland live in concert is to never forget the experience.

It is Cukor's stylistic daringness, his consistent willingness to move the camera, push the depth of field, and crop the elongated frame, that communicates the magic of the Esther/Garland performance and the importance of the "The Man That Got Away" segment to the narrative. Esther's special camaraderie with the band members surfaces as she moves easily among them and the tracking camera establishes spatial connection between her and the various instruments and players. That Esther is the focus of their efforts, the would-be star deserving of attention, is certified by the way in which the camera reframes to keep her in the center of the composition. The explosive dynamism of Esther's performance is felt viscerally when she bursts the top of the frame with her outstretched arms or rushes into close-up before the camera has a chance to pull back.

Again, Cukor's references are painterly. "You're used to seeing the whole of a thing—then suddenly you see a section, arbitrarily, not composed," he explained to interviewer Richard Overstreet in an analysis of the influence David's *Sacre de Napoléon* had on him. "Just a section of something cut off. In the David painting you see a head to one side, bits of other heads cut off here and there when the detail is reproduced in the art book. And I thought why not do that in a movie? We made use of this especially when Judy Garland sang "The Man That Got Away" (pages 28-29).

By the end of the number, Esther has been completely reintegrated into the performing space and almost picture-framed by the instruments that surround her. Bernardoni sees this as Esther's elevation in importance: "But for all of the meaning conveyed by the camera's tracking back, it is its tracking in at the song's conclusion for a rather close shot of Esther and the band that is the single most meaningful camera movement of the sequence, the one that gives the sequence its remarkable resonance. Because the movement results in a shot very similar to the initial shot of the sequence, it suggests the sense of closure, the feeling of wholeness that every true star performance creates. Because the shot is slightly closer than the initial medium shot, the movement also suggest the prominence Esther has earned through her performance and the closer, even somewhat oppressive, scrutiny she is likely to be subjected to in the future"(page 73).

The reaction shots of Norman that bookend Esther's performance remind us of the key role he will play in her career (the song's reference to a "one-man woman" also suggests how influential he will be). Emerging from the shadows to Danny's dismay and Esther's surprise, Norman searches for a way to articulate his enthusiasm. "Do you always sing like that?" he asks Esther. In the face of her confusion, he continues, "I never heard anybody sing just the way you do." Unable to make himself heard over the restarted jamming of the band, he takes her hand and leads her to a serving station just off the kitchen.

The original script had Norman delivering his opinions in a long conversation played across a bar table from Esther, but Cukor restages the action as a running dialogue that extends over multiple sets within the Downbeat Club. Besides providing more visual interest, the change also heightens Norman's excitement. He tries to explain his feelings through the first of some fashionable Hemingwayesque references: "Did you ever go fishing? Do you like prizefighting? Did you ever watch a great fighter?" Cukor's "art boys" have painted the walls light blue and against that subdued background, Norman says, "I'm trying to tell you how you sing."

Still bewildered, Esther asks, "Do you mean like a prizefighter or a fish?" Norman's response comes in three sections. He starts by remarking "Look here" as he opens the door to the kitchen, continues with "there's a certain pleasure that you get" over the banging of pots and pans, and finishes outside the rear exit with "certain jabs of pleasure when a swordfish takes a hook or when you watch a great fighter getting ready for the kill." Each segment of conversation is filmed as a two-shot, Norman always on the left of the frame and Esther on the right. The camera is stationary with Cukor careful to keep all attention on Moss Hart's words—a respect that the director famously displayed toward the writers of all his pictures. "You don't understand a word I'm saying, do you?" asks Norman, and Esther, who recognizes the Hemingway allusions, answers, "No, not yet, but why don't you try bullfights."

Acknowledging the combination of comic banter and earnest seriousness that will characterize their relationship from here on, Norman responds, "You're joking, but that's exactly what I mean. If you'd never seen a bullfight in your life, you'd know a great bullfighter the moment he stepped into the ring." Then, discussing the graceful way a bullfighter moves, he adds, "or a dancer—you don't have to know about the ballet." It all comes down, he concludes, to "a little bell that rings inside your head, that little jolt of pleasure." Finally, standing alongside his white convertible in that same left to right two-shot configuration, he tells Esther "You're a great singer. Hasn't anyone told you that before?"

Astonished at the praise, Esther jokes that maybe Norman is not as sober as they both thought, but he presses on, schooling Esther in a bit of the English theater history that Cukor himself loved so dearly. Her talent, he explains, is "that little something extra that Ellen Terry talked about… She said that's what star quality was. That little something extra. Well, you've got it." Speaking in front of a rear projection that shows a commercial Los Angeles street at night, he tells her she is wasting her time with the band. "I'm doing just fine, Mr. Maine," she counters, asserting how hard she has worked to get the featured singer job.

It is time for the next step, he decides, and then peppers her with a rapid barrage of questions: where is she from, when did she start singing, does she have a family, is she married? Given little chance to react, Esther barely can squeeze out a confused "no," presumably in response to the last two questions. Unattached and on her own, she is pure show business (a point which will be amplified in the "Born in a Trunk" number) and still searching (the "Someone at Last" parody) for connection to family or romance.

As if summoned by Norman's disregard of the band, Danny appears to tell Esther that everyone is leaving. Taking charge of her transportation just as he will her career, Norman guides her into the car and says, "I'll see that Esther gets home." All that the out-gunned Danny can do is remind Esther that the touring bus departs in the morning at 6:00, the same time that Norman is scheduled to leave for location shooting.

The rear projection used for the car ride is imperfect but not distracting. Unsettled by Norman's advice, Esther jokes that she would like to calm down by washing her hair. "When anything happens to me, good or bad," she elaborates, "I make straight for the shampoo bottle," dropping an inadvertent reference to Norman's reliance on a different kind of bottle.

"I understand that perfectly," he responds. "With me it's golf balls. If I'm happy or if I'm miserable, I putt golf balls around the livingroom. It makes perfect sense." Both activities will later be used as visual shorthand to signal emotional turmoil within the characters. Already there is an easy compatibility between Esther and Norman similar to that which we previously saw between Esther and Danny. It helps in softening our suspicion of Norman. So comfortable is Esther that she tells Norman about joining the band, going out on the road, waiting tables. "Wow, that was a low point... I'll never forget it and I'll never, ever do that again, no matter what," she declares, even more significantly than she intends.

At one point, Esther leans back in the seat and admits, "I somehow feel most alive when I'm singing." The comment is revealing. Esther sees herself, before anything else, as a performer capable of delivering the goods no matter how difficult the circumstance. She has already proven that at the Shrine and will again later at the film studio. Unlike the characters in a conventional musical, Esther does not burst into songs that are cued by everyday activities; every one of her numbers is a staged performance presented to an audience or a camera. Sometimes the audience consists solely of Norman, who also sees her primarily as a performer, a creature of show business. It is what he appreciates and loves about her, but it is a limited vision as well. Esther's need for more than just career support is something that Norman is unable to either recognize or provide.

Esther is staying at the Oleander Arms, the same name as the boardinghouse in the 1937 *A Star Is Born*. The actual apartment building, located at the corner of Fountain Avenue and Crescent Heights Boulevard in Hollywood, is seen briefly in some awkwardly matched rear projection footage. "Is there more?" Norman asks as the car pulls up to the entrance. "A whole scrapbook full. Come in," invites Esther.

A dissolve transitions to a two-shot of Esther watching Norman look at her clippings. The door to her room is open, the curtains are billowing at the window and a sprinkler is watering the lawn outside—Cukor doing his best to "blow some air" through the studio set. "What now?" asks Norman concerning Esther's ambitions. "Now I need just a little luck," she tells him. Her goal is to become a recording artist. "Someday," after discovering her singing with the band, "a big record agent will let me make a record, and it'll become a hit and I'll be made." Although she quickly dismisses the idea ("But that'll never happen"), Norman is serious about it and about her. The plan could very likely happen, he concludes, but "the dream isn't big enough."

Leaving the confined room and its narrow ambitions, they walk outside. The lights of Hollywood and its endless possibilities sparkle in the distance. "Quit, don't go," Norman says abruptly. "Let me see what I can do for you at the studio. I'll talk to Oliver Niles right away." Esther is reluctant, arguing that it has taken a lot of effort to get the Glenn Williams gig. "That's right, but it's served its purpose," Norman assures her.

Sitting Esther down next to a fountain in the courtyard, he shares some professional insight: "A career is a curious thing. Talent isn't always enough. You need a sense of timing—an eye for seeing the turning point, of recognizing the big chance when it comes along and grabbing it. A career can rest on a trifle, like us sitting here tonight. Or it can turn on somebody seeing something in you that nobody else ever saw and saying, 'You're better than that, you're better than you know. Don't settle for the little dream. Go on to the big one.'" It is a remarkable speech—conversational, cadenced, inspirational—and Mason gets the rhythm and the rise of it just right. "What makes you so sure?" asks Esther. "I heard you sing," replies Norman matter-of-factly. "But you know yourself, don't you?" he continues. "You just needed somebody to tell you."

Norman will never stop believing in Esther or working to advance her career. He is the Pygmalion who fires the ambition of Esther's Galatea. He is the mentor who gives her a new, more dynamic way of looking at herself. This Norman—responsive, sympathetic, generous, encouraging—is far different from the rude brawler who disrupted the Shrine Auditorium. This Norman is someone the audience can care about. "Don't ever forget how good you are," he advises, telling Esther to sleep on his suggestion and decide in the morning. On his way out, Norman walks around the fountain and stops briefly by its tiled pool, the association of Norman with water another one of Cukor's symbolic references to Norman's fate. Just before he exits, Norman turns around and calls Esther back out of her room. "Hey," he says, echoing Lowell Sherman and Fredric March before him, "I just want to take another look at you." Mason gazes wistfully toward screen left and, in a half wave/ half brush gesture, watches as Esther, the wind blowing her hair, re-enters the apartment.

Esther standing in the doorway dissolves to Norman sitting on the edge of his bed. He is pouring a drink and humming "The Man That Got Away" while the wind ruffles the curtains behind him. True to his word, he has decided to call Oliver about the screen test. Awakened from a deep sleep, Oliver reacts first by asking, "Are you in jail? What have you done?" We hear Norman's muffled voice on the other end of the line as Bickford, like Menjou, sleepily listens to Norman's familiar story and agrees to his requests. In a cut back to Norman's bedroom, he says "Thanks, Oliver. You go back to bed because I want you to be nice and fresh in the morning when I bring her around" and hangs up the phone. Norman returns to humming and to drinking. As Ronald Haver astutely observes, "he absently hums the opening bars of the song; then he stops and begins to think about Esther, and the cello picks up the phrase; as Norman pours himself a drink, a clarinet plays an ascending figure; then the orchestra continues to develop the melody while he ponders the future of all this" (pages 199-200). That future seems clouded by Norman's steady bedside drinking and his earlier, half-humorous "you better make the most of it" comment to Esther about his sober lucidity.

In the most direct thematic link yet between the two characters, the wind blowing strongly through Norman's window cuts to the breeze tugging at Esther's curtains, and the harp which began "The night is bitter/ The stars have lost their glitter" in Norman's room climaxes it in Esther's. Like Norman, Esther is awake and restless. She goes upstairs to talk with Danny, and we see her cross the hallway through the open window of his own bedroom. Just as Norman disrupted Oliver's sleep, she wakens Danny and abruptly tells him, "I'm quitting the band." After lighting a cigarette for him, she stands with her back to Danny and adds, "Norman Maine is going to get me a screen test." The staging is significant; Esther chooses not to face Danny and see in him a duplication of her own uncertainty. Danny is horrified by the news. "Have you been drinking with him?" he demands. "He was making a conventional pass." Esther now sits on the edge of Danny's bed in the left half of the frame; a large mirror reflecting them fills the right half. In another of the mirror motif references to image and identity, Esther insists, "He gave me a look at myself I never had before." The moment is quiet and confidential. Esther, in light pink pajamas, is resolved and Danny, in light blue ones, is resigned.

The camera tracks with Esther as she moves to the doorway. Pausing there, she is framed in the first reddish pink rays of the breaking dawn, which concludes a long, eventful night and heralds a new beginning for Esther. "Oh you fool, you fool," warns Danny while Esther (photographed again through Danny's window) descends the stairs and wonders, "You think so? Then why do I feel like this?" A dissolve transitions to the band bus leaving the Oleander Arms minus Esther a little later in the morning.

The next several scenes constitute an entire editing reel that was chopped from the film after its premiere and has still not been recovered to this day. For the 1983 restoration, Ronald Haver found a complete magnetic master soundtrack but not all of the corresponding visuals. To cover the gaps, he used alternate takes, footage culled from the Warner Bros. stock library, and still photos. The finished product, although a bit uneven in pacing, gives the film back its narrative integrity.

Esther strikes out on her own and loses contact with Norman. Both characters become more fully developed and even somewhat more credible. Still photos of Danny and Esther are accompanied by their farewells and Danny's reminder, "Don't forget who makes the best vocal arrangements for you." Footage of the Glenn Williams Orchestra bus pulling away dissolves to a close-up photo of Norman. In stills, we see Norman, passed out from his post-phone calls drinking, loaded into the back seat of a studio sedan. A critical expository conversation between the driver and Norman's butler reveals that for the next six weeks he will be on location at sea surrounded, they laugh, by the one thing he most hates—water. Another piece of library footage shows the car exiting Norman's curved driveway.

This departure, like the orchestra's, is followed by a dissolve to another still close-up. Esther waits in the Oleander Arms and washes her hair in the stress reduction ritual she mentioned to Norman the previous evening. Photos of Esther shampooing and sunning on the terrace are intercut with close-ups of a phone that does not ring. A swelling reprisal of "The Man That Got Away" on the soundtrack comments subtly on Norman's absence from the scene and Esther's possible status as a "one-man woman looking for the man that got away."

A couple of pieces of more complete and sustained footage show Norman at work on his "sea epic." In an extreme long shot, Norman is plucked from the ocean and hauled into a life raft, which slowly draws closer to the camera. Aboard a larger boat, the director and photography unit film his approach, signaling a successful take and preparing for the next set-up. During a non-synchronous voice-over matched to photos of actor and crew, Norman directs his assistant Eddie to keep searching Hollywood courtyard apartments to find Esther. A two-shot still photo of Oliver and Libby is held for several seconds as Oliver takes a call from the director and learns that the film is behind schedule because Norman cannot work. Wondering, as we are, if Norman is drunk, Oliver is told that instead he is sick. "Bad case of the flu," Oliver relays to Libby, "103° temperature, kept him in the water too long." Unmoved, Libby replies, "Water *would* have a bad effect on him."

Many of the alternate takes that Haver found are entrances and exits, "neutral" shots of vehicles or characters photographed from the back.

A still from lost footage shows Norman on location at sea and directing an assistant to keep searching for Esther.

Destined to be filed and labeled as library footage, they cover transitions as Esther and Norman move in or out of a specific geographic location. And so, after a day of job hunting, Esther trudges up the steps of a run-down house called the Hotel Lancaster and enters the front door. It's a long shot from the street and, minus the "Gotta Have Me Go with You" reference on the soundtrack and any recognition of Garland's figure, could just conceivably have been used as a brief establishing shot in some Warner Bros. police procedural.

    Two photos introduce an intact and intricate comic scene previously thought to have been lost. The landlady, in close-up, informs Esther that someone called about a job, and Esther, at the wall phone, thanks a Mr. Blake and agrees to see him the following morning. Cut to a two-shot of Esther in business dress and hat standing on screen right and staring at a marionette dressed like a combination of Carmen Miranda and a Havana showgirl. She sings, "It's very nice, it's a bargain at double de price" in calypso style as the marionette lip synchs and dances around the miniature stage.

There is a cutaway to the puppeteers manipulating strings on top of the stage, a burst of smoke transition to a long shot of the set, and then a close-up of the marionette singing. Esther is there to shoot a television commercial for "Trinidad Cocoanut Oil Shampoo," a doubly ironic reference to both her tension relief routine and her last place of employment. A tightly composed medium shot of the marionette and Esther on opposite sides of the frame, the puppeteers at the top, the camera in left foreground, and the lighting equipment to the right reveals the considerable care devoted to the filming. For Cukor, another backstage peek at the bustle of show business but this one a slightly satirical gaze at the tawdriness of a new medium competing with his own cherished world of motion pictures.

In the scene's climax, the camera tracks in on the stage as Esther belts out "Take my advice, it's a bargain at double de price," holding the last notes in a prolonged, full-voiced crescendo. Always the performer, Esther gives the crass lyric a power that speaks more to her own longing than to the marketplace.

Trinidad Shampoo does not immediately catapult Esther to stardom because the next photo shows Danny in a hotel phone booth telling Esther, "I squared it with Williams. He'll take you back." Esther puts up a brave front and says she can't possibly leave, but the camera widens out from her still photo close-up to reveal her dressed as a carhop. Like Constance Bennett's Mary Evans and Janet Gaynor's Esther Blodgett before her, she is doing the one job she swore she would never again accept—serving food. Cukor is once more on location, using Robert's Drive-In, which was situated then at Sunset and Cahuenga, for Esther's workplace. As with the Lancaster Hotel, there is a gritty working class feel to the surroundings. It is not Cukor's usual milieu, but he shoots in close with available lighting and conveys a realistic, semi-documentary view of Hollywood to balance the glitzy premieres and fancy mansions. In the surviving footage, the camera tracks with Esther as she serves a tray and then turns to the driver of a convertible to take his order. "What's good to eat?" asks the balding, middle-aged man. "Well," explains Esther, "we have cheeseburgers, lobster burgers, nut burgers, banana burgers, tuna burgers, and our own special super duper super burger." Basically anything, "all burgered up," is available. Similar in tone to the shampoo commercial, the drive-in scene is Hart and Cukor's commentary on the selling of America, their satirical send-up of the nation's mid-century culture of consumerism.

Back from his location shooting, Norman has found the Oleander Arms, but the landlady has no idea where Esther is. Reacting to a still photo of the apartment's front sign, he complains, "Oleander Arms! No wonder I couldn't remember. Why couldn't you call it something sensible?" Over footage of his convertible pulling away from the curb, his voice is heard muttering, "I bet you've never seen an oleander in your life."

Another series of photos follows in which Norman lies on a couch discussing mink coats and trips to Honolulu with Lola. Intercut with the stills is footage of the Trinidad marionette on television singing about

In a piece of recovered footage shot on location, Esther works as a carhop.

shampoo with Esther's voice. "That singing?" questions Norman and a dissolve takes us to his silver white convertible in motion again. The hand of the stock library editor is clearly evident; each time Norman's face is about to appear, the footage is interrupted. We see the car on the street, arriving at the Lancaster, parked at the curb, surrounded by curious children. We see Norman, from behind, climbing the stairs just as Esther did. There are stills of Esther's empty room, of Norman knocking on the door and of Esther drying her hair (again) on the roof. Noise from the kids honking Norman's horn draws Esther's attention, and she calls excitedly down to Norman. An adeptly manipulated photo of the hotel exterior reconnects them spatially as the camera tilts up from Norman on the steps past two neighbors on a balcony and finally to Esther at the edge of the roof. The remainder of the scene plays out in close-up photos atop the Hotel Lancaster. "I got shanghaied away," says Norman. "I tried. Believe me, I tried." The apology and embraces resolve a period of alienated labor for both characters—Esther's waitressing and voice work and Norman's appearance in a routine adventure picture.

On the roof of the hotel, they have returned to the same emotional place they were the night of the Shrine Auditorium and Downbeat Club encounters. Norman is taking charge and giving advice while Esther follows along in admiration. "You look like you could stand a good dinner," he observes. "Let's drive down to the beach and stop off for a hamburger," he suggests as she laughs in private appreciation of the irony. There is a certain crude logic in Warners' decision to hack out everything in between. Norman is still poised to help begin her career at Oliver's studio. What would be missing, of course, is her determination, his anguish, the cultural satire, and the realistic location shooting in blue-collar Hollywood.

The first shot of the untouched footage that follows is an exterior establishing shot of the Oliver Niles Studio. Esther's subsequent experience inside is staged as if she is Alice sliding through the looking glass. An overhead shot has her bundled up in front of a make-up station being scrutinized by three men in lab coats and glasses. Framed on all sides by bright lights and mirrors, the set has the cold, antiseptic feel of an operating room. Shooting into a mirror within a mirror, the camera again confounds the observer and the observed. Through the various reflections, we watch the make-up artists examine Esther, who in turn watches them with fear and anxiety. Sightlines intersect each other in the mirrors. "It's the nose," one of the technicians declares abruptly. "The nose is the problem." His colleague suggests, "Maybe a corrective in the nostril." When

Esther murmurs an objection, she is silenced immediately: "Please, little lady, Mr. Ettinger is thinking. 6:00 in the morning. Just about time for one of his miracles."

The camera tracks backward to frame the tableau in one of the film's "loaded" widescreen compositions. The men huddle on the left of the screen behind a glass divider; mirrors, lights and equipment fill the middle; Esther sits in the make-up chair on the right. In patronizing language almost identical to that directed at Janet Gaynor, one of the make-up guys proposes, "You think maybe the Dietrich eyebrow?" Esther listens in close-up and tentatively arches her brow. "Suppose we try the Crawford mouth to take the attention away from the nose," comes another suggestion.

The factory model notion that stars can be replicated and that defective products can be patched up with supplementary brand name features has direct parallels to MGM's own efforts to transform plump little Frances Gumm into slender and vibrant Judy Garland. "My little hunchback," Louis B. Mayer once famously referred to her in front of a group of important studio visitors.

Discussing the ontology of Hollywood stardom, Susan Hayward writes, "Stars are constructed by the film industry, but stars (although not all) also have a role in their own construction, participate in their own myth-making" (page 339). Thus, Esther agrees to sit still for the make-up experts, to become the empty canvas on which they will design a new yet familiar star in line with the acceptable norms that define female beauty in the developed western world. As a capital asset, she will be fashioned according to specifications ("the Dietrich eyebrow" and "the Crawford mouth") that the studio believes will best sell product. "Stars are somehow baroque in their image-construction," continues Hayward, "since it is so predominantly about illusionism, about 'putting there' what in fact isn't there... The look that has been constructed of them that is up there for all to perceive is also an appearance, a carefully manufactured appearance (of flawless beauty, of rugged handsomeness, for example)" (pages 339-40). The wig, the putty, and the make-up create a semblance of Esther, a fusion of her image with that of some ideal female star.

Norman at first does not recognize the new creation. Passing her on the exterior second floor corridor of the make-up building, he ignores her greeting and says, "Sorry, honey, I'm late for an appointment." Dressed in a gaudy pink gown, she is wearing a strawberry-blond wig and several layers of foundation, filler, powder, and rouge. She calls his name twice and, as he disappears into the make-up rooms, he adds, "Catch me in the commissary." The well-acted double-take is another example of how often Cukor's staging decisions maximize the spatial dynamics of what could otherwise be just a standard piece of physical business.

Reappearing from the doorway, Norman stares carefully and incredulously at Esther. As he approaches her, the camera tracks slowly forward toward him. "Oh no," he laughs, "oh no." He gazes gobsmacked while she protests, "I don't think that's very nice." Norman has to turn away and steady himself from the laughter. "I've been sitting in that chair since 6:00 this morning," she declares. In a camp rejoinder that never fails to amuse gay audiences, he remarks, "You sat an hour too long, honey."

Norman drives Esther to his studio bungalow to repair the damage. Standing around outside is a group of red-uniformed British palace guard extras, reminding us that the illusions here are pervasive and providing Cukor another opportunity to use his favorite color. Inside, Norman places Esther in front of his dressing room mirror; she looks directly at the camera. "Is that you?" he asks, knocking gently against her elongated nose. She shakes her head. "Off it comes," he replies as he removes a strip of putty. Because she has bought into the studio's values, she worries, "My eyes are all wrong, my ears are too big, and I've got no chin." Norman, however, has seen the manufactured knock-offs come and go and shares that Ellen Terry belief in the "something extra." He knows, as Susan Hayward further asserts, that "stars also possess markers of their own authenticity, and as such are involved in their own mythification" (page 339).

Believing as he does in her innate talent, he wants her to look as genuine (itself an illusion) as possible. "But Mr. Maine," she protests, and he answers, "I think at this critical moment you might call me Norman," reminding us of how chastely formal their relationship has been up to this point. He takes the cold cream and smears it over her face to remove the studio handicraft. Once again we see how directly he is involved in her "birth" as a star, how pivotal a role he plays in her creation. "What does it matter how well I sing if my face is so awful?" she asks in one last poignant example of the damage the studio has caused to her (and Garland's) self-image. "Your face is just dandy," he argues.

A dissolve transitions to a shot of the mirror where Norman is powdering the face of a re-emergent and attractive Esther. The camera tracks in to a close two-shot of the couple admiring the finished product; a soft reprise of "The Man That Got Away" commences on the soundtrack. The slightly dreamlike effect is similar to Jimmy Stewart's transformation of

Judy Barton into Madeleine Elster in *Vertigo* and the film's most overt reference yet to the Pygmalion/Galatea motif. "Once more unto the breach, dear friends, once more," Norman says, quoting Shakespeare just as he did backstage at the Shrine with *Richard III*'s "my kingdom for a horse" speech. She suddenly has been hit with a case of stage fright over the screen test she is about to film, and he tells her that it happens to everyone. "Forget the cameras," he advises her. "It's 3:00 at the Downbeat Club and you're singing for the boys in the band and yourself, mainly yourself." And if that doesn't work, he says to lighten the mood, "think of a man sitting in a car and eating a nutburger."

The scene fades to black as Esther bursts out laughing and Norman accompanies her to the door. We don't see her screen test, but unlike with Janet Gaynor's, we don't need to see it. We have already watched her perform a thrilling version of "The Man That Got Away" and we know that she possesses extraordinary talent deserving of stardom.

There is a cut to Esther in a red dress and white hat walking through the studio lot. Passing through a turnstile, she crosses in front of a glass framed photo of Norman and climbs a staircase to the publicity depart-

Norman returns Esther to a more natural "look" and assesses the result in another of the film's mirror scenes.

ment, where she is received with polite disregard. In the considerable time and detail he devotes to the PR department sequence, Cukor both expands the insider's view of a working movie studio and also exposes the assembly line protocol reserved for marginal contract players, especially those recommended by Norman. "I'm Esther Blodgett," announces Esther hopefully, and one of the two female publicists in charge replies,

Esther is about to enter Wonderland.

"I expected a blonde; I don't know why." Dressed in the severe two-piece black and grey business suits usually selected for professional women in 1950s' "office" films, such as *Executive Suite* and *Desk Set*, the women are friendly yet preoccupied with layouts and photo proofs. "Come along, dear. Glad to have you with us," says the more senior publicist in a ritual salutation that will be used several times during Esther's visit. Another repeated joke is Esther's continually ignored offer to display the personal scrapbook she has brought along with her. "Take care of this for me, will you," instructs the supervisor to one of her assistants. "New contract player—Norman Maine," she adds meaningfully. Also assuring Esther how happy she is to have her aboard, the assistant takes her to meet department head Matt Libby.

They enter a photography gallery, where a publicity shoot is taking place. A glamorous model (probably another starlet) poses on a chaise lounge against a background of pink and red fabric and lighting scaffolds. She occupies the left half of the frame with Esther and the publicity assistant crowded into the right corner. There, in the same shot, are three versions of the American woman as depicted in Hollywood films of the 1940s and 1950s: the exotic femme fatale, the asexual career professional, and the gifted girl next door. Unintentionally revealing is the fact that their roles and attributes are all being manipulated by the men who literally are behind the camera.

"Why don't you go in and see Mr. Libby?" suggests the assistant, and Esther starts to make her way through the set. "Get out of the way," shouts the photographer as she gets tangled in some prop white birds dangling from the ceiling. "Leave them alone. It's all right. Get out of the way," he continues until Esther finds another of Wonderland's doors and spills into Libby's office. She finds herself standing beside a huge black and white triptych of the studio's reigning movie queens. One looks like Dietrich, one like Betty Grable, and one like Ava Gardner. Again, the references to Judy Garland's own personal experiences at MGM, where she often felt overshadowed by designated screen sirens like Lana Turner and Hedy Lamarr, are unavoidable. As expected, Libby says, "Glad to have you with us," and Esther wittily replies, "It certainly is a thrill to be here." Even that line doesn't get his attention. Libby sits on the edge of his desk, thumbing through files until, as a kind of afterthought, he suggests, "Would you care to say hello to the big boss? That's the usual procedure." Despite the less than subtle remarks about the standard treatment given Norman Maine referrals, Esther cheerfully agrees to be shuffled along once again. "Come on, I'll take you over to him. May be the only chance you'll get to meet him," he declares. They exit through a hidden door at the opposite end of the triptych and cross a catwalk suspended above two adjoining buildings. Unnerved by the height, Esther hurries after Libby.

Cut to a darkened projection room where a Western is screening at the left of the frame; Libby and Esther enter through a pool of light in the right background. Almost every film about Hollywood has this: the iconic projection room scene. Not only does the imagery (flickering light, cigarette smoke, note-taking secretary) strengthen the mimetic illusion of a real studio in operation, but so also does the narrative moment provide an opportunity for the writer/director to comment on issues of production and identity. There is almost always the implicit respect for the filmmaking process itself that we have seen in all the insider Hollywood pictures. Often, when actors are watching their own rushes, there is also the phenomenon of the subject regarding self as object, resulting in some combination of pleasure, displeasure, or instructive critique. In this case, as we will see, there is a cautionary note about the potential loss of identity. Informed that Libby has brought "the one Mr. Maine arranged the test for, you remember," Oliver Niles turns on a desk lamp to inspect Esther and says, "Nice to see you, dear. Glad to have you with us." Disoriented by the darkness and her journey through the maze, Esther stumbles into the projection beam and remains momentarily frozen there as fragmented images flash across her face. In a stark visual metaphor for the dissolution of self that Esther has endured throughout her introduction to the studio, she seems almost trapped in a close-up of competing identities.

"For one prolonged moment," writes James Bernardoni, "Esther seems lost in the film Niles is watching, just as she is lost in the darkness of the screening room. The suggestion embedded in Cukor's *mise-en-scène* is that at the same time Esther is drawing closer to her formal birth as a star, she is moving toward the loss of her sense of herself as something other than a figure projected on a screen" (page 80).

Finally noticing her discomfort, Oliver directs Libby to "...show Miss, uh, how to get out of here." After crossing and re-crossing the screen, Libby grabs Esther's hand and deposits her outside the projection room. When he belatedly learns her name, he tells her not to worry because the studio will have a new one for her within a week.

Descending the steps, she discovers that she is on a staircase that intersects in a "V" with the same one she first climbed to get to the publicity department. She disappeared into one rabbit hole only to emerge from

A Star Is Born (1954) • 167

Esther and Libby traverse an elevated maze at the studio.

another one right next to it. Looking around in amazement, Esther walks past Norman's photo and takes the exit, only to find herself stuck in the turnstile. The camera tracks in and fades to black.

Comic and painful as they simultaneously are to watch, there is a contextual irony to the scenes of Esther's studio initiation. Already by 1953, the traditional star-centered studio system was breaking apart. No longer would young performers sign on as contract players to be groomed over several years into starring roles. The new order of things would be fresh discoveries or veteran stars making deals for independent projects.

Eventually, Esther is assigned a picture at the studio. Her appearance in that production allows Cukor to further reveal professional tricks of the trade and to stage another of the expensive sight gags which helped to swell the film's budget. The scene opens on a studio train station set with crew members rushing about to finalize preparations. Lateral and forward tracking shots follow the activity as equipment and personnel pass in front of the camera. A deep focus cover shot includes technicians in the foreground, a camera boom in the middle, and moveable lights in the far background. "Esther, waiting for you on the set," calls an assistant, and Esther in a gray skirt, gray short-sleeved sweater, and apricot scarf climbs

Esther momentarily loses her sense of self amid the reflected images of the projection room.

portable steps to a cutaway train car hung with fake icicles. Wardrobe women slide her into a fur coat and the director tells her, "Its farewell, Esther, so give it everything you've got."

We then see the filmic illusion assembled sequentially as it is called out by the assistant director. "Here we go, hit your lights," and there is a cut to various shots of the set lights flashing to life. "Hit your wind," and a large industrial fan is started. "Hit your snow," and crew members above and in front of the train cutaway toss artificial flakes into the flow of air. "Hit your steam," and a hand-held fogging device simulates the engine exhaust.

Cukor's real camera tracks forward toward the set as the fake camera tracks laterally up to the open train window from which Esther is waving a white lace handkerchief. The film's subtextual interplay between reality and illusion plays out as the two different cameras circle each other. The working camera, which has shifted to Esther's point of view from inside the train car, then captures the prop camera as it tracks forward to the window.

"We're getting her face, we saw her face" shouts a camera assistant. "We saw your face" is echoed several different times around the set. It seems that Esther, who was wanted as a hand model only, inadvertently thrust her face into camera range. While she apologizes humbly, the director instructs her once again, "Just the arm and hand. I don't want to see your face."

In a complicated final shot that emphasizes the boundary between the cinematic apparatus and the *mise-en-scène*, Cukor's camera cranes up and away from Esther's waving hand and stops at the side edge of the train car facade so that we simultaneously see both the fake camera moving in for a close-up and Esther bending down out of sight below the window sill. Again, the implied loss of identity, the separation of self from filmic reflection, is conveyed in a single, spatially significant image.

A dissolve opens on Esther queuing up at the payroll office for her first check. In a gag involving sound confusion and profanity, she is told to "go to 'L'" and Garland plays her reaction with a combination of affront, surprise, and relief. When Esther moves along to the window serving the middle of the alphabet, she learns that she has been given the new name of "Vicki Lester." She says it several times to herself, moving from skepticism to amused acceptance. Surrounded, as she is, by extras in gaucho, cowboy, and bellhop uniforms, she realizes that she too has taken on an illusory new identity.

Norman intervenes once again to kick-start Esther's stalled career. Knowing that the studio's latest musical has been shut down by the leading lady's inability to get out of her Broadway contract, Norman lures Oliver to his bungalow on a false pretext and then opens up the French doors so that he can hear a recording on the outside speakers of Esther singing "The Man That Got Away." Sober, focused and very handsome in a medium gray suit, light gray shirt and maroon ascot, Norman directs his charm and acting talents toward getting Oliver to connect all the right dots. Even though he catches on to the ruse, Oliver agrees to cast Esther in the musical and to proceed with production.

Having already communicated Esther's talent, Cukor handles the making of her first picture with remarkable economy. An establishing shot of the studio interior is followed by a single shot of Esther rehearsing a dance number based on the song "Black Bottom." Then, by way of a dissolve, Norman is driving her to the movie's sneak preview. Despite its brevity, however, the studio scene marks an important development in Norman's character arc. In an extreme long shot (a variation of the same establishing shot that Cukor used in *What Price Hollywood?* to introduce Mary Evans's first visit to the studio), the studio door slides open and a small loading truck and trailer enters and approaches the camera. Standing next to the door and dwarfed by its immense size is Norman. He is there to watch Esther rehearse but does so only from the far periphery. His active role in engineering her break begins to recede now as he stands by and observes her success. The diminishment of both his own career and his importance to hers is suggested visually by his tiny figure against the studio entrance and by his distance from the rehearsal space. Just as he has become much more likable and sympathetic to the audience, he also has become less powerful and popular as a star himself.

The car ride to the preview, which threads through a twilight urban landscape of oil pumps and neon signs, is more of Cukor's semi-documentary look at the real Los Angeles. Another gritty blue collar location, it counters the studio's make-believe glamour and reminds us again of Esther's roots. "Cukor seems to use actual locations with the general purpose of undercutting the glamorous connotations of a film about Hollywood," writes Bernardoni. "The locations are not mere background—the characters interact with them, seem to have a real connection to them" (page 81).

Part of the Warner Bros.-ordered cuts, the scene now consists of still photos and found footage. To quiet Esther's jittery nerves, Norman assures her, "I've been through this a hundred times." Nevertheless, Esther has to throw up, and we see the convertible pull up next to one of the oil rigs and she gets out. She crosses behind a pump, disappears from view, and then returns to the car wiping her mouth with another white handkerchief. The footage probably survived because we cannot really recognize Garland in the long shot that therefore could have found its way into the stock library.

Arriving at the theater location, which looks a little like Westwood, Norman self-deprecatingly announces, "We're in luck, Esther. That picture of mine is so bad that anything they see after it will seem just great." His movie, which precedes the sneak, is ironically titled *Another Dawn*. From a corner opposite the theater, there is a cut to Norman and Esther watching her musical from the balcony.

That brings us to the somewhat controversial "Born in a Trunk" number. Filmed after Cukor had completed work and left for a vacation in Europe, the sequence was directed by choreographer Richard Barstow. In fact, many of the professionals involved were different from those who worked on the rest of the movie. The music was not by Arlen and Gershwin but instead by long-time Garland coach and confidant Roger Edens and Leonard Gershe. Irene Sharaff designed the costumes, and Harold

Rossen (*The Wizard of Oz, On the Town, Singin' in the Rain*) took over as cinematographer for Sam Leavitt, who had to leave for a new assignment at 20th Century Fox. Gene Allen and Hoyningen-Huene stayed to work on the set designs.

Arlen and Gershwin had written three songs—"Green Light Ahead," "I'm Off the Downbeat," and "Dancing Partner"—for possible use in the film within a film number that showcases Esther's talent and makes her an overnight sensation. With the film basically completed except for final cutting, scoring, and other postproduction additions, all that was needed was a brisk, three-to-four-minute number that would climax the first half of the film and lead into a planned intermission. Since Garland's comeback vehicle already had exceeded its budget and shooting schedule, the idea was to shoot quickly on available sets and wrap production.

So why then was an elaborate fifteen-minute number that cost $250,000 and took nearly two months to shoot added to a picture that was already more than three hours long? There are various explanations. "The three songs were bad songs," Sid Luft bluntly claimed (Haver, page 189). Ira Gershwin believed it was because choreographer Richard Barstow could not come up with any dance ideas to match the songs. Others have argued that Jack Warner, a former boy singer himself and a big fan of production numbers, simply felt there were not enough songs in the movie. Garland biographers have suggested that Judy wanted her trusted collaborator Edens with her to ensure success and to incorporate bits from her acclaimed Palace show.

Another possible reason, it seems to me, is because an extended narrative production number had never been fronted before by a female star. Kelly had done it with the Gershwin ballet in *An American in Paris* and the "Broadway Melody Ballet" from *Singin' in the Rain*. Astaire was doing it that same year with the "Girl Hunt Ballet" from *The Band Wagon*. Who better to do a female version than the former MGM star that both Kelly and Astaire recognized as one of the greatest entertainers of the century? "Born in a Trunk" would be another opportunity for Garland to prove her pre-eminence to old MGM stalwarts, such as former husband Vincente Minnelli, director of both *An American in Paris* and *The Band Wagon*, and producer Arthur Freed, who famously said of Luft and Garland, "Those two alley cats can't make a picture" (Haver, page 71).

The production number's *mise-en-abîme* begins with an ending: Garland portraying Esther Blodgett playing Vicki Lester playing the part of a newly popular entertainer is finishing a stage performance of "Swanee," a song that Garland often included in her concert and nightclub appearances. The intertextual connections resonate with assorted details from her career history. Dressed in a minstrel costume, the Vicki character sings and dances the last few bars of "Swanee" and then, like Garland did at the Palace, she sits on the edge of the stage and talks to the audience. Her recollections constitute the narrative framework for the production number. Insisting that "it didn't happen overnight," she sings that she "was born in a trunk in the Princess Theatre in Pocatello, Idaho" and worked her way up through vaudeville. The show business baby she is referencing could be Esther Blodgett or even Frances Ethel Gumm herself, who was born to the owners of the New Grand Theatre in Grand Rapids, Minnesota. Her origin story includes a Friday matinee birth, make-up towels for diapers, going hungry, and "dressing rooms and hotel rooms and waiting rooms." Perched on the stage in a medium shot from the waist up and jabbing the air in a trademark Garland gesture, the Vicki character proclaims: "But it's all in the game and the way you play it,/ And you've got to play the game you know."

The number shifts into the flashbacks when Vicki sings: "At first I just stood and watched from the wings. / That's all my mom and dad would allow. / But as I got older, I got a little bolder, / And snuck out for their second bow." We see a little girl behind and in front of various theater curtains and then grown-up Vicki left on stage to sing "I'll Get By" as a solo. She is dressed in a blue satin dress, and the camera tracks in for a close-up. Dissolves move us back and forth between Vicki on the lip of the stage and young Vicki coming up through the ranks—practicing dance steps and searching for work.

Unfortunately, the narrative number starts now to take on a leaden, over-engineered feel as if Chinese boxes had been re-imagined by a Russian constructivist. With the movie theater's stage encasing the stage where Vicki sings, the camera in the flashbacks continually dollies in or out or in both directions successively to emphasize Vicki and to visually signal her importance. Dance movements and song snippets are repeated with different costumes to comment humorously on Vicki's progress. Black, white, red, and gray predominate and are used in stark geometric designs that evoke isolation. Vicki sings: "As time went by, / I looked for jobs / And was kicked from pillar to post." The bright red doors of an elevator set open and Vicki, costumed in a black top, white skirt, and checkered hat and holding a red briefcase, confronts several faceless male mannequins in black suits. The surfaces are sharp-edged, gleaming and empty. Lost in this modernistic space, she laments: "I haunted all the agents' offices / And I almost ended up a ghost."

The agent quest, which is similar to Gene Kelly's auditions in the "Broadway Melody Ballet," provides a clear illustration of how repetition structures the set design and the action. Vicki sweeps into three different agents' offices—one decorated in red, one in gray, and one in white—and sings three different sections of "You Took Advantage of Me." The first two agents shout "no" at her. After hearing her sing "So lock the doors, call me yours / Cause you took advantage of me," the third agent sizes her up and suggestively says "yes." Vicki cries "no" and runs from the office.

The offices and hallway resemble a grid-like modern painting. "All Mondrian," remembers designer Gene Allen (Haver, page 192) and indeed the agent interiors seem to be inspired by the Dutch painter's "Composition" series. Intersecting vertical and horizontal lines against a blank background define the doors, walls, and floor tiles, and the corridor recedes into an angled vanishing point.

After she escapes the lecherous third agent, Vicki gets a job in a "tap show." She and two rows of chorus girls do three versions of "Black Bottom," costumed first in white leotards and black feather hats, then in red leotards and red feather hats, and finally in black leotards and white feather hats.

Vicki's career setbacks are disclosed in a string of physical gags where the lyric sets up a hopeful premise and then a cut undermines it. So, for example, between the second and third renditions of "Black Bottom," she sings: "The star got sick and I was told to go on in her place / But she recovered." In the next shot, Vicki is back in the chorus line where she continues to mess up all the dance steps. Next, she receives an offer to sing in New York and imagines that she will be a "very chic chanteuse." Instead, the quick cut reveals her performing "The Peanut Vendor" song in a garish pink costume against a lime green set and shaking maracas—a real life incarnation of the marionette from the Cocoanut Oil Shampoo commercial. During two attempts to get through the song, a drunk interrupts and asks her to sing "Melancholy Baby" (dubious movie lore has it that Garland's Holmby Hills neighbor and original Rat Pack pal Humphrey Bogart dubbed the male voice).

As expected, in the following shot, Vicki actually is singing "Melancholy Baby." The camera tracks in slowly as she leans against a grand piano dressed in a full-length gown and opera gloves and, in a single long

Esther as Vicki Lester performs the "Melancholy Baby" flashback number in "Born in a Trunk."

take, performs almost all of the old standard. When she leaves the stage, a gray-haired man in a tuxedo approaches her and offers his card. Vicki sings: "He was fresh from heaven all right, / He produced the show that gave me the chance / To sing for you tonight."

And so, with one more dissolve, we return to "Swanee." This is the big finish and there are more people on stage than for any other number in the picture. With its red curtains, floor, flats, and costume accessories, Gene Allen and others referred to this as the "red scene." True to his signature choreographic style, Richard Barstow fills the frame with rows of performers crossing back and forth in front of each other just as he did in the opening Shrine Auditorium sequence. The camera tracks backward from a close-up of Vicki as the chorus—gray and red-suited men with canes and parasol-carrying women dressed in long bustled dresses—enter from both sides of the stage. Vicki catches a cane thrown from off screen and taps it in rhythm with the men. Passing in front of her are six black male dancers with tambourines and a trio of little children. Barstow cuts on movement from medium shots to long shots of the full stage lined with dancers, singers, Vicki, and a final row of band members on a gray terrace. For the final lyric, Vicki holds the last syllable of "Swanee," and the camera tracks in and then slowly pulls out again, as she sings: "Your wanderin' child will wander no more / When I get to that Swanee shore."

The plush red curtain closes and there is a dissolve to Vicki back on the edge of the stage. Surrounded by banks of red roses, she sings: "So I can't quite be called overnight sensation / For it started many years ago / When I was born in a trunk at the Princess Theatre / In Pocatello, Idaho." Again, Vicki holds the last syllables while the camera this time dollies forward and her spotlight irises in to black.

Upon the cut, the doors of the theater are opened and an excited crowd, buzzing with raves for Vicki, spills into the lobby. Many hardcore Garland fans are equally enthusiastic about the "Born in a Trunk" number. It has bits from the Palace show and features a rousing, full-voiced "Swanee" performance. Garland looks great in the Irene Sharaff costumes and shares some of her famous self-deprecating humor. Like *Singin' in the Rain*'s "Broadway Melody," which it very much resembles, the number has circular symmetry and splashy visuals to it. Full of references to painting, theater, and popular music, it strives to be taken seriously. However, also like "Broadway Melody," it is self-indulgent and overlong. There is no narrative or thematic connection between it and the rest of the film as there are with the Arlen-Gershwin pieces, and there is no developing relationship between Vicki and any other character in the number. It is exactly what it seems: a separate artistic endeavor grafted on to an already completed film. The addition might have worked if there was an intermission as originally planned; in fact, the whole unedited original might have been saved if there were an intermission and special roadshow screenings of the film. But there were not and the fact that "Born in a Trunk" was kept and other important narrative scenes scrapped seems particularly misguided.

While the audience members are completing their preview cards, Esther enters the lobby and is showered with applause and compliments. Norman peels off to the side and waits for her in the street. Increasingly, he will be framed in one-shots physically separate from the attention being focused on her. Her reaction, which also will be repeated, is to leave the group and rejoin Norman, in effect creating their own private space sealed off from others. Here, she approaches as he stands before a passable rear projection street at night and thanks him for bringing her to the brink of stardom. They have a few moments alone together before Oliver's entourage pulls them off to Mocambo's to celebrate.

Cukor and his design team built a reasonable facsimile of the famous Sunset Strip nightclub, down to its unique glass-walled bird cages, one of which Cukor fills with pink branches and places in the middle of an outside terrace. This is the second of the film's three major terrace scenes. For Cukor, the terrace becomes a psychologically charged location, a place where the main characters communicate hesitations and contemplate the future. It is where they make profound decisions affecting the direction of their lives.

The first female performer to anchor an extended narrative production number, Judy Garland sings "Swanee" for the finale of "Born in a Trunk."

Cukor deftly orchestrates *mise-en-scène*, camera movement, and framing to emphasize the thematic importance of what takes place on the Mocambo terrace. A deep focus establishing shot encompasses couples dancing behind a red gauze screen in the far left corner of the frame, tables in the middle range, and a diagonal line of Los Angeles city lights (this would be the view looking down on the basin and out toward the coast) stretching from the right back to the right foreground. Libby enters and circles counterclockwise around the terrace to a table where Oliver, Esther, and various studio executives are discussing the evening. Norman stands by himself and observes from a shadowed area.

Delivering piles of preview cards, Libby announces, "You've got yourself a new star, Oliver." Leading her from the table, Norman walks Esther to the edge of the terrace. The camera tracks alongside as they pass in front of the large bird cage which dominates the center of the frame. "It's all yours, Esther," he says as he sweeps his arm along the line of sparkling distant lights. "I don't mean just the Cadillacs and swimming pools. It's all yours." The promise of unlimited opportunity, however, seems at odds with the images of confinement—the couples sealed behind their screen and the elaborate bird cage. Esther likely is trading her independence for the financially rewarding yet physically restrictive control of the studio.

Aware of the many perils, Norman cautions, "Don't let it change your life. Don't let it change who you are." With Cukor's fateful wind ruffling the potted palm tree behind them, Norman also tries to convince Esther that for her own good she should leave him now. "I've done all I can for you," he reasons. "You've come along the road with me as far as you should." When she protests and says she loves him, Norman is even more brutally honest about himself. "I destroy everything I touch. I always have," he says and then adds, "Forget me. I'm a bad loss. You've come too late." Cukor holds on a two-shot to accentuate Esther's belief that she and Norman can build a private world that will protect them from their various inner and outer pressures. "I don't believe that," replies Esther. "It's not too late. Not for you, not for me." As they embrace, Norman whispers, "Don't say that, Esther. I might begin to believe it." The scene ends optimistically on a slow fade-out, but Cukor has planted sufficient verbal and visual warnings to undermine that fragile note of hope.

The next scene, also cut from the original, deals again with the split between Norman's and Esther's movie lives and their private lives and the challenge of maintaining a relationship within that dichotomy. In another humorous manipulation of the means of production, Cukor turns the recording and playback of a song into a very public marriage proposal. Bernardoni is particularly enthusiastic about the scene, rightfully calling it "a tour de force in which Cukor brings the disparate elements of the film—the visual and the aural, the musical, and the dramatic, the documentary and the fictional—to a new height of integration" (page 83).

The camera tracks through a sound booth and dollies in to a window overlooking the recording studio below. A full orchestra flanked by at least four hand-held microphone booms is tuning up; the appearance of Ray Heindorf himself as the conductor and an off-screen voice instructing "we're ready whenever you are" add to the sense of a real working sound studio in operation. A long shot from within the orchestra seems to "catch" Heindorf and Esther beginning the take. Dressed casually in blue pants, blue blouse, and red kerchief tied in her hair, she sings the first bars of "Here's What I'm Here For."

There is a cut to Norman listening at the base of one of the booms and then a second cut on movement from long shot to medium as he takes a seat on a nearby wooden staircase and continues to watch. The opening overhead establishing shot did not include him, but eyeline matches suggest that he is located on the screen left edge of the orchestra. It is also clear from the eyelines and from the lyrics that Esther is once more performing for him and that the words hold special meaning for her. Gazing in medium close-up toward frame left, she sings: "My heart insisted / I seek you out / That you existed / My heart had no doubt."

Cukor cross-cuts twice between Norman and Esther, with her alternatingly highlighted in the MCU and linked in long shot with the rest of the orchestra, just as she often was during "The Man That Got Away." As she finishes the next verse ("What am I here for? / It's time you knew. / Here's what I'm here for, / I'm here for you,"), she rushes out of an extreme long shot of the orchestra and into a medium shot on the steps with Norman. Her movement clarifies his exact physical location on the periphery and, significantly, it is through her agency that he is integrated into the communal space of the musical performance. The chorus continues singing on its own.

Cukor goes to work now staging an elaborate joke based on the disconnect between sound and image. The sound booth technicians phone the boom operator and ask him to swing the microphone above Norman and Esther. Secretly recording the conversation in the kind of prank that Norman himself might organize, the two crew members up in the booth put on their headphones and start to laugh at what they are hearing. Cukor cuts back and forth between a low angle shot looking up at the booth and a frontal medium shot of Norman and Esther. We can hear neither of the conversations, only the singing of the chorus. From a distance, it looks like she is mouthing the words of the song as she smiles at him.

Suddenly, a voice shouts, "Wrap. That's it. Wonderful," and the chorus stops midway through the refrain. Danny calls Esther over to the orchestra to listen to the playback; she obviously has remembered his comment back at the Oleander Arms that he is the best arranger she ever had and out of friendship, respect, and loyalty has gotten him a job in that capacity on her pictures.

The next shot is an unusual one for a director normally so preoccupied with briskly moving along the narrative. It opens on a frame that is empty except for a large studio speaker stamped with the number "12." Norman and Esther enter the shot and stand on either side of the speaker to hear the recording. The camera dollies in for emphasis. A sense of inclusiveness emerges from the blocking—Norman crosses to the left of the frame near her, and Danny enters and takes his place beside the speaker. With the antagonism gone between Norman and Danny, the three characters are united in friendship and collaboration.

When Esther's singing finishes, the playback continues with her asking, "How'd I sound?" and Norman playfully answering, "Just adequate." Realizing that they have been recorded, they plead for the sound to be turned off, but in a cut to the booth overhead, the technician feigns ignorance. While the entire orchestra and crew listen in, Norman refers to "another kind of arrangement, a domestic one" and then casually asks, "Will you marry me?" Maintaining the same bantering tone, she politely responds, "No thank you." The gathered crowd laughs and he shrinks in embarrassment. What seemed previously like Esther accompanying the chorus is actually her singing additional replies to him, with a rising inflection on the last two words: "You're irresponsible, my heart insisted. / You drink too much."

When he hears himself say, "Suppose I become absolutely dependable on all occasions," Norman begins to look truly uncomfortable and sits down. "Would you do all that for me if I said I'd marry you?" asks Esther. In an answer that keeps the tone of this long take light, Norman says, "No, I've had a chance to think it over with all that humming and singing. Too much to ask." Having heard enough, he gets up and good-naturedly says goodbye to everyone, but she grabs him by the shoulders and announces, "Well, wait a minute, my boy, that's much too public a

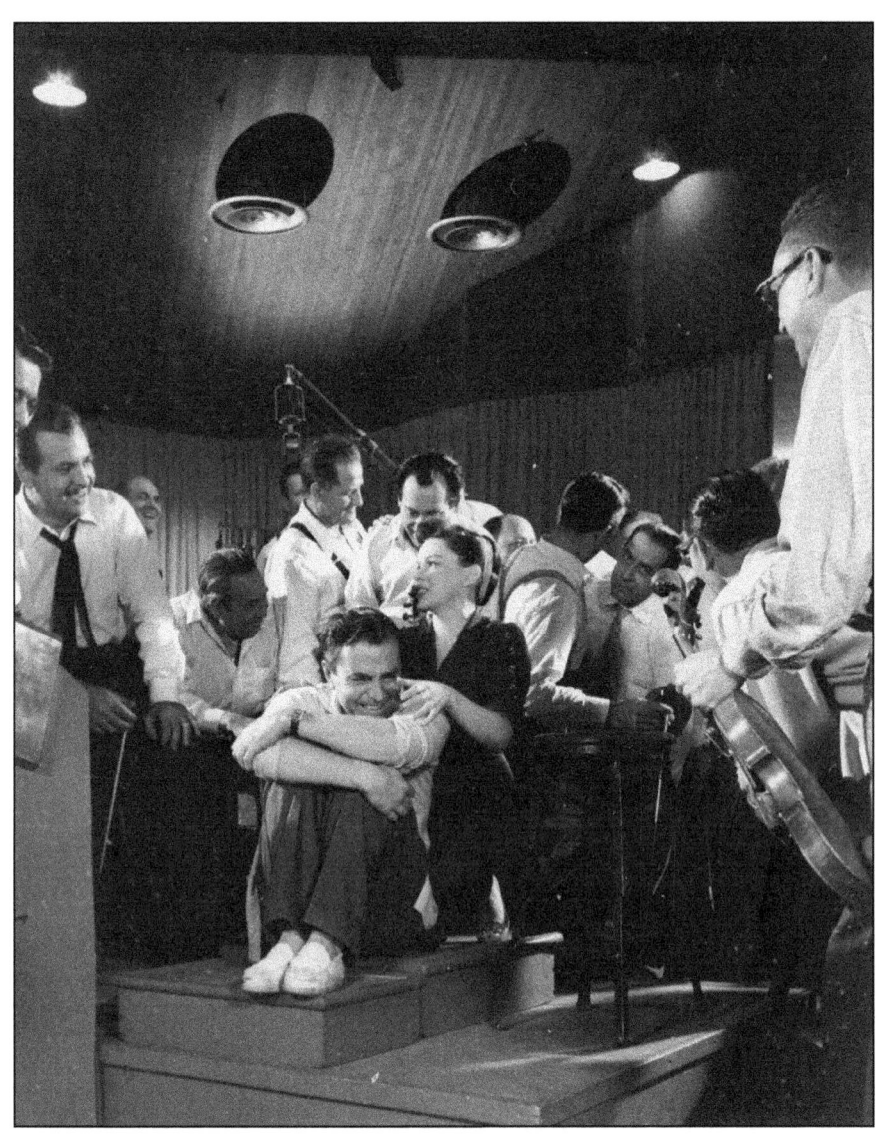

In one of the cut scenes, Esther and Norman react in embarrassment as the band members listen to a secretly recorded playback of Norman's marriage proposal.

proposal for me to say 'no' to. I accept." To the cheers and applause of the crew, they embrace.

The camera tracks out as orchestra members, including a visibly happy Danny, encircle the couple. There is a kind of communal celebration of the proposal, a moment of expansive happiness for Norman and Esther that, for the time being, unites both their professional and personal lives in optimism.

From this point on, Moss Hart borrows generously from the Wellman film, often lifting scenes more or less intact from the original script. The engagement news is such an example. "We're going to get married," announces Norman, as he and Esther surprise Oliver and Libby in the front office. After Norman delivers the resilient jokes about reading the line badly and Oliver considering whether a wedding would be good for the studio, Oliver bestows his "blessing" and Libby offers congratulations despite an otherwise skeptical demeanor.

Perhaps because the script so closely resembles its 1937 forerunner, Cukor handles the action in a very workmanlike manner: master shot, cut-ins for medium close dialogue and reaction shots, stationary camera, closure on long shot. Although tangential to the marriage announcement, Libby has a significant impact on the scene. He expresses an escalating dislike of Norman ("That was quite a decision you made there, Oliver, letting that girl walk into a booby trap") and articulates the studio's view of Norman and Esther as capital assets, one falling and one rising. He refers to her as "the hottest property the studio has right now" and curtly informs his assistant that "Lester and Maine are getting married" in the same way he would discuss the merging of two brand names. For Cukor and Hart, he also becomes a symbol for all the meaningless Hollywood hype that they are satirizing. On the phone to the assistant, he directs her to "see if you can get the mayor to close school that afternoon… get all newsreel and television coverage started right away… get all traffic routed out of Beverly Hills for two miles on each side of the church… the big one… and tell *Life*, *Time*, the AP and UP boys that I'll set up exclusive coverage with each one personally."

As in the earlier *A Star Is Born*, Norman and Esther sabotage Libby's grandiose plans and get married by a rural justice of the peace with Danny as witness. Again, Cukor's scene is almost an exact duplication of Wellman's. The dissolve from Oliver's office opens on a shot of two drunks watching the ceremony from behind bars. Cukor pans from the jail cell to the ceremony and then cross-cuts between a four-shot of all the participants and two-shots of Norman and Esther exchanging their vows. About the only detail changed is that Norman's real name is now Ernest Sidney Gubbins.

Norman and Esther are both dressed tastefully yet inconspicuously in gray suits. As the justice of the peace is about to recognize them, they make a dash for the white convertible parked across the street from the court building. "At least we got away from Libby" and "Libby doesn't even know we left town," they say triumphantly, as Libby himself pulls up in his station wagon.

Shot on location in the tiny town of Piru, California, the encounter contrasts their happiness with Libby's indignation. After giving the 1937 script's speech about being stabbed in the back with a knife bearing the couple's initials, Libby tries to salvage some media coverage, but they ask him not to be angry and then speed away on their honeymoon. "Well, I wish them joy," Libby grimly tells Danny. "Wait 'til they see the press they get. It won't be so funny." When Danny argues that they deserve to have some private happiness, Libby replies that Norman knows better than to further antagonize reporters already tired of his behavior and delighted with his slipping box office. "I've spent ten years covering up for him and smoothing over his insults," fumes Libby. "Double-crossed by a cruddy actor! Well, he needs this more than I do. Ok, just wait your turn, I always say."

Although less detestable than Lionel Stander's Libby, Jack Carson brings a similar seething resentment to the part. Neither version of the character may engineer Norman's downfall, but both feel equally vindicated when it happens.

Wisely, Hart and Cukor do not reproduce the Airstream trailer vignette from Wellman's film. Instead, there is a nighttime dissolve to Norman's car entering the Lazy Acres Motel. Norman and Esther open the door of their room and stop to kiss on the shadowy green threshold. In its darkness and close quarters, the setting is very similar to the Oleander Arms and fosters the same intimate, substantial communication between them.

Despite the exuberance of the studio proposal scene, the film's back-and-forth dynamic between seclusion and engagement seems to favor cocoon-like solitude as the safest place for their relationship to flourish. The motel's interior space continues to shrink in on itself. When Norman accidentally switches on the garish ceiling lights, he immediately dims down to just the table lamps. Doors to the bright white kitchen and bathroom are briefly opened and then closed. At one point, both Esther (to change clothes) and Norman (to retrieve the luggage) exit the frame and Cukor holds on the empty room emphasizing just how small it actually is. The camera stays in close at all times as it follows the couple's every move and links them continually in tight two-shots.

Norman places a coin in the motel radio and hears the announcer say, "And now, folks, Vicki Lester, singing the title song from her new picture, 'It's a New World.'" Both Norman and Esther, who has re-entered the room in a bright red robe, listen to the Hit Parade's #1 song, which we recognize as the soundtrack melody that opened the scene.

"There it is, Esther, you got it just the way you dreamed," congratulates Norman, and she tells him that their marriage means so much more to her. Even in this most intimate of moments, he still thinks of her as a performer and, shutting off the radio, asks her to sing the song just for him. "I've got a private copyright of my own," he says, "including the Scandinavian," a remark which in the context of David Selznick's ongoing assertions about *A Star Is Born's* foreign distribution rights takes on an unintended irony.

Reluctant at first, she kneels down as he takes a seat and begins to sing *a capella* at his feet. The camera follows the song in one extended take, tilting down and then tracking slowly to the left to hold on an over-the-shoulder shot of him on the left and her on the right of the frame.

Of all the Arlen-Gershwin compositions, this song has the most direct thematic connection to the narrative. It is the voice of a young woman celebrating the start of a romance that she believes will create a protective new world for her: "The tears have rolled off my cheek, / And fears fade every time you speak./ A new world though we're in a tiny room. / What a vision of joy and blossom and bloom. / So I'm holding on and I'm holding fast."

Norman pulls her up to him for an embrace and then, on the conclusion, a kiss. As suggested by the *mise-en-scène*, this new world is small, dark, and private, a refuge that may or may not withstand the outside pressures aligned against it.

In comparison to the tranquility of the Lazy Acres Motel, the next setting seems land mined with obstacles. It opens on an extreme long shot of Norman and Esther's new Malibu house across an inlet from the symbolically foreboding waves that Cukor was adamant about threading into the picture. The camera tracks along another terrace as Norman and Esther gather up the guests of their fancy party to go inside and watch a movie. The intrusion of the studio into their domestic space is conveyed visually by a living room that literally erupts with film technology. The drapes automatically close, a painting rises to reveal a projection booth, and a movie screen emerges from the floor. Our view is occasionally obscured; twice Oliver walks in front of the camera. On the second occurrence, he leaves the viewing and slips into an adjacent room. Norman notices and follows; their ensuing conversation is covered in a single, three and a half minute take.

With virtuosity more characteristic of an Orson Welles or an Alfred Hitchcock, Cukor shoots Norman through a glass partition dividing the two rooms and then pulls back to track across the wall until he "meets" him at the door. Norman enters and, seeing that Oliver has turned on a console television in the lower corner of frame left, remarks, "Traitor!" Cukor moves his two actors around in a complex blocking that begins to resemble a dance. Oliver finds a boxing match on television, Norman advances down stage to mix a drink, Oliver rests on the edge of a chair, Norman returns to midground.

There is an uneasy feel to the scene. The image itself is discordant, fragmented at one point by the flickering black and white fight in the lower left corner, the actors in center and the black and white movie visible at the far right edge of the frame. Noticing Oliver's anxiety, Norman asks, "Has this got anything to do with me? What you're worrying about."

Oliver demurs, saying they can discuss things at the studio, but Norman pushes him to share his concerns. With drink in hand, he crosses to the right of the room and Oliver rises from his seat to follow; the camera reframes them in a close two-shot. "The New York boys have been out here for the past week," reveals Oliver in reference to the East Coast parent company executives like Jack Warner's brother Harry or MGM's Nick Schenck, who made all the studios' major financial decisions. Instructive here is how easily Cukor, the adroit *metteur-en-scène*, contextualizes mid-1950s Hollywood in crisis through the television image and the comment about New York moneymen.

"They want me to take a salary cut," guesses Norman, but the news is worse than that. The two friends sit down on a couch backed by a gold/brown Chinese screen and Oliver reluctantly admits, "They've instructed me to buy up the rest of your contract." Unable at first to process this new reality, Norman asks, "But why? My last two pictures haven't grossed as much as they used to, but neither has anybody else's." All of Norman's budget-breaking exploits catch up with him when Oliver explains, "They can't afford you anymore, Norman. You're too big a risk. Those big fat lush days where a star could get drunk and hold up production for two weeks are over."

Standing from the couch, Norman crosses back to the left and Oliver rises to accompany him. The movie screen, visible through the glass partition and a reminder of Norman's fading career, looms between them. In a valiant effort at stoic nonchalance, Norman mentions other studios and concludes, "We had a good long roll of the dice, didn't we, Oliver. Can't complain now."

The camera follows them back to the doorway. "I tried, Norman. I tried very hard," says Oliver with credible regret. Asking Oliver to give him time to "tell Esther in my own way," Norman demonstrates a pull-down ceiling lamp and jokes, "I certainly picked a fine time to build myself a big new house, didn't I?" These closing gestures have a valedictory sadness to them. Sliding shut the door to the television console in the same way that his movie world has been closed, Norman observes, "I sometimes think I was born with a genius, an absolute genius, for doing the wrong thing." As Bernardoni writes, "A star has just died, and Niles's real concern and deep affection for Norman were not able to prevent the death" (page 86).

Barely able to conceal his delight, Libby dictates the press release regarding Norman's departure from the studio. It reads in part: "Mr. Maine feels that his career will be benefitted by a change. We do not wish to stand in his way." To himself, he also mutters, "The wheel goes round and round, and if you just wait long enough." With his feet propped up on his desk, he turns to gaze out the window.

A point of view long shot reveals studio workers removing a billboard advertising Norman Maine in *Black Legion* and replacing it with one advertising Vicki Lester in the ironically titled *Happiness Ahead*. There is no additional commentary on Norman's firing—no shrill headline, no snarky newspaper article. In fact, the complete absence of the gossip column motif from Hart's script makes it even less of a critique and more of a valentine than its two predecessors. Norman's situation is unfortunate but not the fault of Hollywood. Cukor, especially, is having way too much fun showcasing the business he loves than to turn his film into any kind of indictment.

A cause and effect dissolve gives us Norman putting golf balls across the floor of the Malibu beach house. This, as we know from Norman and Esther's first car ride together, is a sure sign of the tension and anxiety he is battling. A persistently ringing telephone call turns out to be reporter Artie Carver, who begins by asking him, "Is it true you're trying to get Vicki to leave the studio because you're sore at Niles for settling the contract?" Their conversation, which includes Norman's angry denial and Carver's request for help in getting an interview with Vicki, is taken almost word for word from the Wellman/Carson script. Adding Carver's note to a list of other phone messages, Norman sits down to a game of solitaire interrupted by the sound of Esther's car arriving outside.

The passionate energy of their greeting is conveyed by Esther rushing down stage to embrace Norman and the camera pulling back as they walk arm and arm into the interior of the house. Aware of her tiring day at the studio, he has prepared dinner and fetches a cart loaded with salad, sandwiches, and milk. While he is in the kitchen, she (also familiar with the backstory) notices the golf balls and seems uncertain how to react. It is further telling that as they prepare to eat, his first comment is "Well, what went on at the studio today, at the old alma mater?" So attached is Norman to his own self-image as a popular movie star that he can think of no other mutually interesting topic of conversation. To take his mind off his worries, Esther jokes about an elaborate scene, a "production number to end all production numbers," that she is shooting. "An American in Paris?" he laughs. She replies, "An American in Paris, Spain, Brazil, Pakistan, the Burma Road," (an intentional ribbing of Vincente Minnelli, director not only of *An American in Paris* but also the wildly opulent Judy Garland-Gene Kelly picture *The Pirate*). "It's got sex, schmaltz, patriotism," she continues. "You should see the things that come up out of the ground and the things that come down out of the ceiling." As prelude to one of the great "spontaneous" dance-around-the-house numbers like "Good Morning" in *Singin' in the Rain* and "Everything Old is New Again" in *All That Jazz*, she says, "I'll put the practice record on and show you."

Counting "The Man That Got Away," this is the third time Esther has sung for Norman's audience of one. With each performance, he has moved closer, both physically and emotionally, to her. For the "The Man That Got Away," he sat far away in the shadows and watched. He was right next to her, the object of her serenade, for "It's a New World." Now, more than just a spectator, he is drawn into "Someone At Last" and encouraged to participate.

This number, running at seven minutes and containing thirty cuts, also differs from the others in the way it is shot. Gone are the long takes and the slow tracks into the frame; in their place are multiple segments, cross-cuts, and abbreviated lateral camera movements. "Someone At Last" is more frantic, even fragmented, than the other two numbers, more a forerunner of Bob Fosse and less an echo of Fred Astaire. Interest lies not so much in Esther's singing and dancing skills but in her ability to improvise film effects from household items.

Grabbing a pole lamp, she yells "Lights," and using the serving cart as a dolly, she calls "Camera." She sings: "Somewhere there's a someone / Who's the someone for me. / Someday there will come one / And my lover he will be." Providing a running commentary on what she's doing in the "real" number she is filming back at the studio, Esther explains, "I'm discovered sitting on a rather simple divan" and "Now we have a stunning shot with a clock." Several times throughout the number, Cukor cuts back and forth between her performance and Norman's amused reaction. "You know I get pretty girlish in this number," she teases as she stops to embrace him.

For Norman's amusement, Esther uses household props to spoof the big production number she is shooting at the studio.

The camera tracks left to follow her around the room and then, when she says "Now here comes a big fat close-up," it slowly dollies in for the iconic *A Star Is Born* movie poster image of Garland cupping her face with her thumbs joined and with her hands fanned outward. A musical number about a musical number in a film about filmmaking starring a veteran performer attempting a comeback elevates the textual duplication which has underscored the narrative from the opening scene at the Shrine Auditorium.

Partly because he was using an "A" camera and a "B" camera to shoot "Someone at Last," Cukor frequently cuts on movement to connect the various stages of Esther's circuit around the room. Shifting back to the right, she "plays" a corded footstool as a harp and enlists Norman's cigarette as a smoke machine. During the extended Parisian scene, she uses palm fronds as a costume, round pillows for a can-can, and an oblong pillow for an accordion. China is suggested by a lamp shade worn as a straw peasant hat, Brazil by a salt and pepper set shaken as *ganzás*, and Africa by a leopard rug worn as a headdress.

Toward the end of the number, the pace becomes noticeably more frenetic. The music tempo speeds up and Esther's behavior seems more manic. Cutting the lights and raising the movie screen, she jumps onto the low-slung mantel and dances a jazz step in the beam of the projector, creating a flickering image that looks like an accelerated silent film. To involve Norman in the playacting, she flops down next to him on a couch and they both pretend to be cowboys firing their six-shooters into the projected light. There is a stain of alarm in her performance, a desperate attempt to hold the troubled Norman close to her and to keep their fragile "new world" from spinning apart. The number's fragmented visual style (i.e., the rapid cuts, the abrupt movements, the melodic breaks) imply that the collapse has begun already.

The song concludes with Norman and Esther tossing pillows at each other and falling to the floor in a passionate embrace, but the euphoria is short-lived. A messenger arrives with a package for Vicki Lester and fails to recognize Norman, who was hoping it was a cabled answer from Alex Korda about doing a picture in England. Compounding the slight, the messenger says (as in the 1937 original), "Sign right there, Mr. Lester." His back to the camera, Norman lingers for a few seconds in the doorway and then braces himself with a shoulder roll. When he turns, there is a look somewhere between pain and anger on his face. He drops the package on a table and mechanically reads off Esther's messages: a request from the

Motion Picture Relief Fund to do a benefit at the Shrine in April, a question from the Academy of Motion Picture Arts and Sciences regarding how many places to reserve for her party at the Awards ceremony, the interview favor for Artie Carver.

Sensing Norman's hurt, Esther cheerfully proposes, "Now that the supper show's over, let's have some supper, shall we?" Norman, however, crosses in front of the camera and recedes into the back left corner of the frame. "I think I'll fix myself a drink," he says darkly. "I'm not very hungry." Up to now, James Mason often has been watching and reacting to Garland's various performances; from this point forward, he takes more of the focus and displays a range of despair, rage, and remorse that keeps us riveted. Apparently Cukor wanted Mason to play Norman more like John Barrymore, and some critics thought the part should be modeled more closely after Errol Flynn. To my mind, however, Mason brings to Norman exactly the right combination of intelligence, humor, self-criticism, threat, and allure.

Excluding some significant changes in Norman's "speech," a shift in locale from the Biltmore to the Ambassador, and some innovative new staging by Cukor, the Academy Awards scene that follows looks very

Esther's frantic finale to the "Someone at Last" parody.

much like it did in the Fredric March-Janet Gaynor version. Even though by 1953 the actual Oscars were being handed out at the Pantages Theater, Cukor keeps Hart's Cocoanut Grove setting perhaps for the aptness of Esther returning to where she sang with the Glenn Williams Orchestra but more likely for the easier logistics of orchestrating Norman's appearance beside Esther from the banquet floor rather than the orchestra pit. A minor key variation on the Shrine sequence, the Awards event has the same documentary-like urgency to it. Handheld shots of limousines and celebrities arriving under search lights at the entrance are superimposed over each other and over an extreme long shot of the Ambassador marquee and a close-up of the official Academy "Auto Pass." There is a similar sense of expectation, only this time the attraction is Esther and not Norman.

And again, Esther is challenged by a clash between her personal and public selves. Nominated as Best Actress for a picture pointedly called *A World for Two*, Esther/Vicki struggles to balance a disjointed universe of mini-worlds: marriage to Norman, friendship and collaboration with Danny and Oliver, professional relations with the movie industry, connections to her fans. The *mise-en-scène* encompasses those multiple realities.

The camera starts with an overhead medium shot of Libby schmoozing with reporters and columnists in the glass-partitioned press room and then tracks along as he passes into the adjacent ballroom. He walks in front of a battery of newsreel and television cameras covering the Best Actor recipient's acceptance speech and makes his way to the Vicki Lester table. A deep focus master shot includes the cameras in the foreground, attendee tables in the middle, and a tiered, slightly elevated stage (from which the actor is speaking) in the background. There is nothing in the frame to alarm us, simply another densely packed Cukor view of insider Hollywood. Even the color scheme is neutral—blue-gray stage curtains and set, blue-gray dresses, black tuxedos.

As the Best Actor wraps up his innocuous speech, the camera tracks in to a medium shot of Esther's table. Danny is on the left, Esther is in the center, and Oliver is on the right; next to her is a vacant seat meant for Norman. "You don't think anything's happened to him, do you?" she asks. "You know what the traffic's like," Oliver reassures her. Just like that the calm evaporates, and we are set on edge by Norman's absence.

Nigel Peters, the previous year's Best Actor winner, takes the stage to announce the nominees for best performance by an actress: Shirley Bander, Vicki Lester, Alice Tenney, and Jane Brandon (each first and last name meeting the two syllable maximum for most made-up Hollywood

A Star Is Born (1954) • 191

Esther/Vicki is named Best Actress in a deep-focus, visually rich shot at the Oscar ceremony. Norman's empty chair is to her right and Oliver Niles (Charles Bickford) is on her left.

names). Cukor cuts back and forth between Nigel reading names and Esther looking nervous. When "Miss Vicki Lester" is announced as the winner, Cukor opts for what should be a tight two-shot but instead is Esther and an empty chair. "Oh, I wish Norman was here," she whispers before climbing the steps to accept her Oscar.

The framing of Esther on stage is a masterful use of the widescreen format and a stunning visual indication that the center cannot hold in her attempt at an orderly, integrated life. She appears on the left side of the frame in a full figure long shot and on the right in a large medium shot on the television monitor. As a fake TV camera dollies in on the stage from the left, the image in the monitor expands to a close-up. Like other scenes in the film that feature a screen, the dual image here suggests disconnect and discord. Looking her most glamorous yet in a low cut, side-slitted black and purple Jean Louis gown, Esther softly remarks, "Out of all the words in the world just two stick in your mind—thank you." Suddenly, the sound of anonymous, solitary applause interrupts her speech. A long shot from the side of the stage (possibly Esther's point of view) reveals Norman staggering down the same stairs he descended so commandingly the night he visited the Grove in search of Esther and the band. Oliver stands to steer a clearly intoxicated Norman toward the table but Norman brushes his arm away; reaction shots show concerned and embarrassed guests. "Congratulations, my dear. I got here just in time, didn't I?" he says unsteadily. "May I borrow the end of your speech to make one of my own?" Once again, as at the Shrine, he is disrupting a public appearance by Esther, but on this occasion she is unable to prevent his total humiliation. For their joint appearance on stage, Cukor continues to reframe a two-shot, Esther elevated a step above and Norman pacing back and forth below. Brilliantly underplayed by Mason, the speech exposes the depth of Norman's desperation and is worth quoting in the cadenced detail Mason gives it:

> "My method for gaining your attention is a little unusual, perhaps, but hard times call for harsh measures. I had my speech all prepared, but it's gone right out of my head. Let me see… it's silly to be so formal isn't it? I know most of you sitting out there by your first names, don't I? I made a lot of money for you gentlemen in my time through the years, haven't I? Well, I need a job now. Yes, that's it… that's the speech. I need a job. That's what I wanted to say… simple as that… I need a job. That's all. My talents, I might add, are not strictly confined to dramatic parts. I can do comedy as well. (a pause). Well play something, boys."

Gesturing to the orchestra, he accidentally strikes Esther across the face. Horrified at what he has done, he starts to sway and she maneuvers him off the stage and to the table, where Oliver pulls out a chair and Libby slides him into it. "Get me a drink, somebody," he says in utter misery. Watch the physical details during this scene and you realize what a consummate film actor Mason was—stepping up and down the dais as he speaks, slipping backward when he sits down, staring at his feet to compose his thoughts, jamming his knuckles in his mouth when he pleads for the drink. Despite an impulse to turn away and avoid the pain, it is impossible to be distracted from Mason's "speech" for even a moment. Through the strength of his performance, what began in celebration ends, on the slow fade to black, in a kind of mourning. The Academy sequence confirms the collapse of Norman's stardom and the ascent of Esther's. As it was for Gatsby, the new world is already behind them.

The next scene, the "Lose That Long Face" number, was, for many years, the stuff of legend, the Holy Grail, among Garland fans and memorabilia specialists. Cut from the original and presumed lost, it was rumored to be in the possession of one or two private collectors and occasionally to be shown upon special invitation to a few lucky acolytes. For the 1983 restoration, Ronald Haver tracked down several leads but had to settle for a heavily edited facsimile based on alternate take fragments. Then, after the restored version had been screened in several cities, an anonymous tip (perhaps from a fan who wanted the pristine number in the new release) resulted in a Los Angeles District Attorney's Office raid on a private collector's vault that netted the "Lose That Long Face" original negative. Haver quickly incorporated it into all future release prints of the reconstruction.

The number's production history is equally tangled. Apparently convinced that the film did not need an additional musical number, Cukor was replaced on the shoot by Warner Bros. contract director Jack Donohue. When Garland learned of the change, she refused to report for work until Cukor got involved. By way of a solution, Cukor returned to sit next to Donohue during filming and critique the various takes. Later on, Jack Warner decided the number was inadequate and ordered Richard Barstow to reshoot it with Cukor once again providing on-set commentary. As a stand-alone, "Lose That Long Face" is entertaining if not exactly ground-breaking. However, when combined with the emotionally devastating dressing room scene that it bookends, it constitutes a segment that in and of itself should have won Garland the Best Actress Oscar.

With her back to the camera, Esther sits in front of a make-up mirror. The reflected image (a sure sign that we will again be confronted with her variant selves) shows her costumed in a baggy red sweater, straw hat,

Norman accidentally strikes Esther after interrupting her acceptance speech.

and applied freckles. After an exchange of friendly greetings, the director asks if she is "ready to go" and there is a cut to the set. It is evident that Cukor himself is directing the pre-number footage because it bares his trademark foregrounding of the cinematic technology itself. Someone calls "Hit the lights" and several successive shots show a battery of variously numbered lights bursting to life and a lighting operator busily flipping switches at his control board.

Esther walks on to the brightly illuminated stage (Ronald Haver reports Gene Allen as recalling that they painted an old *A Streetcar Named Desire* set all white) and is handed a pile of newspapers by a prop man. In a heavily stacked shot with the director and camera boom at the top of the frame and a row of about fifteen gray-costumed chorus members across the bottom, the director shouts, "Roll'em… speed… play back." Cukor, who can so easily draw emotion from the objects in his settings, cuts to a playback record being placed on a phonograph machine and then flash pans to speaker #12, the same speaker that in earlier, happier times broadcasted Norman's marriage proposal. It is at this point that the musical number itself begins.

Esther, as a ragamuffin newspaper vendor, strolls onto another Southern street scene and cheers up the residents with a song about overcoming sadness: "If as, and when you've got a long face / Rearrange it / Don't be contented with the wrong face. / There's a way to change it."

When lightning and thunder threaten, she jumps up onto a loading dock, taking shelter with a little African-American boy and girl and tightly wrapping her arms around them. Ira Gershwin's rhymes are a bit awkward: "Hey there! Say there. / Are you in a vacuum? / All that stuff and nonsense / You can overcome. / A long face gets you nowhere. / You lose that month of May / Like Peter Pan, the sweeter pan / Wins the day."

Garland, however, keeps the melody moving and finds a comfortable phrasing for the words. Motioning to the children, she jumps off the dock and tap dances with them around the street. Together, they collect a line of dancing followers: a baker, a woman and her child, a Colonel Sanders type, and a young man in a gray suit. Within the number's narrative framework, Esther takes the heavy laundry basket from a black washer woman, repositions a kid hanging from a tree, and tosses off two references to Kelly's "Singin' in the Rain" number—nearly bumping up against a policeman and splashing around in a puddle.

Cuts on movement and a tracking camera provide coverage for the considerable geographic distance that Esther traverses (on and off the dock, around a corner, up and down the street). More so than with "Born in a Trunk," the communal nature of the production number is emphasized; the gray, white, and black-costumed chorus men and women continually back her in the long shots and a cutaway features a three-shot of the director, cinematographer, and camera operator observing the performance from an elevated boom.

Accompanied by the two children and also on her own, Garland performs a series of rapid time-steps, a little heavy-footed but perfectly respectable for someone who never trained formally as a dancer. With a running time of just under four minutes, the number's big finish comes as she sings: "If you want trouble double-crossed / Don't give in to a frown. / Turn that frown upside down / And get yourself that long face lost!"

Back atop the dock, Esther strikes an arm-churning Garland pose, and the camera tracks in for a beaming medium close-up. The director calls "Cut," the lights are doused, Esther walks out of the right side of the frame, and the crew prepares to re-set the stage for closer angles.

We frequently have seen Cukor juxtapose moments of happiness with those that are less upbeat. Such is the case here. Waiting between takes in her dressing room, Esther stares forlornly at the reflected images in the mirror. Oliver, who has been traveling on business for three months, surprises her with a visit and notices how worried she seems. "You should get completely away after this one," he advises before asking, "How's Norman?" Her response, a three and a half-minute monologue, is filmed in a single long take by a stationary camera. Despite more extensive use of deep focus and moving camera in *A Star Is Born* than in almost any of his other pictures, Cukor inevitably returns to an uninterrupted, simply designed composition with a single area of focus for scenes of high drama. Stalling Oliver at first by standing to pour some coffee, Esther finally admits that Norman is in a sanitarium:

> "He really wants to stop drinking, Oliver. He's trying very hard. I know he is, but… but, what is it? What is it that makes him want to destroy himself? You, you've known him longer than anyone else. Tell me what it is please. I don't care. Just tell me."

Oliver sits on the left side of the frame, the mirror with Oliver's profile reflected in it dominates the center and Esther is on the right. The mirror, as elephant in the room, represents the Hollywood warp in which both Norman and Esther struggle to find equilibrium. Throughout her

Judy Garland rests between takes on the "Lose That Long Face" number.

speech, Esther chokes back tears, struggles to direct her gaze, and points a finger at Niles, who explains, "Don't you think I've tried to find out through the years—to help him. I don't know, Esther. I don't know what the answer is." Starting to fall apart, she continues:

> "You don't know what it's like to watch somebody you love just crumble away, bit by bit, day by day, in front of your eyes and stand there helpless. Love isn't enough. I thought it was. I thought I was the answer for Norman. But love isn't enough for him, and I'm afraid of what's beginning to happen. Within me. Because sometimes I hate him. I hate his promises to stop, and then the watching and waiting to see it begin again. I hate to go home to him at night, to his lies. Well, my heart goes out to him because he tries. He does try. But I hate him for failing. I hate me too. I hate me too because I failed too. I have. I don't know what's going to happen to us, Oliver. No matter how much you love somebody, how do you live out the days? How?"

To say Garland captures the pain and despair of Moss Hart's words is to undervalue the power of her performance. As she details Norman's deterioration, she breaks into sobs and glances wildly around the room. With the admission of hatred, she shakes her head and gasps for breath. Her words come slowly, painfully. Norman's failure is so difficult to confront that she brings a hand to her mouth as if to stop the memory. And in a kind of punishment for her own failings, she jabs repeatedly at her chest to Oliver's increasing concern. Throughout the scene, Charles Bickford remains the most generous of actors, keeping perfectly still and watching her intently.

Garland's intensity has been well-noted. "Garland played the part with such raw emotions that it was often painful for Cukor to observe," writes Emanuel Levy (page 224). Cukor himself told Gavin Lambert, "A lot of people in musical comedy are like mimics or impersonators, which is not real acting... But Judy Garland was a very original and resourceful actress" (page 53).

Garland's make-up man on the film, Del Armstrong, remembers her ability to sustain the emotion of the dressing room scene through Cukor's many alternate long takes: "I had great admiration for Judy, being able to get up to those highs... So towards the end of the last takes I'd have to come in and furnish the tears for her, and maybe help her get to the point where she was in the last take. She always surprised me in her ability to do this" (Haver, page 171).

Touched by Esther's intimate confession, Oliver promises to visit Norman and offer him work at the studio again. Finally, there is a cut on movement as she is called back to the set and rises to retouch her make-up in the mirror. "You will be careful when you talk to him, won't you? All he's got left is his pride," she says, collapsing briefly on Oliver's chest before rushing out of the left side of the frame.

The coda that follows, unwisely cut from the original, is one of the film's strongest expressions of the grinding divide between a life lived simultaneously in private and before the camera. Standing again on her mark atop the dock, Esther listens to her voice on playback and waits for the proper cue. The newspapers behind her clearly read, "Bright Future Predicted." On the beat, she turns on a huge smile and belts out a variation of the finale—"Go and get your long face lost."

"In one of the most brilliant and poignant moments of the film," notes Bernardoni, "the woman who moments before was on the verge of emotional collapse becomes again the star devoting all of her star power to another take of the happy number that has now acquired an ironic undertone" (page 90). The contrast with Norman is stark. Esther possesses a resilient strength that allows her to engage her different selves and keep on going. He does not. As if to underscore that difference between them, the next scene takes place at the sanitarium.

Cukor always claimed that the sanitarium scene was based on his own visit to John Barrymore, who "…had put himself into some kind of home in Culver City to stop drinking…an old frame house that called itself a rest home." At one point during the visit, according to Cukor, "Jack came in, with a sort of aide called Kelly. He took us into a gloomy sitting room and said, 'Can we sit in here, Kelly? Nobody's going to come through and disturb us by pretending he's Napoleon.' I reported this episode to David Selznick, who was preparing the first *A Star Is Born* with William Wellman. They liked the scene so much they included it in the picture. Then, years later, I found myself redoing it" (Lambert, page 41).

Whether Cukor's recollection is true or not, the scenes in both films are nearly identical. Oliver arrives at a shabby, cheaply furnished house and is asked by a grim matron to wait in the reception area. Similar to Esther's former rooming house and the antithesis of the airy place in Malibu, the interior is dark and cluttered. Descending from the top of the frame, Norman, who looks frail in a bulky beige bathrobe, makes his way slowly and carefully down the stairs. He is accompanied by a tough-looking attendant in a crew cut whom he introduces as Cuddles (Henry Kulky). Despite his weakened condition, Norman summons his mordant humor to put Oliver at ease. "You don't think someone will come strolling through here," Norman asks Cuddles, "telling us he's Napoleon or Julius Caesar, do you?" When Cuddles "attends" to him a little too closely, Norman protests, "Now, Cuddles, Mr. Niles isn't slipping me a case of scotch. He's just going to sit with me." Central to the scene is the friendship between Norman and Oliver, who continues to be portrayed sans any recognizable real-life model as a caring and perceptive studio boss.

Their conversation together on the sun porch (only slightly less dreary) is filmed in another single take. Oliver asks about Norman's accommodation, and Norman replies, "It's positively luxurious (Mason makes the four syllables sound much longer than they are). We even have steel mesh on the windows to keep the draft out." Then, getting to the reason he came, Oliver hands Norman a script and offers him a part in it.

Handling the script like the gift it is, Norman advances downstage to sit at a table and thumb through the pages. Cukor's blocking, with Norman's back to Oliver and his face to the camera, allows us to read the ex-

A Star Is Born (1954) • 199

Norman and Cuddles (Henry Kulky) descend the dreary sanitarium stairs to greet Oliver.

pressions that Oliver cannot see. "Who plays opposite me?" asks Norman. "Well, it isn't exactly the lead, Norman," replies Oliver as he hurries to explain the effect this significant supporting role will leave on audiences. Disappointment clouds Norman's face and he pauses for a moment before turning to Oliver and explaining that he is "pretty well set at another studio." Playing along with the fabrication, Oliver asks Norman to think about the idea anyway and maybe give him some notes on the part. As the two friends walk from the porch, the camera tracks along with them, momentarily reframing Norman when he glances regretfully at the script left lying on a bookcase. Just before Oliver exits the house, Norman suddenly steps forward and clutches Oliver's sleeve. "Thanks for dropping in," he says, in lieu of all the other repressed feelings he is unable to express.

Time passes and a dissolve situates us on location at Santa Anita racetrack just east of Los Angeles. Norman's encounter with Libby in the bar there involves a complicated bit of crowd choreography reminiscent of Hitchcock in, say, *North by Northwest's* United Nations lobby scene. After the appropriate establishing shot (an extreme long shot which pans from the grandstands down across the track as a bugle sounds the call to post), Norman enters and pauses for a moment at the top of a wide staircase leading down into the clubhouse bar. Nearly a hundred bit players and extras are involved in the intricately staged and timed action that follows. During his descent, Norman is passed by several well-dressed people rushing up and down the steps. With the camera tracking out in front of him, he crosses the floor and stops to greet by name (Bert, Marian, Sonny) three people sitting on a couch and checking the racing forms. Barely acknowledging him, they return abruptly to their own conversation and he continues on to the bar, behind which the tracking camera has come to rest. "Hello, Mr. Maine, I haven't seen you around in a long time," welcomes the bartender.

At the same time, Libby enters the far background of the frame and begins to advance. Clarifying in a brief exchange that all he truly wants is "ginger ale and ginger ale," Norman turns to his right at the exact moment that Libby sits down next to him. "Hello, Libby," Norman says warmly and there is a cut on movement from the extended traveling shot to a stationary medium two-shot. With the same venom and mostly the same words that Lionel Stander used in the 1937 picture, Libby answers, "Well, it's Mr. America of yesteryear. Do they let you wander around now without a keeper?" Norman tries to keep the mood light by responding that he's a "trustee," but Libby pushes hard. "I imagine you'll be here all the time, now that you've retired from the hurly-burly of the silver screen," he taunts. When Norman shares how lonely it is in Malibu with Esther working at the studio, Libby says, "I wouldn't squawk if I were you. It's nice having somebody in the family making a living."

Ignoring what is practically a plea by Norman to go easy, Libby unloads his dislike of him and resentment at having to clean up all his indiscretions over the years. "You've got yourself fixed up pretty well," he suggests one more time. "You can live off your wife now," and Norman, who has been painfully listening to the diatribe with his hand to his forehead, turns and sidearms Libby across the neck. Libby punches him to the floor, and a crowd quickly gathers, muttering anonymous comments, such as "Oh, it's just Norman Maine... he's drunk again... he's been drunk for years." Cukor heightens the tension with quick cuts between Libby standing and Norman curled up on the floor and then shifts to an overhead medium shot of the onlookers slowly dispersing and Norman emerging with a hand held to his mouth. Passing each other amid the crowd, Libby walks away from the bar and Norman approaches it. The camera shoots into the mirror behind the bar and the frame is filled with people moving on with their business. There is a cut to a side angle of the bar as Norman sits and orders a double scotch and then a cut on the lifting of the glass to a medium close-up. Mason's body language is remarkable, expressive of Norman's self-loathing, pain, and humiliation. Cradling his temple and jamming his left fist into his cheek, he hunches his shoulders, shivers, and grimaces in something between a silent scream and a stifled sob. Seldom has quiet desperation been so convincingly portrayed on screen.

It is Christmas time, and Norman has been gone for several days on a bender. Oliver, so solicitous of his stars that he makes holiday house calls, is with Esther in Malibu. The brief scene is another single, extended take. Tracking and reframing, the camera keeps Esther and Oliver in a constant yet flexible two-shot. The point is to convey her worried restlessness; it's been four days since she's heard from Norman, and Oliver fears that she is making herself sick. Closing the terrace doors, she crosses the living room and stands near an elegantly decorated Christmas tree on the right. When the phone rings, she is afraid to answer, turning tearfully toward the camera as Oliver takes the call instead. Everything about the scene moves the narrative. Learning that Norman has been arrested for drunkenness, Oliver decides he will go to night court for the arraignment. He moves back left through the room and Esther follows, announcing that she is accompanying him as well. When Oliver warns of the inevitable newspaper reporters, she responds, "What do I care about that now?" Together they step up to the foyer and exit the rear frame, momentarily empty except for the large, somewhat poignantly inopportune Christmas tree that dominates the right edge of the composition.

The next scene, an insert really, is a curious choice for inclusion in a release print already deemed to be overlong. There is no dialogue. Oliver on the right, and Esther on the left, sit wordlessly in the back of a car

In an intricately blocked scene, Norman regains his footing after the brief fight with Libby.

whose driver is not shown. Among the sights as they drive presumably down Sunset Boulevard is Schwabs Drugstore. She opens her compact, shudders, then looks away. Perhaps Cukor's rationale for the scene is to ironically reprise Hollywood landmarks within a more solemn context or to offer up one more mirror image in which Esther confronts the gritty realities at odds with her manufactured movie star image. Either reason seems redundant this far into the film.

The night court is different in style and substance from the scenes around it. For one, it is heavily edited, containing thirty-four separate cuts during its four-minute running time. Consequently, there is an uneasy tenseness to the scene commensurate with the uncertainty over Norman's ultimate fate. Events are spiraling beyond even Esther's ability to control them. Second, the action here, unlike the rest of the film, takes place outside the protective cocoon of studio, home, and night life. Oliver is unable to influence the judge, who tells him that Norman will get a fair hearing just like everyone else.

The setting is drab, the lighting flat, and the colors muted. In memory, the episode seems to have been shot in black and white. This is a hard-knock world beyond the pull of studio privilege and influence. To emphasize the impersonality of the judicial bureaucracy, Hart and Cukor spend considerable time on the dispensation of cases, the processing of detainees, and the reasoning of the judge.

We first see Norman as he ascends in a wire-meshed lift from the cells to the courtroom. Disheveled and badly in need of a shave, he is among a group of similarly destitute drunks. Cukor tracks in on the bars of the lift and then sets up a side angle medium shot of the judge's bench and the line of prisoners. Once Norman spots Esther sitting with Oliver, Cukor cuts several times between them, with Esther ultimately breaking a hesitant smile and Norman hanging his head in shame.

After he sentences a confused and hung over little man (Percy Helton) to sixty days, the judge (Frank Ferguson in the familiar role of a mid-level authority figure) moves on to the case of Ernest Sidney Gubbins, who is charged with crashing a car under the influence and, among other things, resisting arrest: "Were you Norman Maine, the actor?" he asks disbelievingly, the use of the past tense accenting the finality of Norman's collapse. Appalled at Norman's squandered opportunities and his disregard of public safety, the judge lectures him severely: "You've come pretty low, haven't you? There's not a man here who's had the advantages you've had and look what you've done with them. You're nothing but an irresponsible drunk."

Just as he is about to sentence Norman to ninety days in county jail, Esther steps forward (despite Norman wordlessly warning her off) and begs for leniency. "I recognize you, Miss Lester," says the judge, proving that there may be a little studio juice left after all. "Please," she continues, "I promise this will never ever happen again. I'll be responsible for him, I will, if you'll please just not send him there." In a kind of plaintive variation on the marriage vows, the judge asks, "Do you realize the responsibility you'll be assuming to the court and to the people of this city?" and she responds, "I do." After a long pause, the judge decides, "Sentence suspended. Prisoner remanded to custody of wife."

As Rick Altman points out in his book *The American Film Musical*, the Norman-Esther relationship has reversed itself completely. Norman, he writes, "began as her father (at first he makes decisions for her), at the center they are equalized (marriage), she ends as his mother (taking him into custody and making his decisions)" (pages 266-67). Additionally, Esther's formal assumption of responsibility for Norman caps the various references to him as a misbehaving child that began back in the Shrine

Auditorium sequence. In a shot that would be right at home in a prison drama, Norman, who has been processed for release, slowly emerges from the bottom of the frame in the elevator cage, pauses to adjust himself, and exits the rear door.

Outside, Oliver and Esther greet him in a few moments of consolation before reporters and photographers swarm into the shot from all edges of the frame. The fact that Cukor does not follow with a lurid newspaper insert indicates once again that the gossip industry is not the same target here that it was in the 1932 and 1937 films.

Cukor dissolves instead to Norman deeply asleep at the Malibu beach house. Like the climax of an opera, the Malibu scene reprises and resolves many of the film's major motifs: the wind and wave images, the terrace setting, the fragmented reflections, the contrast of light and dark, and the theme of protector/dependent.

Esther emerges from shadows to straighten Norman's bedcovers. A sea breeze blows briskly through the open window, and a ray of light picks out his face in the center of the frame. As she exits the bedroom, there is a cut to an extreme long shot of the house exterior with waves washing in to the shore. Wind and water seep visually and aurally into almost every shot, the former emblematic of Norman's restlessness, the latter of his fate.

Waiting outside on the terrace that in happier times contained party guests, Oliver turns and watches Esther through floor-to-ceiling sliding glass doors which reflect the breaking waves. Her figure seems somewhat vague, somewhat superimposed, among the reflections. There is thematic resonance here (Esther's struggle for psychological integration) but practical necessity as well. Cukor is shooting on a studio set; the waves are rear projections that look more convincing mirrored against the windows, and the wind rustling her chiffon scarf is a stream of air pumped in via sound-insulating canvas tunnels from fans outside the studio. Esther and Oliver walk downstage toward the edge of the terrace facing the ocean. "He's asleep," she reports. "He's been sleeping most of the day." When he advises, "That's the best thing for him," she begins to cry and says, "He looks so helpless lying there. Smiling in his sleep, just like a child." It is the same infant-in-his-bed view that Norman's butler shared much earlier with Libby. A gust of wind blows some papers from the terrace and Cukor à la Douglas Sirk pans with the scraps and cuts to show them swirl past Norman's window. In a medium close-up, Norman wakes and listens to the voices from the terrace. We can hear Esther say, "I love him" and "I know you'll understand what I have to tell you."

Oliver as solid protector escorts Norman and Esther from night court.

There are a total of seven cuts back and forth between the terrace and the bedroom as Norman overhears increasingly more painful information. The shots of him grow longer in duration. In a two-shot back on the terrace, always a location for major decisions, Esther tells Oliver, "I can't do any more pictures. I'm going away for good with Norman." Turning aside, she walks behind him and crosses the terrace; the waves become visible on the left edge of the frame. He, of course, argues against the idea: "You're at the very height of your career, Esther, the very peak of your success." Her answer to this is that "there wouldn't be any career without Norman."

More cross-cutting between Norman and the terrace occurs while they debate who is responsible for her success. Each successive shot of Norman is the same medium close-up with him in the same frozen position. His reactions are conveyed silently, the focused pool of light on his face in contrast with the darkness that threatens to engulf him. When Esther, assuming some of the guilt for his alcoholism, says, "Maybe if I'd have been with him, some of these things wouldn't have happened," Oliver frankly asserts, "Esther, I have to tell you this. I hate to but I must.

There's nothing left anymore." His words continue as an overlay to the shot of Norman internalizing the painful truth. "It happened long before last night. Long before we let him go at the studio. Twenty years of steady and quiet drinking do something to a man. It wasn't just bad pictures, it was him. And there's nothing left anymore. He's just a shell of what he once was," concludes Oliver. During the speech, Norman slowly opens his mouth as if to gasp and tightens his forehead. After a brief cutaway in which Oliver concedes that Esther is not wrong to try to help Norman, Cukor returns to Norman for the conversation's conclusion.

"James is a highly talented man but a reserved, rather enigmatic person," Cukor confided in his lengthy interview with Gavin Lambert, "and I knew that his last scene in the picture, when he breaks down and decides to commit suicide, would be a case of letting him find things out for himself. So I let the camera stay on him for a very long time, and all his feelings came out and he became so involved, in fact, he could hardly stop" (page 53).

The decision to hold the camera on Mason was an astute one. As Esther confirms that she and Norman will leave Hollywood, and Oliver says, "I'll arrange it. Bye Vicki Lester, good luck Mrs. Norman Maine," Norman reacts in palpable physical agony. He pushes his head back, clenches his eyes shut, and then arcs his whole body upward. Starting to weep, he rolls to his side in a semi-fetal position and buries his face in the pillow. It is, like the tormented drink at Santa Anita, a stunning piece of wordless, in-close acting.

Esther is sitting alone on the terrace, the waves washing in behind her. Norman opens the interior bedroom door and stands in front of the sliding windows. More so than Esther was, he is completely lost among the reflections of the ocean, a ghost-like figure with no corporeal substance. The film's repetitive use of mirror images serves now to reveal his final dissolution. Dressed in a white bathrobe, he lingers in the center of the frame and watches her. Among the cross-cuts is a medium close-up of him looking directly at the camera, followed by a point of view shot of the ocean horizon at sunset. As string music swells on the soundtrack, he girds himself for one last performance and greets Esther. For her benefit, he momentarily becomes the chief decision-maker again, proclaiming that the mood around the house should brighten and that he will be adopting a new athletic lifestyle that includes daily swims in the ocean. "I shall want some hot soup and sandwiches," he instructs her, and then adds, "But the thing I'd like more than anything else, I'd like some singing around the house." In an optimistic replay of their honeymoon banter, he inquires if he "still own[s] the copyright," and she replies, "Yes, even the Scandinavian." Promising to sing in the kitchen and open the window so he can hear, she recedes into the rear of the frame, caught briefly in a strip of light that links her visually to the pool of bedroom light that illuminated him. Thus, we reach the gaze-centered, farewell tagline, first introduced at the Oleander Arms, durable through all three versions of the story and nearly as resonant as *Casablanca's* "Here's looking at you, kid." Calling her back, Norman softly, almost whisperingly, remarks, "I just wanted to look at you again."

Cukor follows this with repeated shots of Norman framed against the setting sun and the ocean. In one intricate yet essentially redundant composition, Norman exits screen left and walks toward the waves while the camera dollies in to the superimposed window reflections where he completes the same actions again. He appears to be overwhelmed with water on all sides.

Off screen, Esther sings the now impossible "It's a New World," and a cut on movement continues Norman's walk toward the shoreline of an actual beach (shot on location at Laguna). Removing his bathrobe, he wades out toward a horizon streaked with the iridescent orange and pink sheen of sunset. Finally, in that familiar synecdoche of melodrama, the camera pans off the ocean to his submerged bathrobe swirling in the riptide. Appropriately, Norman leaves Esther just the way he met her—during one of her performances.

Norman's death provokes frantic albeit disingenuous activity within Libby's office. The establishing shot there opens on an assistant holding a newspaper with a front page banner headline that reads "Ex Film Star Victim of Accidental Drowning." Libby takes several phone calls, each conversation more bogus than the last one. "We had big plans for him, all set for a comeback," he tells one reporter, and "Oh, yes, it was very sad. It was a great personal loss to everybody," he lies to another. Libby's real interest is to maximize publicity for the studio, helping the *Herald Express* with its "front page spread" and providing "pictures of the home and beach" to another paper. Although Carson's Libby does not make the crudely insensitive comments uttered by Lionel Stander's character, he quotes Eliot's "This is the way the world ends, not with a bang but a whimper" as a way to diminish Norman's stature. The drink in his hand during working hours also suggests that he may be a functioning alcoholic himself, hypocritically condemning Norman for some of his own issues.

Norman walking into the ocean toward a symbolically setting sun.

The funeral, probably orchestrated by the publicity department, deteriorates into a tawdry mob scene. Shooting on location at the Church of the Good Shepherd in Beverly Hills, Cukor brought a couple hundred extras and waited for the rare southern California day with drizzle and clouds. He gets the surging threat of the crowd exactly right. Filling each frame with people and often shooting from low angles, he cuts rapidly between shots, some of which are taken by hand-held cameras. There is a jumpy documentary realism like that captured outside the Shrine at the opening of the film.

When Esther, supported on each arm by Danny and Oliver, emerges from the church, the crowd charges across the lawn and pushes up against the steps. Excitable disembodied voices shout things like "You'll get over this" and "Yeah, give us just one look." Danny and Oliver fight their way through the mob, but an arm in a white raincoat reaches into the left side of the frame and snatches the veil from Esther's face. Traumatized, she begins to scream, and the grim little scene fades to black. To the extent that there is any critical target in Cukor's celebration of Hollywood, this is it—boorish, hysterical fans who invade the privacy of stars like Vicki Lester.

Libby feigns sorrow over Norman's death and capitalizes on publicity for the studio.

 Oliver is next seen walking with Libby outside a studio sound stage. Their conversation provides an expository update on Esther and an opportunity for Oliver to undercut Libby's so far unanswered Norman-bashing. Pressed by Libby for news that he can give reporters, Oliver insists that no announcement will be issued regarding Esther, who is in seclusion and not taking calls, until he has had chance to speak with her. In reference to the Hollywood tradition of naming studio buildings after stars (a practice which Paramount, for example, still maintains to this day), Oliver tells Libby that Norman Maine's name will remain on his bungalow as long as Oliver runs the studio. "You know, Libby," adds Oliver, "you missed a lot not knowing Norman Maine." Libby protests, "Not knowing him? I spent my life knowing him. I knew what he was going to do before he did it. I knew him backwards." Speaking for Hart and Cukor, Oliver replies, "You didn't know him at all. He was quite a guy."

 Esther's seclusion is more extreme than even Oliver suspects. Attended to by a soft-spoken butler, she sits alone in the darkened beach house library and stares at a small blaze in the fireplace. She has withdrawn into a sealed refuge like the honeymoon motel room where she felt safest and happiest with Norman. Isolation, even with its overtones of

Esther escorted at Norman's funeral by Danny (left) and Oliver (right) just before she is assailed by a riotous crowd.

death, seems to her now the best way to preserve his memory. In a shot that foregrounds the fundamental artifice of set design, the camera tracks "through" the wall separating the foyer from the library as the butler enters and asks if there is anything else he can do before going to bed. Kept off screen for a few moments to build suspense, Esther is seen first in profile and then straight-on, each composition unbalanced and off center, reflective of Norman's absence and her distress.

After the butler leaves, she remains motionless in a shaft of light until the doorbell rings and voices are heard behind her. Danny enters from the rear of the frame and, in a cut on movement that bridges into an ordered two-shot, takes a seat opposite her. He is there to escort her to a benefit appearance that she promised ironically to make at the Shrine Auditorium. She demurs and he keeps at her. "You told them you'd be there," he insists. "That, that was before," she protests. He asks, "Are you just going to sit here forever?" There is a cut to a slightly different angle (to facilitate the subsequent single take tracking), and she explodes, "Yes, tonight, tomorrow night, and for as long as I like." Pounding her arms on the chair and standing, she screams, "I don't want sympathy from you or anybody else."

With more force than he has shown to this point in the picture as well as his career, Tommy Noonan delivers the Grandma Lettie speech minus all the pioneer references. You don't deserve it. You're a great monument to Norman Maine, you are," shouts Danny. "He was a drunk and he wasted his life, but he loved you, and he took enormous pride in the one thing in his life that wasn't a waste—you. His love for you and your success, that was the one thing that wasn't a waste."

She turns her back to the camera and walks away, but Danny circles around in front of her and keeps hammering. "Maybe what he did was wrong. I don't know," he says in recognition of what really happened in the ocean, "But he didn't want to destroy that, the one thing he took pride in. Now you're doing the one thing he was terrified of, you're tossing aside the one thing he had left... you're tossing it right back into the ocean after him."

Sobbing, Esther walks toward the door, her face still turned away from the camera. Danny concludes by arguing, "You're the one thing that remains of him now, and if you just kick it away, it's like he never existed. Like there never was a Norman Maine at all." Slowly, she relaxes her shoulders and turns to him and the camera. She is composed and resolved. Smiling weakly and grabbing his hand, she asks, "Will you wait for me." This is an important moment for the film, whose form and content have been patterned dualistically on the rise and fall, the birth and death, of stardom. Norman's collapse became his literal death, which threatens now to dominate Esther with its overtones of darkness and seclusion. Danny here must be the agent who returns Esther to life, performance, and engagement with others.

The dramatic imperatives of the scene, the right blend of intensity and restraint, are why Garland wanted Cukor to direct her comeback in the first place. She wanted his ability to sit quietly with his actors, talk them through motivation, and help them access inner resources. However that alchemy works, Garland and Noonan make believable the heightened emotions which so easily could have slipped into travesty.

Garland's brilliant performance in the scene forms the basis for an oft-told Cukor anecdote, which bears repeating here for the insight it provides into Garland's talent and self-effacing sense of humor:

> "Toward the end of shooting we had to do a scene where she's in a state of total depression after her husband's suicide. While we lined it up she just sat there very preoccupied... Just before the take I said to her very quietly, 'You know what this is about. You

really know this.' She gave me a look, and I knew she was thinking, 'He wants me to dig into myself because I know all about this in my own life.' That was all. We did a take... a friend, played by Tommy Noonan, comes to see her to try and persuade her to go to a benefit performance that night. He chides her about not giving in to herself, he even gets deliberately rough with her—and she loses her head. She gets up and screams like someone out of control, maniacal and terrifying. And when Judy Garland did this, it was *absolutely* terrifying. She had no concern with what she looked like, she went much further than I'd expected, and I thought it was great...So he grabbed her and held her and spoke his next lines with great force and energy. The lines were meant to shame her—and her reaction was unforgettable. She turned around and you saw that all the anger and fear and madness had disappeared. Her face looked very vulnerable and tender, there were tears in her eyes. So I said, 'Cut!' and then, 'Quick let's do it once more.'... So Judy did it again—differently but just as stunningly... when it was over, I said to Judy, 'You really scared the hell out of me.' She was very pleased, she didn't realize what an effect she'd made. And then... she said, 'Oh, that's nothing. Come over to my house any afternoon. I do it every afternoon.' Then she gave me a look and added, 'But I only do it *once* at home.' (Lambert, pages 53-54)

Even without the anecdote, viewers sense that Esther's outburst and recovery are bringing them remarkably close to the real Garland.

The film achieves the symmetry of the musical numbers by ending where it began—at the Shrine Auditorium. Backstage hums with a familiar preparatory activity. Cukor's deep focus tracking shot through the wings is astonishing. As he explores the exotic surroundings, the camera reframes on one bizarre tableau after another. The mélange of historical and cultural allusions is somewhere between Carnevale di Venezia and Día de los Muertos. Opening on a composition packed with formally dressed guests and showgirls, he pulls away slightly and then dollies into a crowd of performers behind them. A flamenco guitarist is playing a melancholic solo ("Amor Flamenco"); on either side of him porcelain-faced *damas* in lace dresses and mantillas slowly fan themselves. Then, like Renoir following chateau party guests in *Rules of the Game*, Cukor center frames on the guitarist and tracks leftward with him to the edge of the screen, where he serenades a tall Spanish woman dressed all in black. In the background are a toreador and a French aristocrat (or maybe he's an American colonialist). Seated close to the floor on the right is a bird-like woman with orange hair, an exaggeratedly long nose, and a very pointy chin. Although the frame is filled with people, the atmosphere is languorous, mournful, even funereal. The guitarist seems to be playing at a masked wake frozen in time.

Cut to several black and red costumed chorus girls rushing up a rear staircase where the camera "discovers" Danny and Esther and reverse tracks as they descend into the backstage wings. Pausing to greet one of the performers, Esther is positioned at the right edge of a long brick wall. We notice the "E.B. and N.M." heart that Norman drew there even before Esther does and fear for her reaction. Touching the initials, she starts to fall apart, but Danny embraces her and leads her up a set of steps to the main stage.

An extreme long shot from the audience offers a view of the stage's closed red curtains. The emcee (Wilton Graff) enters in a spotlight and announces, "We're all of us aware of the tragic circumstances which prevent Vicki Lester's appearance here tonight." Just as he is extending sympathy, Danny walks out on stage and whispers new information. "Vicki Lester," exclaims the emcee, "will appear tonight."

Cukor pushes hard for a big emotional payoff to the finale. The stage and house lights are cut. A medium shot of Oliver in one of the boxes (indicating Esther's probable return to the studio) is followed by two quick shots of the expectant audience. While the curtain rises on a half-lit blue stage, the emcee breathlessly hyperbolizes, "Here she is, ladies and gentlemen, a star that burns bright and high." Esther, dressed in Jean Louis's version of a Christian Dior high-waisted, floor-length New Look gown, acknowledges the audience's reception in a medium long shot. Stepping back on stage, the emcee explains that the benefit is "being broadcast all over the world" and asks, "Your fans are hoping you'll say a few words to them, won't you?" A medium shot, a pause, then with growing intensity, Esther says, "Hello, everybody, this is Mrs. Norman Maine."

In a succession of quick shots from several different angles, the audience rises in waves for a standing ovation. A choral overlay reprises "It's a New World," and the camera slowly cranes outward from the medium shot of Esther alone on stage. To make the movement even more emphatic, Cukor dissolves to a set-up further back in the Shrine Auditorium and

Esther reacts emotionally backstage at the Shrine to the lipstick initials previously drawn by Norman.

continues the long, slow crane-out from there. The moment serves two important thematic purposes. Esther's words legitimate and memorialize Norman's contribution to Hollywood, and the camera movement reintegrates her back into the wider community of colleagues and fans. Her new world now will return her to performance and stardom. Applause continues forcefully as the screen fades to black.

That *A Star Is Born* itself would receive the same enthusiastic reception seemed all but assured by opening week audiences and newspaper reviews. Premiere crowds in Hollywood and New York thronged the theaters, closing traffic for blocks and filling the streets. *Time* magazine gushed that Garland "...gives what is just about the greatest one-woman show in modern movie history" (Morella and Epstein, page 166). Bosley Crowther, writing for *The New York Times*, concluded that Cukor "...gets performances from Miss Garland and Mr. Mason that make the heart flutter and bleed" (page 165). Summing up the film's strengths, *Life* magazine stated that *A Star Is Born* is… "a brilliantly staged, scored, and photographed film, worth all the effort" (Haver, page 211).

At a little over three hours and with short subjects included, the film could have been shown about four times a day if screenings started around noon. By adding an intermission and charging special roadshow engagement prices, *A Star Is Born* could have been marketed successfully. In fact, ten years later, Jack Warner would do exactly that with Cukor's *My Fair Lady*, and the film would go on to be a box office success and to win Oscars for Best Director and Best Picture.

However, Benjamin Kalmenson, head of distribution, believed that profits could be maximized more effectively by cutting about half an hour from the picture and squeezing in more daily screenings. Speaking as one salesman to another, Kalmenson convinced parent company president Harry Warner that he was right, and Harry, always eager to play alpha male in the family, ordered younger brother Jack to make the cuts.

Working off notes from the sales department, editor Folmar Blangsted removed whole scenes, sequences, and reel sections. Audiences and critics, who saw the cut version at test screenings, protested, but the deed was done. At Warner Bros.' distribution offices around the country, full-length versions were trimmed according to studio instructions and the excised footage shipped back to Burbank. Even with the cuts, business was very good during the opening month, but by the winter holiday season, attendance fell off dramatically. Somewhere along the way, the legal issue with Selznick was settled (foreign distribution rights for Warner Bros. with $25,000 and remake rights to *A Farewell to Arms* for Selznick), but it hardly seemed to matter. The film was nowhere near making a profit.

In February, *A Star Is Born* was nominated for six Academy Awards—actor, actress, art direction, song ("The Man That Got Away"), scoring, and costume design. Then, as now, a Best Actor or Best Actress Oscar would bring in additional profit (roughly a million dollars for each major category in 1955).

Because Garland, who was expected to win, was due to give birth about the same time as the awards ceremony, a special television hook-up was assembled in her hospital room so she could talk to host Bob Hope if/when her name was called. The other actresses in competition were Dorothy Dandridge for *Carmen Jones,* Audrey Hepburn for *Sabrina,* Grace Kelly for *The Country Girl,* and Jane Wyman for *Magnificent Obsession.* When the awards were presented on March 30, 1955, *A Star Is Born* failed to score a single victory. After Garland lost the Oscar to Grace Kelly, the television crew packed immediately and left her alone, consoled, she always claimed when telling the story, by the birth a day earlier of her son, Joey.

According to studio records quoted by Haver, the film still had not earned back its negative production cost by the end of 1955. Its domestic and negative gross hovered around $6 million. No further pictures ever were made under the abrogated Warners/Transcona deal.

And so, the truncated *A Star Is Born* disappeared into local television movie matinee purgatory, revered by Cukor fans for the opening Shrine sequence and by Garland fans for her "The Man That Got Away" number, until the early 1980s. It was then that Ronald Haver, assisted by Gene Allen, Fay Kanin, Douglas Edwards, Bruce Davis, and others, assembled a restoration based on found footage, alternate takes, stills, and a serendipitously discovered complete soundtrack. The restored version premiered to great acclaim in New York and Los Angeles during the summer of 1983 and enjoyed an extremely successful roadshow engagement, as well. The 1983 version, in letterbox format, was also widely available on Warner Home Video.

We will probably never find the complete original print lying around in a vault somewhere. We will probably never have exactly the same experience those early audiences had in 1954. What we do have, however, is enough. Enough to show us Garland, James Mason, George Cukor, and the entire production team working at the height of their creative abilities. Enough also to give us a dazzling insider Hollywood film that deals intelligently and imaginatively with issues of performance, perception, and identity.

5

A Star Is Born
(1976)

It now seems inevitable that Barbra Streisand would star in a second musical remake of *A Star Is Born*. Arguably the premier American female pop singer of her generation as was Judy Garland of hers, Streisand, in the mid-1970s, was looking for a contemporary picture that would allow her to sing, dance (a little), act, and be funny. Along with some box office failures, she had made an extremely successful drama (*The Way We Were*, 1973, Columbia, directed by Sydney Pollack), a successful screwball comedy (*What's Up, Doc*, 1972, Warner Bros., directed by Peter Bogdanovich), and two successful costume musicals (*Funny Girl*, 1968, Columbia, directed by William Wyler and *Funny Lady*, 1975, Columbia, directed by Herbert Ross), but she had not yet made a successful youth-oriented film in which she played a hip, modern woman and had a chance to display her full Garland-like talents as a total entertainer. *A Star Is Born*, she hoped, would be that picture.

Another similarity with Garland's *A Star Is Born* is that the Streisand project was to be co-produced by Streisand, her romantic partner at the time, Jon Peters, and Warner Bros./First Artists. Like Sid Luft, Peters was his own unique Hollywood creation. A tough kid from Burbank, who had served time in reform school for petty larceny, Peters, by the time he met Barbra Streisand, had amassed about $10 million in net assets as a trendy hair stylist, salon owner, and beauty product entrepreneur. Through his relationship with Streisand, he would also become both a record (Streisand's *ButterFly* album) and a movie producer. It was Peters who pushed Streisand (three years older than her new boyfriend) to dress and look younger, and it was Peters who read the new *A Star Is Born* script and insisted that she (and he) should make it.

Peters especially liked the fact that the script, by the well-regarded husband and wife writers, John Gregory Dunne and Joan Didion, changed the characters from movie actors to sexy young rock musicians. But the rockers Dunne and Didion originally had in mind did not include Barbra Streisand. In an article titled "Gone Hollywood" first published in *Esquire*, Dunne wrote, "It was at one o'clock in the afternoon on the first day of July 1973, when I turned to my wife, while passing the Aloha Tower in downtown Honolulu on our way to the airport, and said sixteen words I would often later regret: 'James Taylor and Carly Simon in a rock-and-roll version of *A Star Is Born*'" (page 37).

That neither Dunne nor Didion had ever seen the previous iterations of *A Star Is Born* was not considered by them to be a drawback. That Taylor had acted only in Monte Hellman's low budget film *Two-Lane Blacktop* (1971, Universal) and that Simon had never appeared in a movie at all was similarly deemed a non-issue. The goal was to explore life on the road, concert tours, and groupies. The *A Star Is Born* angle was just a hook to get Warner Bros., who now owned the rights to the two previous versions, interested. Another selling point was that Taylor and Simon were married in real life and both recorded for labels associated with Warner Bros., which meant the company could recoup the cost of film production and reap an additional tidy profit on the sale of a hit soundtrack album alone.

After its sudden conception on Oahu, the *A Star Is Born* remake had a long and complicated gestation. Dunne and Didion pitched the idea to Dick Shepherd, head of production at Warners and their former agent, and he green-lighted it as a studio project. For three weeks, the Dunnes traveled with Jethro Tull and Uriah Heep to master the milieu and then hunkered down for six months to write a first draft of the script that briefly was called *Rainbow Road*.

At that point Warners took up the issue of who would direct the picture. "Our first choice to direct," commented Dunne, "was Warren Beatty, whom the studio did not see as a director, our second Mike Nichols, whom the studio did not see as a director on this picture, and after that we kept our mouths shut. Our agents sent the script to Peter Bogdanovich, for which transgression we fired them; his opinion of the script matched ours of his pictures" (page 41).

Ultimately, Warner Bros. agreed to let actor-director Mark Rydell work on speculation with Dunne and Didion to develop a second draft and to line up two stars to play the leads, Carly Simon and James Taylor already having declined to be involved. If Warners liked the results, the company would sign Rydell to a very lucrative directing contract. Dunne remembered the rewrite this way: "It took one more draft and another six months to make us thoroughly sick of the project. I recall the second six months only as an endless argument, carried on over commissary lunches and studio meetings, usually about who the pay-or-play elements should be" (page 41).

Halfway through the second six months, Warner Bros. took Rydell off the project and replaced him with John Foreman as producer and Jerry Schatzberg as director. (Five years later, Rydell finally would direct his own rock and roll musical drama, *The Rose*, in which Bette Midler as a self-destructive Janis Joplin-like singer combines both the rising and falling star into a single character.) Schatzberg, the successful director of *The Panic in Needle Park* (1971) and *Scarecrow* (1973), and Foreman, producer of 1973's *Serpico* (all three films starring Al Pacino), worked on additional draft revisions and shopped the script to a string of actors and actresses.

Kris Kristofferson, a major country-western performer, who had appeared in films like *Pat Garrett and Billy the Kid* (1973) and *Blume in Love* (1973), came on board early in the Norman Maine part (now called John Norman Howard) despite some half-hearted talk about securing Elvis Presley or Mick Jagger for the role. For the Esther Blodgett (now Esther Hoffman) part, the script was submitted to Liza Minnelli, Diana Ross, and Cher. Of the three singers, only Cher, who signed with Warner Bros. Records in 1974, and who would marry rocker Greg Allman in 1975 just days after finalizing her divorce from Sonny Bono, was interested in the part and knew anything at all about the raucous world of rock. In fact, according to writer Randall Riese, she campaigned heavily for the role and "agreed to submit herself to one audition after another" (page 402).

It is tantalizing to think of Kristofferson and Cher starring in the Dunnes's original script, but that possibility was never to be. Jon Peters, sometime during the summer of 1974, read the revised draft and convinced Streisand, who had already passed on the first version of the script, to reconsider. This, he argued, would be the hip contemporary film where she would appear as the sexy young woman she was and would attract a whole new demographic of fans. The more he talked, the more she liked the idea.

Once Streisand became officially involved, everything about the project changed. As part of her agreement with Warner Bros., control of the picture would pass to First Artists (the company she had formed with Paul Newman, Sidney Poitier, and Steve McQueen), distribution rights would remain with Warners, soundtrack rights would be relinquished to Columbia, where Streisand was signed, the budget would be increased to $6 million, and, in maybe the biggest jaw-dropper of all, Jon Peters would produce. Surprisingly, Warner Bros. conceded to all the terms, perhaps because the studio believed, in the words of one of its executives, "It doesn't matter if the picture is good. Shoot her singing six numbers and we'll make $60 million" (Spada, page 347).

For Streisand, a lingering problem continued to be the script. She wanted more emphasis on the romance, a stronger part for Esther, and less attention to the drug-fueled ambiance of rock concert tours. "Two weeks after Barbra Streisand came in," declared Dunne, "we again asked our lawyer for an out" (page 42). To avoid breach of contract and to preserve their profit points in the picture, Dunne and Didion wrote yet a third version of the script, which still preserved more of their vision than Streisand's. Under pressure from Streisand, Warner Bros. negotiated a settlement with the Dunnes, releasing them from the project, which had now been rechristened *A Star Is Born*, in exchange for screen credit, a $125,000 fee, and a hefty ten percent of the gross. "In the long run," notes Randall Riese, "for John Gregory Dunne and Joan Didion, those sixteen words uttered in Honolulu would pay off very handsomely" (page 405.)

With virtually complete control over the film now assured, Streisand and Peters went to work shaping it into the vanity project they had always imagined. To infuse the script with what he believed would be appropriately au courant dialogue, Peters hired novice twenty-something writer Jonathan Axelrod, stepson of playwright and film director George Axelrod. In a series of private story conferences that infuriated Schatzberg, Axelrod absorbed Streisand's and Peters' ideas about how to make the script more about themselves. "The world is waiting to see Barbra's and my story," Peters announced to *New Times* reports Marie Brenner in January of 1975 (Riese, page 405).

Consequently, into Axelrod's draft went conversations and incidents from their life together, Streisand's opinions of the press and of fans, and Peters's notions of how to make John Norman Howard even more macho. At one point, Axelrod proposed reversing the male and female roles with Esther the declining star and John Norman the rising one, so as to give Streisand the more dramatic part, an idea which star and producer briefly supported before deciding it detracted too much from the romance. The love relationship was essential, especially as it afforded endless opportunities to show Barbra in intimate situations and sexy, flattering clothing.

Sometime during the lengthy rewrites by the "committee of three," Kristofferson backed out of the project over refusal to give him above-the-title starring credit with Streisand. Like something out of a Hollywood film satire, Peters then lobbied to play the John Norman Howard part himself, despite the fact that he couldn't sing and had amassed only a single screen acting credit as a child extra riding a donkey in Cecil B. DeMille's *The Ten Commandments*. Arguing that there was no way to "shoot around" these deficiencies, Schatzberg won the battle but soon forfeited the war; he bowed out of the production, feeling that he "couldn't

Barbra Streisand saw the Esther Hoffman role as an opportunity to play a young, hip, independent and powerful female character.

direct Barbra properly under the circumstances" (Spada, page 348). Axelrod followed a couple months later when his final draft failed to satisfy Streisand and Peters. Lacking a writer, director, or leading man, the game of musical chairs shifted into overdrive.

John Gregory Dunne estimated that fourteen different writers, including Axelrod, worked on the script after he and Didion departed. Next up was the husband-and-wife writing team of Bob and Laurie Dillon, followed in no exact order by Jay Presson Allen, Buck Henry, Arthur Laurents, Alvin Sargent, and one more married team—Renée Taylor and Joseph Bologna. According to Streisand biographer Anne Edwards, Laurents advised the star that the only good script was the original one by Didion and Dunne but that he knew she would never do it "because it's tough" (page 369). Barbra, he continued, "wanted what I guess all insecure women want—to be romantic princesses" (page 369).

Equally vexing was the director question. Not surprisingly, Jon Peters proposed himself for that position also, telling Marie Brenner, "Directing is a thing I've done all my life! It's getting people to do what I want them to do" (Spada, page 349). For several weeks Streisand seemed to support the idea until she realized probably that a $6 million picture needed someone with a bit more experience at the helm and announced instead that in addition to *A Star Is Born* Peters would also be producing *The Life and Times of Bruce Lee* for First Artists. With Peters "promoted" to new projects, several top-tier directors were approached for the *A Star Is Born* job, including Bob Fosse, Arthur Hiller, Hal Ashby, Sidney Lumet, and Robert Altman, all of whom turned it down, some more adamantly than others.

Under pressure from Warner Bros. to begin shooting no later than January of 1976, First Artists finally revealed to the press that Frank Pierson had been signed to write and direct *A Star Is Born*. Fifty years old at the time, Pierson had written several film scripts, among them the very successful *Cat Ballou* (1965, Columbia, directed by Elliot Silverstein), *Cool Hand Luke* (1967, Warner Bros./Seven Arts, directed by Stuart Rosenberg) and *Dog Day Afternoon* (1975, Warner Bros., directed by Sidney Lumet). On March 29, 1976, during shooting of *A Star Is Born*, Pierson would win the Best Original Screenplay Oscar for *Dog Day Afternoon*. Although he had directed only one feature film, an adaptation of John le Carré's *The Looking Glass War* in 1970 for Frankovich Productions and Columbia, Warner Bros. was high on Pierson and agreed to his demands to direct as well as rewrite *A Star Is Born*. Streisand gave her own formal approval when Pierson promised to collaborate fully with her and to accept input on the film's overall direction.

One of Pierson's first changes in the script was to de-emphasize the career competition between the two main characters and to heighten the romance. In regular story conferences with Peters and Streisand, he listened to their autobiographical suggestions on how to develop the narrative. According to Anne Edwards, "a love scene in a bathtub encircled with burning candles, the only light in the room, was taken from their personal experience, as was the romp in the open field on the fictional antihero's ranchland. And when it came time to create the sets, Streisand had the fictitious Esther's apartment decorated as though it was hers, bringing carloads of furniture, fabric, and other things from her attic and cellar storerooms… to make the set feel as though it were once someplace where she had lived" (page 372).

Pierson also conferred with Streisand and Peters on the non-existent leading man dilemma. They needed someone who could sing, act, look good with Barbra, and still seem genuinely ravaged by substance abuse. During one session, Streisand proposed doing the film as a straight drama and getting Marlon Brando, an idea which also appealed to Peters until Pierson reminded his producers that the studio's support had always centered on the profitability of Barbra actually singing in the movie. Bob Dylan, who also had appeared in *Pat Garrett and Billy the Kid*, was briefly considered but apparently studio executives did not feel he and Streisand made a believable romantic couple. This same objection, coupled with the opinion that he had not been commanding in either Nicolas Roeg's *Performance* (1970) or Tony Richardson's *Ned Kelly* (1970), scuttled the second look at Mick Jagger.

Much more serious was the reconsideration of Elvis Presley. Peters and Streisand even flew to Las Vegas to meet with the King of Rock and Roll. The three of them spent several hours drinking wine and talking about the part, but in the end (depending on which star biographer you believe), Elvis either passed because he didn't want to share the screen with a powerful female entertainer or Barbra hesitated because Elvis in real life was too similar to John Norman Howard to be able to play him in the film. In either case, Elvis stayed in Vegas, and Streisand and Peters came back to Los Angeles.

Finally, despite almost losing him again to schedule conflicts, Streisand agreed to Kristofferson's insistence on equal billing and her new leading man signed a formal contract. Both Pierson and Streisand felt it was the right decision.

Kris Kristofferson as the Jim Morrison-like rock star John Norman Howard.

Given corporate insistence on Streisand's singing, the search for a musical supervisor became critically important. Just months before the mandated start of filming there was still no score. Streisand's attempt to transfer a successful recording collaboration to the project had not turned out well.

For her album *Lazy Afternoon*, which was released in October 1975, she had enjoyed a creatively productive working relationship with the young, British-born singer and composer Rupert Holmes. A former pianist and song writer for The Cuff Links and The Buoys, he released a solo album in 1974 called *Widescreen* that attracted considerable attention and established his reputation for clever, heavily orchestrated "story songs" and romantic ballads. Holmes later would go on to write the pop hit "Escape" aka "The Piña Colada Song" and to collect multiple Tony Awards in 1986 for the book, lyrics, and score of *The Mystery of Edwin Drood*. Streisand was one of the people impressed with *Widescreen* and hired Holmes to produce and write songs for *Lazy Afternoon*. The album received positive critical reviews, charted at #12 on *Billboard* and was certified Gold within the year.

Hoping to build on her rapport with Holmes, Streisand invited him to Los Angeles to serve as music director on *A Star Is Born*, replacing predecessors Jack Nitzche and Richard Perry. Stymied by the competing drafts of the script, Holmes composed about a dozen songs that Streisand felt did not hang together dramatically and that Peters rejected outright. Offended by what biographers Randall Riese and James Spada both refer to as Peters's angry display of temper, Rupert Holmes returned to New York City, once again leaving the production without a composer.

Enter cocky, 5' 2" songwriter Paul Williams. Known already for hit songs, such as "An Old Fashioned Love Song" (Three Dog Night), "You and Me Against the World" (Helen Reddy), and "Rainy Days and Mondays" and "We've Only Just Begun" (the Carpenters), Williams met with Streisand and Peters to discuss what they intended as a single climactic song for the film, but he ended up being signed to do the entire score with his composing partner Kenny Ascher. Additionally, Williams's contract stipulated that his material could not be changed without his personal consent.

With only ten weeks left before filming was scheduled to begin, Williams and Ascher frantically set to work on the score. As part of the working relationship that developed, the composers would finish a song and bring it to Streisand for suggestions. Her input was constant. "There was so little time," Williams later explained. "Every time the phone rang, it was Barbra, and she wanted to know how we were doing, and she wanted to have another meeting. And all of that was time that Kenny and I didn't have time to write. There *was* some tension [between us] about that" (Riese, page 414). Down to the wire, Williams and Ascher shut themselves up in Williams's house for three days with phones unplugged and pounded out the music. Ultimately, the score would also contain two of Rupert

Holmes's songs and contributions by Donna Weiss, Alan and Marilyn Bergman, Leon Russell, and Kenny Loggins.

Led by a first-time executive producer and producer and a second-time director, *A Star Is Born* began production on February 2, 1976, Warner Bros. having agreed to extend the start date by one month. The most experienced person involved was sixty-nine-year-old cinematographer Robert Surtees, who had won Academy Awards for *King Solomon's Mines* (1950), *The Bad and the Beautiful* (1952), and *Ben-Hur* (1959), as well as nominations for ten other pictures including *The Graduate* (1967), *The Last Picture Show* (1971), and *The Sting* (1973). Not only was he experienced in dramas, comedies, Westerns, war films, epics, and thrillers, he had also photographed a series of glossy musicals including *Oklahoma* (1955), *Doctor Dolittle* (1967), *Sweet Charity* (1969), and George Cukor's quirky *Les Girls* (1957).

Incredibly, James Spada quotes Frank Pierson as claiming that neither Streisand nor Peters knew who Surtees was—"What does he know about backlight?" Pierson says Streisand asked him (page 355). The choice of cinematographer was just one of many issues that caused disagreement between producers and director. It was not a happy set. Kristofferson quarreled with both Streisand and Peters, Streisand quarreled with Pierson, and Peters quarreled with everyone.

So involved was Streisand with the direction of the film, Kristofferson has commented, that he frequently did not know whose instructions to follow. Pierson and Streisand argued about camera set-ups, blocking, lighting, and locations. After one blow-up, Streisand apparently attached a video camera to Robert Surtees's boom so she could instantly review how a scene was being played and shot. "You two have got to get your shit together," Kirstofferson is reported to have told his leading lady and director. "I don't care which of you wins, but this way, with two commanders, one sayin' retreat, the other advance... it's demoralizing the crew and puttin' me into catatonia" (Spada, page 357).

Kristofferson's acuity was also affected by the massive amounts of tequila, beer, and weed that he was ingesting. Streisand worried that Kristofferson's carelessness and what she perceived as Pierson's indifference would ruin the production on which she and Peters had staked their Hollywood futures. Amazingly, however, given the high drama and dissension behind the camera, filming was completed in just under three months—on schedule and within budget. Streisand pushed to have a screen credit as co-director, but Pierson adamantly refused.

Paul Williams (center), at the picture's premiere in Westwood, was brought on board late to serve as composer/music director.

Pierson's directorial approach was to shoot *A Star Is Born* like a rock concert documentary punctuated with dramatic interludes. Stylistically, it is *Monterey Pop* meets *Five Easy Pieces*. Pierson, in fact, begins with a concert sequence. Over the Warner Bros. and First Artist title credits, we hear the voices of roadies preparing the stage: "Is this thing working?" and "Are you getting anything?" as the sound equipment is checked. Then, to signal immediately that this is not a traditional Streisand musical, a stage manager announces, "We don't want to keep repeating these things, but there are just one or two of you assholes out there who won't listen. Now we're asking you to take your seats."

The first visual image is arena spotlights, an update of the klieg lights that opened the 1954 *A Star Is Born*, sweeping the ceiling. The camera pans down off the lights and into a rapidly edited series of handheld crowd shots. People clap, someone crowd surfs, a fight breaks out, a little girl with a balloon wanders through the aisles alone. Audience members start to stomp their feet and the camera tracks past them at ground level. Mixed in with the crowd coverage are shots of the crew adjusting speakers and instruments; Gary Busey as Bobby Ritchie (John Norman Howard's road manager) walks on stage and hurls an object back into the crowd. Ritchie keeps frantically checking his walky-talky for updates on John Norman's whereabouts. The star is late and the ticket-holders are restive. Slowly, in contrast to the montage, the title, starring, and major production credits are superimposed over the visuals. A black limousine pulls forward to completely fill the frame, and a heavily buzzed John Norman exits and is hustled into the area by his entourage.

Like Cukor in the 1954 *A Star Is Born*, Pierson opens with the Norman character, immediately establishing his unreliability, dissipation, and volatility. The handheld camera stays on Kristofferson as he rushes through the interior corridors on his way to the stage. In a signature gesture that will be repeated throughout the film, he removes his shirt and dons another one for the performance. Bobby Ritchie gives him a hit of coke and then again, just before climbing steps to the stage, a slug of whiskey. "Are you a figment of my imagination," John shouts to the crowd, "or am I one of yours?" It is the lead-in to one of John's supposedly crowd-pleasing hits, a Williams/Ascher song called "Are You Watching Me Now?" He sings: "Watch closely now. / You'll observe a curious exchange of energy / Are you a figment of my imagination, / Or am I one of yours?"

The camerawork is fast and frantic—close-ups and low angles of Kristofferson mixed with cutaways to the crowd, band members, and backstage. There are multiple references to Jim Morrison in John's bare-chested sex appeal, his erratic singing, and lyrics: / "Your eyes are like fingers, / They're touching my body and arousing my soul. / Ridin' the passion arising inside me, / How high can I go?"

Toward the end of the set, à la Morrison, he stops the song, complaining that he's done it too many times and attracting some boos from the crowd. "If you feel that way about it, go to hell," he tells them. Once again removing his shirt and replacing it with a leather vest, he pulls on a Halloween monster mask and launches from the "go to hell" lead-in to a song titled "Hellacious Acres." The symbolism of John's split identity is hard to miss: changing clothes like changing skins, wearing figurative and literal masks, singing lyrics that proclaim "Go to hell, after dark, / It's a sin-filled city, an amusement park. / It's a one way ticket to the other side. / It's a Dr. Jekyll and a Mr. Hyde." Revealing his disdain for the entire scene, John concludes the song with his middle finger thrusting aloft the microphone.

The post-concert activity is equally chaotic. Groupies are shuttled in and out of cars, Bobby Ritchie argues with John about returning to the hotel for some rest, people rush in and out of the camera frame. "Where to?" asks John's driver as they depart alone. "Back about ten years," comes the answer.

They end up instead at a small Hollywood nightclub (shot on location in Pasadena). Esther is singing there with two black backup singers in a group called the Oreos, a name which, in the mid-1970s, probably passed as racially progressive and witty. Just like James Mason's Norman Maine before him, John will first experience and appreciate Esther as a performer.

Bothered by a persistent fan, John tries to watch unobtrusively from an upstairs balcony. Esther is presented in direct contrast to Howard; she is sober, neatly dressed, precise in her blocking, young-looking, engaged with the other musicians, and completely aware of her surroundings. The Oreos are singing one of the surviving Rupert Holmes songs—"Queen Bee"—about black widow spiders, wasps, queen bees, and mother bears. The lyrics address an aspect of Esther's character that was especially important to Streisand—that she be viewed as stronger and more independent than either Gaynor's or Garland's Esther: "So, in conclusion, it's an optical illusion / if you think that we're the weaker race. / Men got the muscle, but the ladies go the hustle, / and the truth is starin' in your face." To escape the fan, John takes a seat at a reserved table near the stage, where he gets into a loud discussion with the waitress over the club's lack of a liquor license.

The "meet cute" here works basically the same as it does in the 1954 version: John Norman chaotically intrudes on Esther's ordered performance and threatens to destroy it. Like Garland at the Shrine, she physically intercedes with him, but rather than incorporating him into the

Esther performs as part of a singing trio called the Oreos.

number she shoots angry glances and aggressively emphasizes the lyrics. "You're blowing my act, OK?" she snaps as she stands next to his table at the end of the song. "OK," he smiles, focusing intently on her movements.

"Everything," the second song she performs, also with words and music by Rupert Holmes, speaks to Esther's professional and romantic goals: "I want to learn what life is for. / I don't want much, I just want more. / Give me the man who's gonna bring / More of everything."

Granting her all his attention, John is accosted by an even more obnoxious fan (played by Robert "Freddy Krueger" Englund), who sits uninvited at his table, pours him whiskey from a flask, and loudly demands that he "get up there and sing a song for [his girlfriend] Sheila." Enraged when John refuses and tries to silence him, the fan starts a fight that soon spreads through the club and chases the Oreos from the stage.

Kristofferson accomplishes what James Mason only approached—the inadvertent yet foreboding wreckage of a public performance by Esther. As the bar gets more violent, she helps him escape out a rear exit, and he convinces her to let him and his driver take her home. "F-ing star," shouts an unhappy bar patron as the car pulls out of the parking lot.

Esther lives in an old Hollywood neighborhood. Although this *A Star Is Born* is nominally about rock, not movie stars, the use of Los Angeles locations is one of the elements that qualifies it as a film about Hollywood. Another is the fact that by the 1970s the movie and recording industries were closely intertwined in gigantic entertainment conglomerates. At one time or another, practically all of the major Hollywood studios owned a subsidiary record label. MGM Records, for example, was formed in 1946 and absorbed thirty years later into Polydor Records. In 1958, both Warner Bros. and 20th Century Fox established record companies bearing the studio names. Through a series of corporate acquisitions and mergers, Warner Bros. Records grew into Warner Music Group, one of the four major international music conglomerates and bought in 2011 by Access Industries. 20th Century Fox Records was sold to PolyGram in 1982 and absorbed into Casablanca Records. The biggest success of all was Universal Pictures Music, which morphed through deals involving Decca, MCA, Seagram, PolyGram, and other companies into Universal Music Group, the world's largest music corporation. Paramount Records, formed in 1969 and sold to ABC Records in 1974, became part of Universal Music Group. Somewhere in his career trajectory, a major recording star like John Norman Howard would have worked for one of these companies, bankrolled by the same corporate executives financing Hollywood movies.

During the drive to Esther's apartment, John tells her she has the kind of talent recognized and capitalized by the Hollywood entertainment machine. "You're a hell of a singer," he explains, comparing the thrill of hearing her to the adrenalin rush of hooking a deep sea marlin. It is essentially the Moss Hart speech from 1954 minus the additional references to boxing and bullfighting. John also begins a running commentary in the car focused on her physical assets. "God, you've got incredible eyes," he remarks. On the steps to her apartment, he first adds "You've got a beautiful mouth" and then "You've got a great ass," a line that Jon Peters claims he spoke to Streisand when they first met. Several critics have noted a strange pattern in Streisand's later films of the male leads continually assuring her how beautiful she looks, and certainly in *A Star Is Born* there is evidence of it.

Along with the talk of physical appearance, the film gives us plenty of complimentary Streisand close-ups and several gratuitous shots of her derrière packed into tight pants. Attractive and seductive, Esther is also virtuous. John Norman wants to spend the night, but she tells him to come back in the morning for breakfast.

In a further example of his rootlessness, John spends what's left of the night sleeping in the back seat of his limousine. When he bangs on Esther's door bearing a pizza, he is disheveled and weary. In comparison, she looks fresh and well-rested. Her apartment is neat, bright, and cozy. The couch and the drapes are a matching shade of pink. There are lace runners and mementoes on the tables.

When John asks for something to drink, Esther first offers him orange juice. The orderliness of her life once again contrasts starkly with the chaos of his, a paired duality that will be preserved throughout the film. Film historian Rick Altman sees this masculine/feminine polarity, elaborated through a series of secondary distinctions, as the primary narrative animus of the American musical. One partner in the couple may be hard-working, the other frivolous; one may be solitary, the other sociable. Through a series of repeated parallel actions (e.g., singing performances in the case of Esther and John), the differences are mediated and balanced. "The musical's typical romantic resolution, which depends on the harmony of a couple originally at odds," writes Altman, "is thus matched by a thematic resolution in which opposite life styles or values merge" (page 51). The conflict/resolution pattern begins in Esther's kitchen when John egoistically assumes that she will accompany him to a stadium concert gig. "You just save us a place on the chopper," he tells Bobby during a phone conversation, "I'm bringing someone with me." She objects and says she wasn't even asked. He apologizes for having "the manners of a hog" and she agrees to go.

There is a dramatic cut to overhead shots from the helicopter as it swoops down on thousands of fans waiting in a large outdoor stadium. The sequence was shot on location at Sun Devil Stadium in Tempe, Arizona, and caused considerable consternation between and among Kristofferson, Peters, Streisand, and Pierson. The idea was to fill the stadium with 50,000 rock fans (mostly students from Arizona State University required to pay $3.50 to attend), who would see acts like Santana, Peter

Frampton, and Montrose and also serve as "extras" for shots of Kris Kristofferson performing as John Norman Howard.

It was producer Jon Peters's job to arrange the concert, but, just a couple weeks prior to the date, few details had been settled. Ultimately, he hired legendary rock promoter Bill Graham, who quickly stepped in to sign acts and oversee physical operations. Music producer Phil Ramone, who had been contracted to handle the soundtrack, worried that the film crew was experienced only with prerecorded sound playback and not with the live recording that would be used for Kristofferson. "But when Kris goes out on that stage," he is quoted by Spada as saying at the time, "we'll be filming it, sound and all. What you hear in that stadium is what you'll hear in the film. What we don't get we'll never get. It's like driving on slick pavement" (page 360). Kristofferson was also concerned about the sound, feeling that he had been given way too little time to rehearse with his band. Streisand had first refused to use Kristofferson's own band at all but then had relented, only to monopolize their time rehearsing her material. A day before the concert, Kristofferson was edgy and unprepared. And, as usual, Streisand was upset with Pierson for not setting up shots the way she wanted and for maintaining a resigned "whatever happens" attitude in the face of potential disaster.

Tensions came to a boil during rehearsals that were witnessed by about 150 entertainment reporters who had been flown in to Arizona on a publicity press junket. Randall Riese reports that onstage microphones inadvertently broadcast a heated argument between Kristofferson and Streisand to the note-taking guests. Angry at her for telling him how to read a line, he shouted, "Who's the director?" Pushing on, Streisand responded, "Look, you're not doing what I tell you to do. Listen to me when I talk to you, goddamnit." After he told her to "f-off," Kristofferson was accosted by Peters, who demanded, "You owe my lady an apology." In an exit line and an authentic inside Hollywood moment that should have been used in the film itself, Kristofferson answered, "If I need any shit from you, I'll squeeze your head" (page 420).

The actual day of filming was equally strained. Frustrated by long technical delays in the shooting, the crowd grew noisy and impatient. Responding to her own impulsive hunch, Streisand went on stage to talk to the fans, singing several songs and pleading for understanding. Everyone agreed that things got better after her appearance.

Once John Norman's helicopter lands outside the stadium, he and Esther are hurried into an ambulance van and chauffeured to the stage.

During the brief ride, he again peels off his shirt (and pants, too, this time) and changes into brown suede for the performance. The behind-the-scenes turmoil is similar to that of the opening concert. He is late, plied with whiskey and cocaine by Bobby, disdainful of the audience, and sloppy in his presentation.

Present now at the same time in the same environment, Esther continues to provide contrast. Dressed in a long white crocheted sweater, matching white cap, and jeans, she is upbeat and friendly. She is concerned about John's lateness and encourages him not to be rude to the audience. Reaction shots show her disapproval of the substance abuse and of a suggestive pat on the rear by one of the band members. Visually, she is separated from the others. Bobby has placed her backstage next to a speaker, where she is seen in cutaway one-shots. Introduced as John Norman Howard Speedway, John and his band take the stage, and Pierson reverts to documentary-like handheld camera shots of the crowd and the performers. Fans smoke grass, squirt wine, dance, and sit on each other's shoulders for better views. Opening again with the "Are you a figment of my imagination, or am I one of yours?" question, John launches into his opening song. When he gets to the "Are you watching me now?" line, he

John Norman gives a sloppy outdoor concert in Arizona.

turns and looks at Esther, and Pierson uses the song as a prompt for several eyeline matched cross-cuts between the two of them smiling at each other.

Interested more in Esther than the song, John moves toward the wings, coaxing her to come out on stage with him. Shocked by his lack of professionalism, she pushes him away, and then runs down off the stage platform. At that point, to the confused dismay of band and crowd, he abandons the song and follows after her.

Down below the stage, things quickly turn worse. Borrowing a motorcycle from a biker who has kissed him on the lips and said, "Man, you're beautiful," John peels around in the dirt and then accelerates up a ramp and back onto the stage itself. The crowd goes crazy. "You're going to kill yourself," shouts Esther. "I'm just giving them what they want," he replies before he plows through wires and equipment and plunges in slow motion down into the pit. A low-angle shot reveals Esther with others peering anxiously over the edge of the stage and then being pushed by security back up out of the frame. A stadium speaker announces the end of the concert plus the location of medical facilities for anyone needing attention. While lines of people struggle out of the stadium, both the helicopter and the van leave without Esther. In a final shot that effectively summarizes her isolation, the camera cranes up and away from her as she stands alone in an empty parking lot.

So far in the film there have been three extended musical sequences, and not one of them has featured a true rock and roll song, a problematic omission for a movie that is supposed to be chronicling the rock scene of the mid-1970s. It is a contradiction that particularly bothered Kristofferson. Even before filming began, according to James Spada, "An angry Kristofferson asked for a meeting that included [Paul] Williams and took place in an empty rehearsal stage on the Warner Bros. lot in Burbank. It quickly became clear that Kris hated Williams's music and wanted to use his own" (page 354). Streisand refused the request, claiming she wanted something that sounded more like Bruce Springsteen although, ironically, Williams's compositions are not even remotely similar to Springsteen's.

"Kristofferson's songs (not of his composition) are painful to hear," writes Anne Edwards, "and although Streisand is supposed to become a rock star of the magnitude of a Janis Joplin, the songs that make an impression are close to the old Streisand mold," (page 385)—songs that are more Las Vegas than Woodstock. Even Paul Williams now admits, "I am not a rock and roll writer" (Riese, page 429). None of this mattered to the record-buying public, however, because the soundtrack album of *A Star Is Born* hit #1 on the charts and sold over 5 million copies in the United States alone.

From the long shot of abandoned Esther, Pierson cuts to a medium close-up of John Norman floating by himself in a swimming pool. "This time only seventeen people were hurt, John," intones an off-screen voice that turns out to be producer/personal manager Brian Wexler (director Paul Mazursky), who is one of more than a dozen hangers-on keeping him company around the pool. Among those guests are band members, groupies, publicity manager Gary Danziger (Oliver Clark), assorted other staffers, and the omnipresent enabler Bobby Ritchie, who reels John ashore for a fresh batch of Bloody Marys. The news is all bad. Future concert dates have been cancelled because of John's unreliability, expenses are skyrocketing, and the government is demanding payment of a $186,000 tax bill. "I can put you into the Indian Relief Benefit if you can get there on time," advises Wexler.

Pierson's go-to structural blueprint for scenes with John has been to escalate tensions like this and then close on chaos. That is exactly what he does again here. A helicopter carrying radio disc jockey Bebe Jesus (M.G. Kelly) roars in over the pool for some kind of crazed "exclusive." Shouting through a loudspeaker, Bebe invites John to "rap" with him; instead, John grabs a gun and fires it toward the chopper. The guests scatter and the chopper retreats. As he slips inside the house for a drink, John Norman catches a glimpse of himself in a mirror above the bar and stares critically at it for some time. The camera lingers on his reflected image. It is, however, a shot without context; nothing up to this point has indicated any capacity on his part for extended self-analysis.

Match-cutting on the reflections, Pierson shoots the Oreos through the glass windows of a recording studio. Like Garland's Esther singing about cocoanut shampoo, they are there to record a commercial for "Meow Chow" cat food, but the jingle's lyrics are so absurd that Esther is unable to complete a take without laughing. "This is terrible, you can't do this," she tells the producers, and they agree—the Oreos are politely dismissed from the job. As they are packing up, John walks past the windows in the background; a reverse-angle shows him failing to recognize the Oreos standing with their backs to him on the other side of the glass. He is carrying a carton of Jack Daniels bottles as a peace offering for Bebe Jesus, who also broadcasts his show from the studios. Bebe, however, refuses to accept the apology and, shifting into his fake DJ voice, goes on air to explain that

A Star Is Born (1976) • 237

Surrounded by hangers-on, John Norman "recovers" poolside.

"Bebe don't take no jive from no burned-out superstar." Framed on the opposite side of Bebe's window, John Norman says, "Hey, I said I'm sorry" and listens briefly to the hysterical rant. Finally hearing enough insults, he shoulders the box of whiskey and heaves it into the window. "Send the bill to my business manager," he deadpans before calmly disappearing down the hallway, where he once again passes Esther's recording booth.

This time, of course, they meet. In a shot that Cukor would have liked, they see each other in the reflections, she dressed all in white and he in a black coat and dark jeans. The nature of their conversations has been thrust, parry, counterattack, and so it continues here. She accuses him of causing wreckage everywhere he goes, he wonders why she didn't respond to his eight phone calls, she insists she tried three times and then couldn't get through anymore, and he confesses that his number is changed every six weeks to prevent fans from pestering him.

Once outside the studio, he convinces her, for the third time in the film, to accompany him on a journey. Why Esther would get into a red sports convertible with an alcoholic who has driven a motorcycle off a stage and has just hurled a carton of whiskey bottles through a window is not particularly clear, unless it is the line that one can only hope was not written by Joan Didion, which is, that John Norman bought the car because it reminded him of Esther, "fast and out of my league."

John drives Esther up in the hills to his gated Hollywood mansion that is guarded by two noisy German shepherds. Domestic space continues to define character. His house is enormous yet also cold, empty, and unfinished. The rooms do not seem to have any traditional function—one houses a piano and might be used for recording "…if we ever get the acoustics right," another looks like a bar or game room, where boxes of leftover Chinese food litter the tables.

The conversation is as desultory as the home tour. When John pours himself a drink, Esther asks, "Are you an alcoholic?" "Probably," he answers before admiring her one more time: "You're cute. You are f-ing cute." Moving to the second floor, they linger on a staircase landing crowded with paint buckets and brushes, while he grabs a can of black spray paint and, like James Mason borrowing Garland's lipstick, scrawls her name on the wall. The gesture seems to impress her, less so the waterbed in his room. "Who cleans up around here?" she asks. "I don't know," he answers in further evidence to her of his carelessness. In a profile two-shot, he affectionately caresses a curl of the Afro-like hairdo that Peters advised would make Streisand look years younger.

It is their mutual love of music, however, that finally clinches the romance between John and Esther. Back downstairs, she picks out a tune she has composed at the piano and he sits down next to her to improvise some lyrics. After giggling over the double entendre implications of "Then you came inside my life," they compliment each other's talent and he raises her hands to his lips. In another profiled two-shot (a composition which will, in fact, become emblematic of the film and the basis for its advertising imagery), they engage in a prolonged, passionate kiss. From there, in slow motion, John carries Esther to his bed. What is significant in the lovemaking that follows is that she rolls on top and is the first to remove her belt and blouse—another example of female aggressiveness and independence that Streisand insisted be included. The camera pans to darkness.

Then, Pierson pans off that transition to the couple immersed in a bubble bath lined with beer cans and candles, one of the autobiographical details taken from the real-life Peters/Streisand relationship. It is also a scene that incensed Peters when Kristofferson slipped into the tub wearing nothing at all. Filming temporarily was halted until Peters calmed down and Kristofferson agreed to wear flesh-colored trunks. The scene itself is appropriately romantic—softly lit, mostly silent, held for an extended period of time. Toward the end, Pierson cuts to a close-up in which Esther applies a strip of glitter to John's eyebrow, puts rouge on his cheeks, and murmurs, "You're so pretty." With this bit of business, the film underscores the gender bending it has been playing with all along: the biker's kiss, her sexual control, and his androgyny.

That, however, is the problem; the film only "plays" with and teases the concept as just one more hip feature to make it seem contemporary and relevant. Unlike, say, a John Schlesinger whose movies such as *Midnight Cowboy* (1969) and *Sunday, Bloody Sunday* (1971) centered more profoundly on questions of sexual identity, Pierson drops the seed but leaves it undeveloped, just as he does with potential motifs like the mirror images. The scene ends on more double entendre. "Let's do it again," requests John, but it is several days later and he is giving Esther guitar lessons. They are now an authentic couple engaged in collaborative creative work.

That collaboration takes them to a recording session with Bobby and John's band. Bobby is miffed that John has been concentrating on Esther's songs and not his own material. Even more irritating is her advice on how the band should be accompanying her. "They're fantastic musicians, but it's just not what's in my head," she tells John Norman, and he seems to understand the more "classical" effect she wants.

Visually, Pierson begins to move John to the periphery, as he does here with a deep-focus shot where Esther and Bobby converse in the sound booth and John can be seen through the window behind them translating her desires to the band. "I'm good for him," she tells Bobby, arguing that John has gone several days without drinking and is sleeping through the nights without downers.

"But he ain't working," Bobby reminds her. Instead, there is a cut to a close-up of a microphone and Esther steps into the frame to sing "Evergreen," the film's romantic ballad that became a monster hit. With music by Streisand and lyrics by Paul Williams, it received an Oscar for Best Song, won Grammys for Best Female Pop Vocal and Song of the Year, and sold over a million copies as a single. Like "The Man That Got Away" was for Garland, it became a staple of Streisand's concert performances and a fan favorite (President-elect Clinton requested it at his inaugural gala).

Pierson shoots the "Evergreen" performance in a single extended take. The camera tracks circularly to the right for ninety degrees and then slowly back again. John is gradually incorporated into the performance, as well; first his hand enters from frame left to hold Esther's and then his head and shoulders appear. He kisses her hand, sings a few bars of the song, and listens to the take on headphones. Always the initiator, she pulls him toward her at one point and kisses him quickly on the lips. The words address the unlikely yet strong relationship between the two contrasting personalities: "Two lights that shine as one, / Morning glory and midnight sun. / Time we've learned to sail above. / Time won't change the meaning of / One love, ageless and ever evergreen." For the finish, she holds the last note and he leans in to kiss her again. It is a bravura Streisand performance, a bit self-indulgent but full-voiced, powerful, and dramatic.

A sound overlap of applause takes us to the audience of the Indian Relief Benefit concert. Tilting down off the balcony, the camera sweeps across the orchestra seats to the stage, where John Norman Howard Speedway appears in an extreme long shot. For a third time, as tiresome to us as it is to him, John begins with the "Are you a figment of my imagination or am I one of yours?" hook but can only get through a couple lines of the song. In the wings, Esther, dressed in a masculine grey pantsuit and vest, and Bobby exchange worried glances. But John has a plan; he drags her out on stage and tells the unhappy audience, "Now shut the f-up and give the lady a chance."

Reverse front and back close-ups of Esther at the microphone are intercut as she starts to sing softly, barely audible over the noise of the crowd, until she gains confidence and stuns everyone with the power of her voice. She is singing Williams and Ascher's "The Woman in the Moon," another anthem to feminism: "I was raised in a 'no you don't' world, overrun with rules. / Memorize your lines and move as directed. / That's an age old story, everybody knows that's a worn out song, / But you and I are changing that tune / We're learning new rhythms from the woman, / I said, 'The woman in the moon.'"

Mysteriously, Esther's Oreo back-up singers appear, and her spontaneous appearance turns into a full-blown, polished performance with lighting changes and choreographed dance steps. Cutaways show John, the backstage crew, and the audience all delighted with Esther's act. For the finale, she holds the microphone triumphantly aloft in the spotlight, and the crowd applauds wildly. She rushes off stage to embrace John Norman and then returns for an encore.

The next song, in what turns out to be a little Streisand mini-concert in the middle of the film (recall the Warner Bros. executive predicting that they could shoot six Barbra Streisand numbers and make $60 million), is "I Believe in Love" by Kenny Loggins and Alan and Marilyn Bergman. Nowhere near being a rock tune, it is nevertheless a lively, fast-paced pop pleasure, and Streisand handles it perfectly. The tempo is quick and the lyrics dense: "But I don't want to find myself one day / Waking up and looking at Monday / With some what's his name left from Sunday / I believe in love, what?" Esther's easy mastery of the song makes her look even more impressive. Moving around backstage, John keeps monitoring the crowd reaction and encouraging her. With quick cuts and camera zooms, Pierson intensifies the song's climax and then shows the audience rising in waves to give Esther a standing ovation.

The acclaim continues backstage, where Esther is mobbed and congratulated by Brian, Gary, Bebe, and various other industry reps. It is the film's archetypal "a star is born" moment complete with celebrity sycophants. John watches proudly from the sidelines, marginalized already by enemies like Jesus, who shouts, "Esther, you're dynamite, but get rid of the creep." John and Esther exit in the red convertible.

The next several scenes are all reinterpretations of the Wellman and Cukor films: the "it's all yours now" celebration of Esther's ascent, the secret wedding, the honeymoon house, and the collapse of John's career. As they drive along what looks like a nondescript boulevard in the San Fernando Valley, Esther asks, "What just happened?" He tells her that she has made it, that a major road tour is next, and that she will be on "a full tilt boogie from motel to motel." When he asks her what else she wants, she reverses gender expectations again and answers, "I want to marry you." Like the two Norman Maines before him, he tries to talk her out of it. "No, you don't, I drink too much, I throw my money around, I owe the government 180 grand," he explains. But her belief that they can overcome the obstacles is stubborn. "I want you, Johnny," she says simply. Repeating the same surrender made by Fredric March and James Mason, Kristofferson replies, "Don't bullshit me, Esther. I'll start believing it."

With no need to clear their plans with a studio executive, they proceed directly to the civil marriage ceremony outside a country courthouse somewhere. The scene is going for unconventional but ends as perfunctory. The ceremony takes place next to a fountain in front of the court building rather than inside. The justice of the peace is a black woman. The bride and groom are both dressed informally in white, and they have no friends or witnesses with them. Rushed and abbreviated, the vows substitute the word "obey" with the word "cherish." There is, however, no dramatic urgency to the scene, no attempt to evade fans or to confound publicity manager Gary Danziger. The whole thing seems like a gag. When they are pronounced husband and wife, they giggle together and more or less fall out of the frame. A few spectators look on from the background as the action simply deflates.

Pierson then cuts to John and Esther speeding along an Arizona highway in an open jeep (the emotionally freighted car trip is the film's most dominant recurring motif). Arriving at a vast empty expanse of high desert, John introduces it as his "88,000 acre, non-working ranch" and the future site of their secluded new home. Marveling at the blue sky beauty of the place, Esther spins and twirls like a Maria Von Trapp of the flatlands. Dressed in a long Spanish-style skirt, a black blouse slit to the waist, and a floppy black hat, she follows him as he shows her where the house will be built. Sticks and strings indicate the floor plan. Initially, Streisand had resisted filming in the Arizona desert, preferring to use Peters's Malibu ranch for the getaway abode. Pierson, on the other hand, wanted to surround the house with wide, photogenic vistas, and this is one creative battle with his star and producer that he ultimately won.

In all three *A Star Is Born* films, the acquisition of a new house functions as a metaphor for the recently married couple's establishment of a hopefully secure new life together. As Gaston Bachelard first observed in *The Poetics of Space*, "…a house constitutes a body of images that give mankind proofs or illusions of stability" (page 17). To dream of the house, according to Bachelard, is to return to an earthly paradise that is enclosed, protected and intimate.

John and Esther do more than dream about their house; they apparently build the whole structure by themselves. In a series of dissolves, he operates a bulldozer, she drives a truck filled with furniture, and together they erect a windmill. The construction montage also provides an opportunity for a Streisand fashion show. In an all-white ensemble of Superman t-shirt, gym shorts, and knee-high socks, she supervises the soil grading.

Dressed as a nineteenth century Brooklyn street urchin, she unloads the truck. Wearing a suede vest and jeans, she sprays John and his sleeveless white t-shirt, jeans, and fedora with a garden hose. Completed in record time with no subcontractor delay issues, the finished product is some kind of minimalist adobe hybrid, far roomier inside than the exteriors would indicate. There is a large open living space, a kiva fireplace, and a bedroom loft. The furnishings are fashionably Southwestern.

The only thing disturbing the couple's idyll is John's reluctance to go on tour with Esther, a disagreement that highlights the film's bewildering treatment of artistic labor and the marketplace. It is collaborative creative work coupled with a mutual appreciation of each other's artistic talents that first sparked the romance between John Norman and Esther. Making music and building a house together obviously bring joy and affirmation. Even separately, however, Esther believes strongly in the value of the work she does and has repeatedly asserted female control and agency. So, other than missing his company, it does not follow that she should be so afraid of touring by herself. She was already a working professional singer when he caught her Oreos act in the Hollywood nightclub. Norman's attitude toward his own work is equally muddled. His contempt for the music industry's hype and commercialism makes sense, but his skill in producing her first recordings suggests a depth of talent and a work ethic not revealed in the lackluster concert performances.

Much of this confusion may be explained by Streisand's control of the film's final cut and her elimination, as Anne Edwards has claimed, of scenes showing "Kristofferson's character before his decline, when his great strengths as a performer, his emotionality, the sensitivity, the intimacy he created with an audience, explained his stardom and Esther's respect for him" (page 382). Streisand always has refuted such charges, but certainly none of John's backstory appears in the final film. Similarly unclear is why, given his disdain for the commercial imperatives of touring, his knowledge that his style of music is different from hers, and his belief that she will be better professionally on her own, he suddenly reverses his position and agrees to perform on the tour.

Presumably it is because of the volatile love that plays itself out in the Arizona desert. The antics there seem more appropriate to smitten adolescents than to adults in their twenties and thirties. Esther gets angry over John's refusal to tour, and he rushes outside to careen around on his motorcycle. "How are you going to cherish me in traction, you dumb bastard?" she shouts just before he (in a second foreshadowing of his ultimate fate) crashes the cycle and catapults himself into a mud hole. Dressed in silky white pants and blouse, she runs to him. He seems unconscious, but then suddenly opens his eyes and pulls her into the mud. (Randall Riese reports that a few crew members, fed up with the demands and behavior of their star, mixed real animal waste with the mud smeared onto her pantsuit.)

When she refuses to kiss him during the mud wrestling and tells him that she doesn't "like hairy men," he dashes into the house to cut his beard. Begging him to stop, she whispers, "If you die, I'll kill you" and they embrace. "Oh hell," he says, resolving the travel issue, "I'll go on your goddamn tour."

There is a dissolve to John and Esther riding horses across the windswept landscape. Streisand now is wearing an orange turban and an orange, white, and purple serape. "Do you realize how long it's been since you've seen anybody but me?" she asks, reminding viewers that for the past ten minutes or so we have watched no one else on screen but them.

As if on cue, three black sedans speed along the horizon toward the adobe ranch house. It is Brian and the various staffers to discuss her tour. In his capacity as agent/promoter/manager, Brian combines the Oliver Niles and the Matt Libby parts. He is both reasonable and unlikable. Brian levels with John Norman about how concert hall owners regard Esther and him. "They love her," he says, "you, they're suing." Under an appropriately overcast sky, Brian continues, "You blew it, you blew it. Your songs don't work. You're causing people a lot of trouble, a lot of people are getting hurt." John's appearance on the tour with Esther will only have a negative impact on her career. "Her single is #6," argues Brian, "she's up for a Grammy, she's ready to fly on her own."

Realizing the truth of the argument and tactfully claiming he wants to work on his own new music, John again bows out of the tour and goes inside to deliver the news. Esther is doing a photo shoot. "You changed your mind, you're not gonna do the tour," she guesses, reading his body language and falling into a mournful expression that the photographer callously appropriates for the shoot. The click of the camera shutter merges through an abrupt transition similar to Cukor's cuts into a battery of flashing cameras photographing Esther during a concert on the road.

Front and side close-ups of Esther at the microphone alternate with shots of the crowd. For a third time, she sings, "I believe in the best of both worlds," an upbeat signature line to contrast her optimism with the hallucinatory darkness of John's "figment of my imagination" lead-in.

Esther takes the stage during her own successful concert tour.

Also intercut are clips of Esther being interviewed in the most rock documentary-like footage seen so far—shaky camera, grainy stock, and erratic zooms. She is discussing recording sessions in imagery so at odds with the romantic glossiness of the rest of the film that it can only be explained as Pierson's concession to whichever audience members might still think they're watching a movie about rock and roll performers.

A montage that follows seems to have the same *raison d'être*. More interviews, snippets of Esther in concert (seemingly shot the same day as John's motorcycle bit at Sun Devil Stadium), magnetic tape sliding through recording equipment, crowd reactions, and backstage photos. Even more perplexing for the narrative is the fact that John shows up in the interviews and informal pictures as if perhaps he went on the tour anyhow.

Somewhat anticlimactically, the issue of the tour itself—its impact on her career and its forced separation of the newlyweds—suddenly ceases to be a point of dramatic interest since the very next shot after the montage is John dropping Esther off for a rehearsal of a television special she is shooting in Hollywood. Ironically, they're now talking about him reuniting with Speedway, recording new music, and initiating his own tour.

What becomes most interesting in the plot now is how it updates the 1937 and 1954 scripts. The iconic tag line is planted when John calls Esther back to the car. "I was just taking another look," he tells her before speeding off to the recording studio. It is there that he learns his career has slipped irretrievably away from him. His band, which is now called Freeway, is recording without him. "We thought you retired, Slick, now that the old lady's working," Bobby tells him.

The band has a hit, a "#5 with a bullet," and John watches them play through the studio windows but declines Bobby's offer to go in and meet with them. Like Norman Maine salvaging his pride at the sanitarium with Oliver Niles, he says he has offers to go out on his own with "new, different stuff."

Back in his Hollywood mansion, John drinks and takes phone messages for Esther. "No, this isn't her secretary, no, this isn't her answering service," he explains to one persistent caller. As he wanders around the house, he attempts to write music again, and, among the film's many missteps, this is one detail that it gets right. With an acoustic guitar and a tape recorder, he tries out notes and phrases that will eventually become the song "With One More Look at You."

The process of artistic creation in Hollywood films—painting, composing, writing—is usually presented as a single epiphanic moment. Compare, for example, MGM's 1941 *Lady Be Good*, directed by Norman Z. McLeod, where married songwriters Robert Young and Ann Sothern sit down at the piano in evening clothes and effortlessly bang out the title tune. Here, however, John mulls over a line, "your loving touch has made me strong again," and records the chord progression, before putting the project aside for future consideration.

A close-up of a pensive John Norman cuts to a long shot of Esther entering the darkened house. Echoing Gaynor and Garland, she rushes in from her day of rehearsal, eager to see her husband and hopeful of his own good news. She asks him a string of questions: "How did it go with the guys?" and "Are you going out with them?" and "Did you play your stuff for them?" Changing the subject, John suggests they have a picnic in bed, a sexy reimagining of the sandwich and milk supper from the earlier films.

But the mood is interrupted by another phone call. "It's probably for you," he says almost bitterly. "Which reminds me—Jameson wants you to do an interview show on the 12th, and you've got a wardrobe fitting and an insurance examination the day after tomorrow." She disregards the messages, but he continues, "Let me finish before I forget. They want to know how many places you want at the table at the Grammy Awards. " Scrapping the picnic, he makes himself a drink instead.

The award debacle occurs at the Grammys rather than the Oscars. Arrayed across tiered platforms like in the old Earl Carroll Theater on Sunset, the audience sits at tables facing the stage. As we have seen, films that incorporate real Hollywood rituals like the Academy Awards or the Grammy Awards not only give viewers the illusory sense of being let in on a privileged experience, but they also provide intertextual commentary on their stars' careers. Watching the Garland and Streisand versions of *A Star Is Born* today, we ponder why one performer was rebuffed by her peers and the other rewarded. Talent, we assume, was one of only several factors at work in the decisions. Streisand, like Garland previously, sits in a fictional audience as a fictional nominee for the same award that she will later be nominated for in real life.

"Now, to present this year's Grammy Award for the best performance by a female artist," announces the emcee, "here are Rita Coolidge and Tony Orlando." Adding to the self-referential context is the fact that singer Rita Coolidge was married at the time to Kris Kristofferson. When Esther's name is called, she receives a standing ovation and takes the stage to give her prepared acceptance remarks.

John's disruption of the speech is less deliberate than it is clumsy and accidental. Arriving late and drunk, he can't find a seat and gets into an argument with a guest who tries to restrain him. "Sorry, babe, I can't find my place," he explains loudly. "They don't seem to have a place for me down here." When Esther begins to thank him, he stumbles onto the stage and interrupts by saying, "Hey, don't do that to me. You did something all by yourself and you don't owe anybody a goddamn thing for that. Not me and certainly not them." His comments are combative and defiant, more like Fredric March here than James Mason. He is not humbly asking for a job but rather spewing his disdain for phony well-wishers and for himself. "What about the one for the worst performance?" he asks in reference to the awards. "You all know I deserve it, I want it, so where the f—k is it?"

A burst of flashbulbs fills the screen as Esther helps John off the stage and out of the theater. At the escalators, they are accosted by more reporters and more paparazzi. In the confusion, he accidentally strikes her and knocks her down. "Hey," shouts Bebe, "how does it feel to uncork on the old lady?" John wheels around and punches him in the face, setting off a whole new explosion of camera flashes. "Shut off those goddamn lights," screams Esther. "When is it ever enough, goddamn it? Don't you ever have enough?"

John Norman disrupts Esther's Grammy acceptance speech as Tony Orlando (playing himself) looks on.

This version of *A Star Is Born* has the same targets of criticism as the Selznick/Wellman film. It is not an exposé of the music industry any more than it is a study of rock and roll performers. It has nothing to say about exploitative contracts, royalty skimming, or radio pay-for-play schemes. It does not address the inequities faced by women or minorities. Rather, Pierson and Streisand are directly attacking media vultures like Bebe and boorish fans like the one played earlier by Robert Englund. The real crimes are invasions of celebrity privacy and distorted magazine stories. For Streisand, who faced daily onslaughts at the gated property she shared with Peters in Malibu, the critique of intruders held obvious personal resonance. She herself often had asked, "When is it ever enough?"

John's self-destructive behavior weighs heavily on Esther. In the backstage restroom they escape to at the Grammys, she asks, "What are you going to do for an encore? Set yourself on fire?" He has no response, and she says sadly, "I love you, Johnny, but it's not enough, is it?"

With a quick cut to the TV show rehearsal, her distraction continues. Singing a song with the foreboding line, "you and I are changing," she struggles with the blocking on a set of stairs and asks if she can just stand still and sing. "Could you please stop the playback?" she asks an unresponsive production crew. Like young Fanny Brice peering out in the theater darkness at the unseen Flo Ziegfeld, she calls, "Hello, anybody hear me?"

Brian has arrived, and she takes a break to discuss her marital troubles. The *mise-en-scène* is surprisingly sparse and bare. Where Cukor would have filled the screen with the bustle of production, Pierson keeps his frame flat and relatively empty. Partly this is to keep the budget down but also it is to suggest the growing isolation felt by Esther. Angrily, she asks Brian to help her draw John out of his seclusion. "There's a lot you can do for him," she declares. "You can give him your time, your support, you can earn your 25%." Brian agrees to listen to John's new music and, if he believes it is good, to record it. During the conversation, she also returns to her obsession with John's physical beauty: "Sometimes I look at him when he's sleeping and he has no pain in his face, no hurt. He's so beautiful." It is almost as if she is resentful that he is as pretty if not prettier than she is.

Brian listens to the music at the house in the desert and claims to like it but tells John, "I think we need to give them some of your golden oldies, stuff that made you a household word." To save face once again, John replies that the music is not available because he is going to record it himself. "I want to start my own label. I want to be a mogul like you," he says in the film's only reference to the relationship between the individual artist and the means of production.

For no clear reason other than to further contrast the propriety of the desert with the profligacy of the city, John returns to his Hollywood mansion, where he finds a young reporter named Quentin (Marta Heflin) swimming in his pool and offering her body in exchange for an interview. He takes her inside the house and in response to the grandeur, she actually says, "far out, out of sight, blows the mind." Speaking for every discerning viewer, John drolly comments, "You really have a way with words. I can't wait to see what you write."

Giving Gary Danziger as a sexual reference, Quentin repeats that she'd "really like this interview" and then adds, "with Esther." As John downs a drink, he replies, "Perfect." Maybe it is this humiliating rejection of his own celebrity that propels him to accept the offer. Maybe it is his loneliness and desperation. In any case, going to bed with Quentin makes him much less sympathetic than either the 1937 or the 1954 Norman Maine, infidelity being the ultimate offense in romantic melodrama. Recall again Streisand's contractual right to approve the final cut and her five months of working with editor Peter Zinner and his assistants to re-edit Pierson's version. Anne Edwards quotes Zinner as remembering, "Primarily she felt that her character needed more time on the screen. She felt that some of the sequences were too heavy with Kristofferson. I would say that she made major changes not so much with the story line, but as far as the characters were concerned. Her character became much more pertinent" (page 382).

Frank Pierson is even more specific regarding the damage done to John Norman's part: "Kris's character often seems an unpleasant drunken dangerous bore...I see she has speeded up the film by cutting his establishing scene, moments of boyishness, of feeling the pain of his existence, that makes us feel for him and with him; she has cut his reactions... the sadness, the wonderful wasted quality Kris brought the part, the exhaustion, and the playfulness with which he courts her...is diminished or gone" (Edwards, page 385).

Some of that banked sympathy and good will would have helped to mitigate John Norman's betrayal here toward the end of the film. Esther comes home early and discovers John and Quentin in bed together. Further illustrating how immoral entertainment reporting can be, the script has Quentin fumbling for her tape recorder as if nothing has happened and testily asking, "Hey, is she gonna' talk to me or what?" Streisand and Kristofferson play the scene in completely different ways—she on a screaming rampage, he subdued and in pain. Important as always to Streisand is that her Esther not be the self-sacrificing victim that she perceived the two earlier Esther Blodgetts to be. Just as she never offered to abandon her career to care for John, here too she fights for her own survival. "I've had it with you," she snarls with a defiant lifting of the chin. "You can trash your life, but you're not going to trash mine."

Tossing a potted plant at the name "Esther" still spray painted on the wall, she rushes downstairs and takes a pool cue to John's bar bottles. Present is much of the iconography of a Sirkian melodrama—the grand staircase, the cavernous mansion, the violent shattering of expensive glassware—and it seems to belong to a suddenly different film.

John follows after Esther, who slaps and punches him hysterically. "Fight, protect yourself, you bastard. I'll kill you, I'll kill you," she shouts. Some of George Cukor's much-vaunted skill in working with actresses would have been beneficial; the performance is shrill, false, and over the top. By contrast, Kristofferson is actually quite believable. Wrestling her to the ground, he plaintively tells her, "I tried to tell you. It's no good with me." When she says, "Don't touch me. I don't like you anymore," he watches her silently for several seconds and slowly turns away with tears in his eyes. "Where the hell are you running to now, you f-ing coward?" she demands and he quietly answers, "I don't want to do this to you anymore."

Something seriously has gone wrong with the performance dynamics when most viewers now find themselves identifying more with the adulterous drunk than the deceived heroine. Still, Streisand pushes it— "Then fight for me, goddamnit. Because if you keep walking I'll hate you and I'll hate you forever."

Curious in all their fights is that neither John nor Esther really tries to change. Unlike the Norman Maines, he does not offer to enter rehab and she, as we have seen, does not offer to scale back her career. They reach an impasse, which gets resolved by their overwhelming physical passion for one another. Such is the case here. With even more tears, he whispers "I love you Esther." She responds, "Well, I hate you," and they embrace.

The kiss, which is preceded by her biting his tongue and shoulder, is again the emblematic profile portrait, John on the left and slightly higher, Esther on the right. The similarity to portraiture is revealing. As art historians long have demonstrated, trends in how painted and photographed portraits are structured reveal social, political, and even economic values. Renaissance marriage portraits, for example, provide heavily coded insights into the competing demands of conjugal expectations and lineal responsibilities. In the highly eroticized "portraits" of John and Esther, physical attractiveness is seen as the most important factor in defining a personal or even professional relationship and possessive embrace of the female, despite narrative markers to the contrary, the key dynamic therein.

The camera slowly tracks in on the kiss, dissolving to a long shot of John and Esther riding together on the same horse across another desert landscape. As expected, the natural purity of their Arizona ranch is restorative. With "Evergreen" reprising on the soundtrack, the camera pans in a leisurely 180° arc to follow the path of the horse. They are clothed in native Southwestern gear—he in a light brown buckskin jacket and she in another serape. Sometime during the previous few days, they have settled their romantic and artistic conflicts by resolving anew to tour together. The serenity of their embrace in front of the house's Navajo rug tapestries is disturbed only when he tells her that she was right about not letting him trash her life. It "sounded like you knew who you were," he remarks. "I'm Esther Hoffman Howard," she answers in a premature telegraphing of her

252 • *A Star Is Born and Born Again*

John Norman's emblematic sensual embrace of Esther became the film's iconic advertising image.

proud acknowledgement of his influence on her. While she smiles in a long held medium close-up, he says, "That's right. Don't you ever forget."

The imagery that follows is somewhat confusing in its mixture of menace and innocence. Esther's face dissolves to the sun setting ominously behind the mountains (cf. the beach sunset in Cukor's film), an image which then itself dissolves to a bare-chested John watching her peacefully asleep in the early morning. He changes into a black shirt and covers her with his buckskin jacket. Having forgotten that he is to pick up Brian at the airport, she struggles awake and offers to go along, an idea that he gently but pointedly dismisses. "I'll have breakfast waiting like a good little wife," she promises sleepily. Lingering for a moment at the bedside, he watches as she opens an eye to ask, "What?" The famous farewell line, which has been passed along from Lowell Sherman through Fredric March to James Mason, is pared down here to a three word minimum. "Just looking, babe," responds Kristofferson with the same longing and regret as expressed by his predecessors.

The issue of John Norman's suicide was another point of contention during production. Because he identified with the John Norman Howard character, Jon Peters did not want him to kill himself and leave Esther all alone. He also felt it might negatively influence box office. Citing successful films like *Anna Karenina* and *A Tale of Two Cities* where the main characters precipitate their own deaths, Pierson argued that John's suicide was essential to the narrative. All of John's comments and actions, he insisted, led logically to this conclusion. The compromise was to have him die in an auto accident, which, as filmed by Pierson, still evokes suicide anyway.

A variation of the portrait embrace amid the Southwestern serenity of the couple's hideaway home.

Exiting the house with a can of beer in hand, John greets his dogs and takes what looks like a last survey of the property. Still holding the beer, he gets into the red convertible and pops one of his own tapes into the tape deck. "Are you a figment of my imagination" blares into the quiet desert air. A long shot of the car speeding away from the ranch cuts to a close-up of an awakened Esther looking frightened by the noise of the engine. He replaces his tape with one of her singing "Lost Inside of You," the song that they wrote together in the early stages of their courtship. In a kind of cinematic *danse macabre*, a helicopter shot tracks parallel to the car, sweeps down to reframe John gripping the wheel, and then hovers behind as the convertible accelerates out in front of it. Pierson builds conventionally to the crash with a dozen or so quick cuts. Long shot of the car crossing over the yellow line. Another long shot of the car ignoring a stop sign and disappearing around a corner. Close-up of his face followed by a POV of the highway speeding past the camera. A slow zoom-in on John that gives way to a ground level shot of the car approaching and then a cut back to his face. An over-the-shoulder shot of the road matched to the sound of squealing tires leads to close-ups of his face and of his hand switching into an even higher gear. Just as the song ends ("now I'm lost inside of you"), the red convertible crests a hill in an extreme long shot, and the camera holds for several seconds on the empty road and horizon.

Another helicopter (a visual motif which has accrued overtones of both privilege and threat) lands by the side of the highway. Nearby is the wrecked car, turned on its side and showing "WANTED" as the lettering on its license plate. A police radio relays the information that the car was traveling 160 miles per hour at the time of the crash. Even though John can only have driven several miles at most from the ranch, it is Esther, accompanied by Brian, who incongruously disembarks from the chopper. Wearing his buckskin jacket, she runs to John's body still laid out next to the car. In a close-up with Brian positioned behind her, she kisses his face and requests, "He needs a blanket, get him a blanket, please." Even as she touched all the wrong emotional chords during the infidelity scene, Streisand hits all the correct ones here. Less is more in terms of both the dialogue and the acting. Wetting her finger in her mouth, she wipes his face and tells the attendants, "Would you please not stare at him please." She begins to cry softly and quietly, whispering "I'm so scared, Johnny. I don't know what to do." As she cradles his head, she says, "Hold me, please hold me." Because of Streisand's restraint, the confusion and grief are believable. "We've got to move him," explains one of the responders. While she is lifted up out of the frame, she adds, "Be gentle with him. Don't hurt him. Don't hurt him." Despite admonitions from the police, a persistently ghoulish photographer keeps taking pictures of the body. "Just one more," he asks in a perversely ironic and unintentional paraphrase of John Norman's farewell line.

The shot of John's body being lifted into an ambulance dissolves to a shot of a funeral procession on the freeway. Voice-over radio commentary has Bebe Jesus hypocritically pontificating: "John Norman Howard. Bebe Jesus calls him one of the greats, one of the all-time greats." There is no service, just a dissolve to Esther alone in a rocking chair that is framed against a darkened window. Almost immediately, the conclusion of the film starts to go wrong. Hearing John's voice echo through the Hollywood mansion, she rushes downstairs to search frantically for him in rooms that are being emptied by movers. "Hey, lady, how do you shut this thing off?" asks one of them, handing her the tape recorder on which John was composing "With One More Look at You." She sits in one of the ornately paneled rooms to listen to the song and argue hysterically with John's voice on the tape. The underplaying of the crash scene gives way here to exaggeration. "You are a very selfish person and a liar, you son of a bitch," she rants, "because you promised me and you lied." As the camera tracks in for the kind of very tight close-up that Streisand told Pierson there were not enough of in the film, she rips up the tape and breaks down sobbing. Later, more calmly, she whispers, "I'm sorry, Johnny. It's just that there are so many things I wanted to tell you."

A dissolve opens on Esther and Brian entering the stage door of a theater. Apparently, she is there for a benefit performance, but the decision not to include a scene where she is argued out of her self-pitying funk diminishes the sense that this is her tribute to John. Uniformed in a white pantsuit that symbolically suggests she has regained her power and control, she walks directly on stage. An unseen voice announces, "Ladies and gentlemen, Esther Hoffman Howard."

By not having Esther introduce herself and acknowledge the connection to John, the film misses the big emotional payoff, the moment where she defiantly declares her pride in her marriage and in her husband. Instead, after the crowd stands for an ovation and holds memorial lighters in the air, Esther begins softly to sing "With One More Look at You." Framing her in a centered close-up, the camera holds on Streisand for the next seven and a half minutes in a single, uninterrupted take. Unlike the way Cukor explores and analyzes Garland's performance in the long take used for "The Man That Got Away," Pierson's camera remains stationary, reframing only slightly to keep Streisand gazing out of the left side of the frame. She cries, and lighting changes glide across her face, but little else, certainly no thematic point, happens. Midway through, she segues into John's signature "Are You Watching Me Now?" and the pace accelerates from ballad to anthem. An alternate ending was filmed with multiple camera set-ups and extensive cutting between them. Both versions were shown to preview audiences, and reportedly the more heavily edited version emerged in the feedback cards as the clear favorite. According to editor Peter Zinner, "I felt that the edited version was stronger. The other one was too long. It went overboard. Seven and a half minutes is too much of a load for one person, no matter how good you are" (Riese, page 425). Streisand seemed to agree but at the last minute changed her mind and went with the one-take.

For the song's conclusion, Esther holds the microphone with one hand, the stand with the other, and thrusts her head aggressively upward. The film freeze frames on that image and the credits scroll over it. Including the credit shot, there are over ten minutes of the close-up footage so highly valued by Streisand. Among the end credits are one that reads "Musical Concepts by Barbra Streisand" and one that states "Ms. Streisand's Clothes from... Her Closet." The executive producer and star had also wanted co-credit for directing and editing but either lost or abandoned those battles.

A Star Is Born premiered on December 18, 1976, in Los Angeles and opened nationally on Christmas day. Continuing to work on the final edit right up to the deadline, Streisand still concerned herself with details as the finished product was being shipped to theaters. She wrote a note to exhibitors that read: "In setting your usual level of sound, please make sure that Reel 1 and Reel 2 are allowed to play *as loud as possible*. The color is also at its best at 14½-foot candlepower... Barbra Streisand" (Edwards, pages 386-87).

The post-premiere review from industry cheerleader *Daily Variety* was extravagant in its praise, but most east coast and national critics savaged the picture. "If there's anything worse than the noise and stench that rises from [the sound-track] album," wrote Rex Reed, "It's the movie itself. It's an unsalvageable disaster. This is why Hollywood is in the toilet. What the hell does Barbra Streisand know about directing and editing a movie? So many people have disowned this film that I don't even know who to blame" (Spada, page 366).

A Star Is Born (1976) • 257

Dressed in Esther's white power suit, Barbra Streisand delivers the seven and a half minute single long take finale.

Pauline Kael singled out Streisand, arguing "The director and the writer, those credited and those unaccredited, must be partly responsible, but the sinking feeling one gets from the picture relates largely to her. One is never really comfortable with her, because even when she is singing she isn't fully involved in the music; she's trying to manage our responses" (Riese, page 429).

John Simon was even more brutal in his attack on Streisand: "And then I realize with a gasp that this Barbra Streisand is in fact beloved above all other female stars by our movie going audiences; that this hypertrophic ego and bloated countenance are things people shell out money for as for no other actress; that this progressively more belligerent caterwauling can sell anything—concerts, records, movies. And I feel as if our entire society were ready to flush itself down in something even worse than a collective death wish—a collective will to live in ugliness and self-debasement" (Spada, page 366).

Review headlines played maliciously on the film's title. "A Star Is Born: Dead on Arrival," read one. "A Star is Still-Born," joked another. "A Star is Shorn," mocked one of the national magazines.

Despite the often petulant critical backlash, the picture was a huge commercial hit. On opening day in some cities, fans waited in long lines amid snow storms to see it. Within the first ten days of release, it grossed about $10 million, a huge box office figure for 1976. Eventually taking in around $150 million, the film went on to become Streisand's biggest moneymaker and one of the most commercially successful musicals of all time. The soundtrack album, as mentioned earlier, was equally successful. Both the album and the "Evergreen" single climbed to #1 on the charts, with the album selling more copies than any other soundtrack up to that time. Another barometer of the film's popularity was the five Golden Globe nominations and wins it received for Best Picture Musical or Comedy, Best Actress Musical or Comedy, Best Actor Musical or Comedy, Best Original Score and Best Original Song. Although it was nominated for Academy Awards only in the "technical" categories of cinematography, sound, music score, and original song, its sole win for "Evergreen" generated additional publicity and kept the *A Star Is Born* phenomenon dominant in the minds of consumers.

Beyond the critical and commercial considerations, *A Star Is Born* accomplished the goals of its makers. It established Jon Peters as a legitimate and respected movie producer. Following this debut effort with *The Eyes of Laura Mars* in 1978, he would go on to produce or executive produce nearly forty more films, including *The Main Event* (1979), *Die Laughing* (1980), *Missing* (1982), *Flashdance* (1983), *Rain Man* (1988), *Batman* (1989), and *Superman Returns* (2006). It gave Barbra Streisand the valuable behind-the-camera experience she would draw on when finally directing herself in *Yentl* (1983), *The Prince of Tides* (1991), and *The Mirror Has Two Faces* (1996). It enabled Frank Pierson to parlay his second feature film directing credit into future assignments on *King of the Gypsies* (1978), *Citizen Cohn* (1992), *Truman* (1995), and *Conspiracy* (2001). Finally, the picture made a pile of money for Warner Bros., First Artists, Jon Peters, Barbra Streisand, John Gregory Dunne, Joan Didion, and every other player with a piece of the action.

As a living record of her musical performances, it also showcases the power of Barbra Streisand, the consummate pop singer. Full-voiced and confident, she commands the screen. "I Believe in Love," "With One More Look At You," and "Evergreen" are a pleasure to watch. What the film doesn't do, however, is smoothly integrate the original Robert Carson/William Wellman story into a contemporary setting. Streisand makes Esther less victimized and more independent but not very convincing as an inexperienced, rising star. The concert sequences, while well-photographed and realistic, do not mesh with the glossy melodrama of the romance. Opportunities to deconstruct the music industry or develop promising thematic ideas also pass unfulfilled. Of the four related films dealing with the vicissitudes of Hollywood success, this version remains, unfortunately, the weakest.

6

Conclusion

Writing about the American movie capital in 1950, anthropologist Hortense Powdermaker observed, "In Hollywood there is far more confusion and anxiety than in the society which surrounds it. Even in its most prosperous periods when net profits were enormous, far surpassing those of other businesses, everyone was scared. Now, when diminishing foreign markets, increasing costs of production, competition with European pictures, and changing box-office tastes threaten the swollen profits of past prosperity, fear rises to panic. Anxiety grips everyone from executive to third assistant director" (page 309).

To be sure, there is a sense of unease permeating each of the four films analyzed here. Mary Evans and the two Esther Blodgetts struggle to earn a living while they attempt to break into the movies. At one time or another, each of them works as a waitress—Mary at the Brown Derby, the first Esther at a catered party, and the second Esther at a drive-in. Esther Hoffman also toils away in low-paying gigs before getting her big break. Once they are established in the entertainment business, all four women battle to balance the competing demands of marriage and career.

The men who helped to engineer those careers bitterly suffer the collapse of their own. One of Hollywood's most successful directors, Max Carey loses his studio contract and ends up hanging around Mary Evans's sets as some kind of unpaid personal assistant. The two Norman Maines are fired by their bosses and unable to sign with anyone else. James Mason's Norman practically begs for a job during his public humiliation at the Oscars. Worried about their images as leading men, both actors refuse to accept supporting roles as a way back into the industry. Rock star John

Norman Howard is abandoned by his backup band and has his comeback music rejected by the producer who used to manage him. Even the executives in all four films are plagued by anxiety. Studio bosses Julius Saxe and Oliver Niles, numbers one and two, worry about bad publicity, bankers, and the bottom line. Their need to show a profit trumps their loyalty to troubled old friends unable to overcome their alcoholism. All-purpose entrepreneur Brian Wexler frets constantly about cancelled concert appearances, potential law suits, and record sales.

Yet in each of the four films, as in most self-referential Hollywood pictures, love of show business overshadows everything else, including the angst. *What Price Hollywood?* and the 1937 and 1954 versions of *A Star Is Born* are unabashed tributes to the creativity and energy of Hollywood. The tragic ends of Max Carey and Norman Maine are not the fault of the studios but of their own inner demons. Each man, disdainful of the hype, comes to miss the excitement inside those sound stages. For Selznick, Wellman, and Cukor, the world of moviemaking is an extraordinarily imaginative and professional place. Cukor's camera, in particular, with its deep-focus compositions, its overflowing frames, and its seamless tracking shots, celebrates the spectacle of Hollywood. Pierson's handheld

Love of moviemaking conquers all.

camera and quick cutting convey a similar enthusiasm for the nervous energy of pop music concerts.

Equally important is the fact that the career aspirations of each female actress/performer are legitimated and even glorified. Becoming a star is depicted as a laudatory preoccupation. "To be a star," writes Edgar Morin, "is precisely the impossible made possible, the possible made impossible. The most talented actress can never be assured of becoming a star, but an unknown pretty face may be given a leading role from one day to the next" (page 51).

The star-making process is somewhat mystified in *What Price Hollywood?* and the three *A Star Is Born* films. Admittedly, we see the remarkable talent of Judy Garland and Barbra Streisand when they sing, but even with them and certainly with Constance Bennett and Janet Gaynor, the special quality that captures the public's attention and thrusts them into stardom remains illusive. As Morin notes, "A remarkable technique of encouragement-discouragement: accession to stardom depends upon luck; luck is a break, and a break is grace" (page 51).

The stardom itself in each of the four films is more tangible. Some variation of "It's all yours now" is uttered to Mary Evans and the three Esthers, often with the glittering lights of Hollywood stretched out behind them, and endless opportunity is promised to them for creative expression, material success, and public approbation. When personal troubles threaten to remove the four risen stars from their success, each ultimately pledges to return to her career and continue shooting films, making records or giving concerts. For Janet Gaynor's Esther Blodgett, that return even has patriotic overtones of the American frontier attached to it. The only taint is not the alcoholic mentor, whose importance is proudly acknowledged, but the callous tabloid reporters, photographers and fans who intrude on the star's privacy.

In an essay titled "Stardom as an Occupation," Barry King explains, "It should always be recalled in considering stars that they are highly selected phenomena. Before any star—out of the large number present—can meet with public approval he or she must be selected by those governing the current organization of production. Indeed, it is a consistent position that the former is governed as a possibility by the reality of the latter" (page 180). In other words, stars like Mary Evans and Vicki Lester are manufactured by the corporate structures which control the means of production and distribution. In *What Price Hollywood?* and the 1937 and 1954 *A Star Is Born* pictures, the controlling structure is a studio patterned on one of the Hollywood minors (production and distribution but not exhibition) like Universal or Columbia and commanded by a single powerful boss. Apart from the narrative details regarding screen tests and the assemblage of the star's image, each film also reflects economic and organizational trends appropriate to its particular moment in Hollywood history. That is, as contemporary films, they mirror contemporary business models.

Gregory Ratoff, as Julius Saxe, operates his studio like a cranky great-uncle running the family department store. He is very hands-on, making spontaneous decisions about publicity, story ideas and budget revisions. An eastern European émigré and silent film pioneer, he probably moved into the movie business from the rag trade. Here he is in an excerpt from the Gene Fowler and Rowland Brown script (considerably altered during filming) arguing with director Max Carey over how many extras to hire for a scene:

> SAXE: Why you say that's all for today?
> CAREY: (very nasty) Because I said three hundred extras on the set at nine o'clock and they're not here.
> SAXE: (with growing indignation) Yes, and you said three hundred extras on the set yesterday morning and you weren't here! What kind of monkeyshines is this— You're driving me crazy! I should pay three hundred extras seven dollars and a half a day while you sleep off a drunk! D'you know how much is three hundred times seven and a half?
> CAREY: No, and neither do you. I'm a director, not a bookkeeper. And if you want me to finish this masterpiece, give me what I ask for and stay off the set!
> SAXE: Three hundred extras is too many… a thousand times too many! I give you twenty-five.
> CAREY: And you expect me to shoot an Embassy Ball with twenty-five people! Maybe you want me to play it in a telephone booth.
> SAXE: All right. This once I give in to you. You can have a hundred and fifty extras. (he stamps off)
> CAREY: (calling after him) Make'em all twins!
>
> (pages 23-24)

Conclusion • 265

The interchange could be Carl Laemmle fighting with von Stroheim at Universal over *Foolish Wives*, except the reference to a "masterpiece" would not have been tongue in cheek.

Although appearing only five years later, Adolphe Menjou's Oliver Niles manages a studio that is more factory line and less sideshow. He has various department heads like Matt Libby in publicity to handle all the production and personnel details. The studio facilities and equipment are more lavish, and the stakes are higher. There is the sense of unseen banking partners pressuring him for profit. By 1954, studio economics have changed radically. Less avuncular and more uptight, Charles Bickford as Oliver Niles presides over an industry in transition. A titular studio boss only, he worries about directives from "the boys back East," moneymen like MGM's Nick Schenck and Paramount's Adolph Zukor who made the real financial decisions. Contending with competition from foreign films and television, he is acutely aware of escalating costs and shrinking profits. Stars may still be signed to long term contracts but there are also plenty of deals, as Norman Maine suggests, to be made with independent producers like Alexander Korda. The 1976 *A Star Is Born* does not even mention studios or record companies. Stars like Esther Hoffman and

Long term studio contracts are a thing of the past.

John Norman Howard move from one concert tour or recording contract to another. Their business affairs are managed not by an executive but by a cadre of personally hired advisors and consultants. The closest thing to a mogul is Brian Wexler, who, rather than running a brick and mortar entertainment company, makes his money by promoting, producing, and managing independent clients.

The economic imperatives and industrial practices referenced in the four fictional narratives somewhat characterize the production circumstances of the films themselves. *What Price Hollywood?*, for example, was a traditional studio product, directed by George Cukor and executive produced by David O. Selznick, both of whom were under contract at the time to RKO. As head of production, Selznick reported only to David Sarnoff, president of the New York-based parent company Radio Corporation of America, and functioned more or less as studio boss. Constance Bennett was also signed to RKO and was cast in the picture as part of her contractual obligations. Selznick's *A Star Is Born*, on the other hand, was one of the first films he made for his own company, Selznick International Pictures. Operating out of the old Thomas Ince Studio on Washington Boulevard in Culver City, Selznick International maintained a skeletal administrative staff and released its product through United Artists. Both Fredric March and Janet Gaynor were hired under lucrative one-picture contracts to play Norman Maine and Esther Blodgett in *A Star Is Born*. The 1954 George Cukor version, as we have seen, was an independent project co-produced by Warner Bros. and Judy Garland's personal company Transcona (part of a trend most successfully realized by Burt Lancaster in which stars set up their own picture-making corporations). Cast and crew were all contracted for the single assignment and control of the final cut resided with Warner Bros. When Warners partnered with Barbra Streisand's Barwood Productions for the 1976 *A Star Is Born*, the balance of power had shifted. Warner Bros. provided studio space, equipment, and financing, but Streisand had final approval on all the major cast and crew hires and on the film's final edit. Both parties made a lot of money on the results. By whatever means in the various films they were selected, the actual stars (as well as the diegetic ones) were always intended to maximize profit for the products in which they appeared.

Tied to the economic parameters of stardom are less obvious sociological ones. As Barry King reminds us, "What is particular about the star is that he or she is not so much an actor… but a self or personality that behaves. To say that a star behaves does not mean that they are themselves, but rather that stars do not, as it were, surrender their public personality to the demands of characterization" (page 160). Those public personalities are representational, as well, reflecting social norms, values, and roles. Stars show us who we are or would like to be at a particular moment in history. "From ideological criticism," writes film scholar Jeremy Butler, "star studies has fastened onto the basic presumption that ideology consists of the taken-for-granted values and concepts that underpin a particular society. Moreover, it is argued that these values exist in a systematic relationship to one another and that they have 'real' social causes and effects. Ideological values are presumed to be generated by a society's economic and social infrastructure and related to the ways that society treats individuals of different classes, races and gender. As a result, star studies has sought to analyse the meanings of star images in relation to ideologies of class, race, and gender" (page 345).

Going a step further, Susan Hayward points out that ideology operates within a national context and that a country's film stars embody its specific cultural and gestural codes. In her book-length study of Simone Signoret, for example, she traces how the star, the first foreign performer to receive an Oscar for Best Actress, was cast in parts that reveal changing French attitudes regarding female agency. "During her acting career," notes Hayward, "Signoret embodied roles that can only be described as ones that offered the spectator a series of challenging sexualities, feisty femininities, and, later on, a cross section of maternal bodies that had lost none of the former two qualities" (page 238). In her early films, she was the erotic beauty, often playing prostitutes and schemers. She was valued for her "incendiary eyes and long, slim legs" (page 27). Then, with her marriage to Yves Montand, she became the star as political activist, passionate and *engagé*. The Academy Award victory confirmed a period of international stardom, where Signoret was viewed widely as an independent, sophisticated, and sexually assured woman of the world. Finally, as her looks faded and her weight increased, she refused to deny the aging process and commanded respect for her maturity and intelligence.

Similarly diverse portrayals of American women run through *What Price Hollywood?* and *A Star Is Born*. The real stars' personas and their fictional characters overlap in signifying recognizable "types" dominant at different times in popular culture. Constance Bennett/Mary Evans is a fast-talking, urban realist. Pretty and style-conscious rather than beautiful, she uses her brashness and street smarts to navigate the early days of the Great Depression. Similarly aggressive blonde working girls appear in

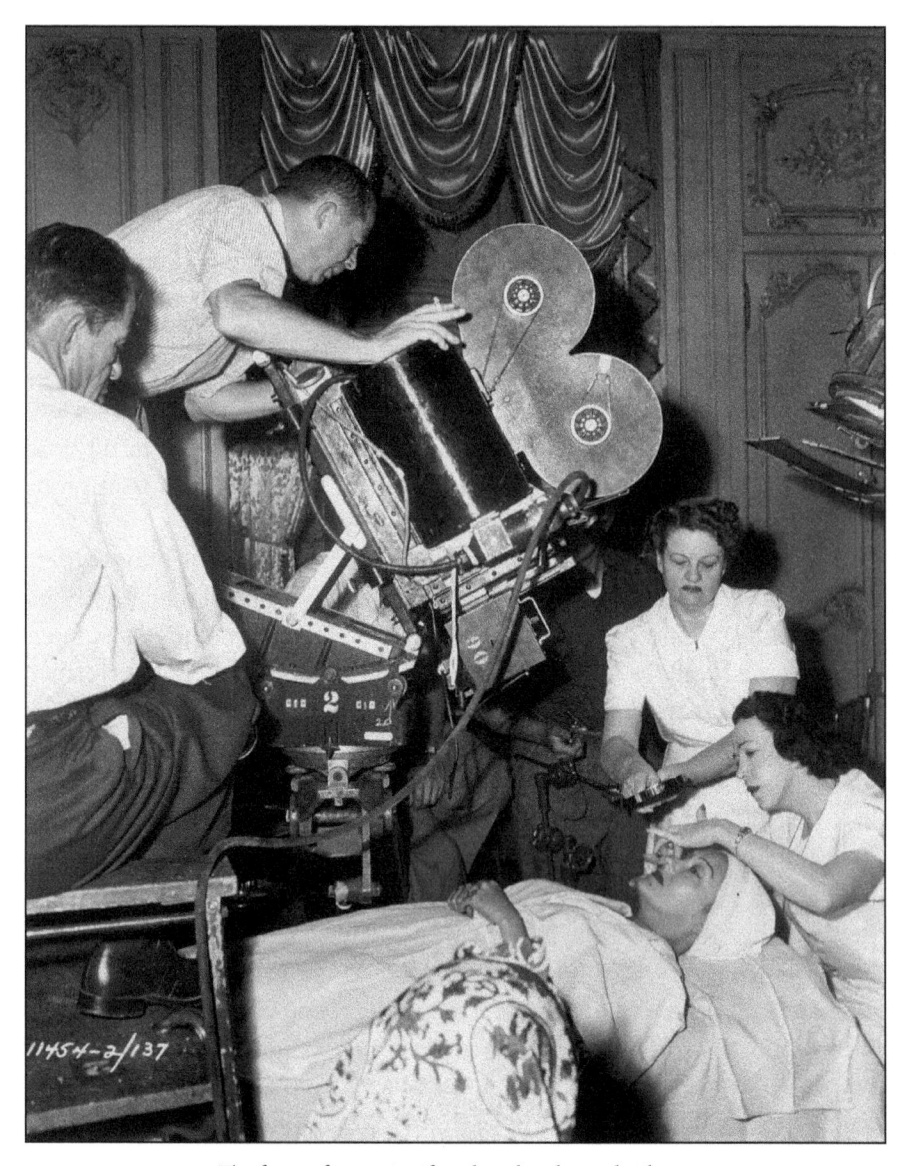

The faces of stars signify cultural codes and values.

the popular social melodramas and backstage musicals at Warner Bros. Entirely different is the brunette Janet Gaynor/Esther Blodgett heroine of the later 1930s. Where Mary Evans would confront a strong-willed male, this Esther reconciles and submits. Less abrasive and more demure, she represents small town American virtues of husband, hearth, and home. Think Jeanette MacDonald shuttling between Paramount and MGM or Irene Dunne in *Showboat*. This Mrs. Norman Maine's honeymoon, in fact, is a camping trailer expedition through the California high country. Judy Garland's Esther Blodgett, to a certain degree, mediates conflicting gender attitudes of the mid 1950s. "This is an essential allure of the star," Jeremy Butler perceptively observes, "the resolution of contradictions that cannot be resolved in the social sphere, in 'real life'" (page 347). Garland is both professional and domestic. She values her career and her marriage. There is still a hint of the homespun MGM girl-next-door to her but also a new-found elegance and sophistication. She seems to exist above the mid-century Hollywood star-image divide between the voluptuous (Marilyn Monroe) and the waif-like (Audrey Hepburn).

As we have discussed in some detail, Barbra Streisand as Esther Hoffman is a whole different kind of star and woman. Independent and liberated, she initiates sexual encounters and remains (literally) on top. Refusing to abandon her career for a husband, she maintains strict professional standards in the pursuit of goals that have not been determined by powerful men. Her pointed reference to herself as Esther Hoffman Howard speaks directly to the influence of 1970s feminist politics in the United States and in Hollywood.

The ever-evolving images of women in *What Price Hollywood?* and *A Star Is Born* are grafted onto a narrative core based on one of the most androcentric stories in mythology—the tale of Pygmalion and Galatea. In Ovid's *Metamorphoses*, Pygmalion is a sculptor who, despairing of the prostitution in Cyprus, carves his ideal image of a woman out of ivory. So beautiful and realistic is the statue the he names her Galatea and quickly falls in love with her. At a festival for Aphrodite, he prays to the goddess that he might find a wife who would be the flesh and blood embodiment of Galatea. Returning home, he kisses the statue and discovers that she has come to life. After educating and refining Galatea, he marries his creation and together they have a son named Paphos. Although the most direct descendants of Galatea are the Eliza Dolittle characters in Shaw's *Pygmalion* and Lerner and Lowe's *My Fair Lady*, also related are Mary Evans and the various Esthers. Substitute an alcoholic film director or actor for Professor Henry Higgins and make Eliza a talented yet undiscovered actress/singer and you have the basic "star is born" formula. For even broader appeal there is a hint of Cinderella in the nondescript maiden who blossoms overnight and finds her prince.

At least two different versions of *A Star Is Born* have been made in India, the Kairali-language *Bharatham* in 1991 and the Hindi-language *Aashiqui 2* in 2013. In *Bharatham*, the rising young star and the fading alcoholic star are brothers trained in the family tradition of Carnatic music. As the older brother continues to appear drunk at his concerts, the younger one takes over and achieves great popularity. Recognizing what he has lost, the older brother struggles to reform but dies in an accident. A major Bollywood musical drama directed by Mohit Suri, *Aashiqui 2* follows the 1954 and 1976 *A Star Is Born* plots almost exactly. Rahul is a legendary pop singer who discovers the beautiful and talented Aarohi singing in a bar. Despite his alcoholism, Rahul recognizes her potential and promises to help. She quits her job but a mix-up prevents Rahul from contacting her. Once they are reunited, he gets her a recording contract and advances her career as his own suffers. Upset by gossip that he is living off his protégé, Rahul goes on a binge and lands in jail. Bailed out and nursed by Aarohi, Rahul overhears her tell a friend that she plans to abandon her singing career to care for him. Realizing he has become a burden, he leaves and commits suicide. Vowing at first to never sing again, Aarohi returns to the stage as a tribute to Rahul and uses his name when giving her autograph to a fan.

Despite these successful reimaginings, *A Star Is Born* still seems to me to be an essentially American myth. The idea of traveling west to compete for success on the last frontier is a cherished pioneer paradigm. So also is the belief that, in a society where class is supposedly determined more by talent than by birth, anyone can achieve riches and recognition. And, in the tradition of Horatio Alger and Jay Gatsby, there is the underlying assumption that as an American you can effortlessly redefine yourself, morphing smoothly from Esther Blodgett to Vicki Lester.

The question today is whether this Hollywood archetype still has any mileage left in it. Certainly Hollywood the place does not hold much resonance or even interest. "I looked around and it was gone," Robert Wagner told Turner Classic Movie host Robert Osborne during a recent screening of *A Kiss Before Dying*, "it" referring to the gilded old Hollywood he used to know. Currently, Paramount is the only studio located within Hollywood that retains its original name and facilities; the old Columbia, RKO, Monogram, Goldwyn, and Republic properties continue to be carved up and retitled. Hollywood Boulevard itself, even with the installation of the Walk of Fame in 1958, was already trashy and disreputable by the mid-1960s. Despite the construction in 2001 of the Hollywood and Highland shopping complex and the adjacent Dolby Theatre (originally named for the pre-bankruptcy Eastman Kodak Company and used mostly now for the annual Academy Awards ceremony), the area in no way invites wonder or fascination.

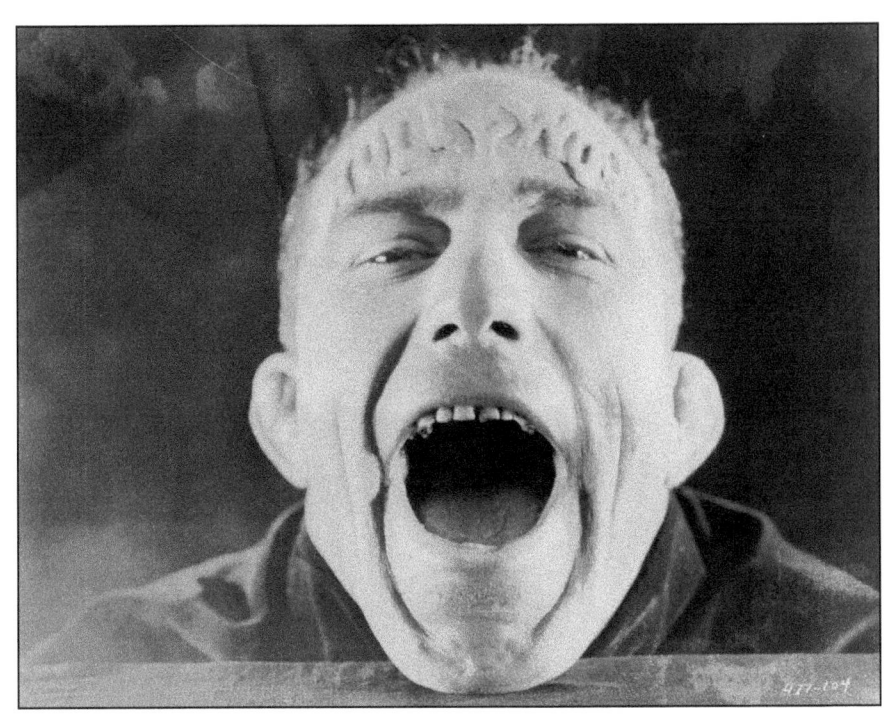

A less than glamorous image from James Cruze's lost 1923 film *Hollywood*.

Perhaps the narrative itself has more ongoing potential. John Gregory Dunne and Joan Didion obviously thought so since they used it again as the framework for their 1996 *Up Close and Personal* script, shifting from movies to the television news business and recasting Norman and Esther as a veteran news producer (Robert Redford) and an up-and-coming young reporter (Michelle Pfeiffer). Believability was always a major challenge for the various "star is born" stories. Now, with multiple media platforms and 24/7 social networking, a scenario involving the casual discovery, corporate grooming, and overnight success of an unknown star requires an even greater leap of faith and logic for young audiences.

But there still is something universal and timeless about the professional and romantic complications of a couple where one partner's career is rising and the other's is falling. How to support a beloved yet troubled mentor suffering from addiction without wrecking one's own life is a question as relevant today as it was in 1932. In addition to updating the relationship (a same-sex or interracial couple?) and the business model (no studio contract players or moguls), any creative overhaul of the archetype also would have to confront the darker realities that Selznick and

Cukor so carefully avoided. We know too much about the egos, greed, sexual abuse, corporate mismanagement, and general deception of Hollywood to accept anything else. The image of kindly Oliver Niles, never a credible studio boss to begin with, has long since been replaced by that of David Begelman, the former Columbia and MGM president who extorted and bilked Judy Garland and who embezzled payments meant for Cliff Robertson. The only way back into *A Star Is Born* will have to be more honesty about what really lies behind the shimmering facade.

Works Cited

Altman, Rick. *The American Film Musical*. Bloomington, Indiana: Indiana University Press, 1987.

Bach, Steven. *Dazzler: The Life and Times of Moss Hart*. Cambridge, Massachusetts: Da Capo Press, 2002.

Bachelard, Gaston. *The Poetics of Space*. Boston: Beacon Press, 1969.

Behlmer, Rudy, ed. *Memo from David O. Selznick*. New York: The Viking Press, Inc., 1972.

Bernardoni, James. *George Cukor: A Critical Study and Filmography*. Jefferson, North Carolina: McFarland and Company, Inc. Publishers, 1985.

Butler, Jeremy G. "The Star System and Hollywood," in John Hill and Pamela Church Gibson, eds., *The Oxford Guide to Film Studies*. Oxford: Oxford University Press, 1998.

Clarens, Carlos. *Cukor*. London: Secker and Warburg Limited, 1976.

Didion, Joan. "Some Dreamers of the Golden Dream," in *Slouching Towards Bethlehem*. New York: Dell Publishing Co., Inc., 1968, pp.3-28.

Dunne, John Gregory. "Gone Hollywood," in *Regards*. New York: Thunder's Mouth Press, 2006, pp.37-42.

Edwards, Anne. *Streisand: A Biography.* Boston: Little, Brown and Company, 1997.

Finch, Christopher. *Rainbow: The Stormy Life of Judy Garland.* New York, Grosset and Dunlap, Publishers, 1997.

Fowler, Gene and Brown, Rowland. *What Price Hollywood?* New York: Frederick Ungar Publishing Co., 1959.

Fricke, John. *Judy Garland: World's Greatest Entertainer.* New York: Henry Holt and Company, Inc., 1992.

Haver, Ronald. *A Star Is Born: The Making of the 1954 Movie and Its 1983 Restoration.* New York: Harper and Row, Publishers, 1990.

Hayward, Susan. *Key Concepts in Cinema Studies.* London: Routledge, 1996.

Hayward, Susan. *Simone Signoret: The Star as Cultural Sign.* New York: The Continuum International Publishing Group, Inc., 2004.

King, Barry. "Stardom as an Occupation," in Paul Kerr, ed., *The Hollywood Film Industry.* London: Routledge and Keegan Paul, 1986.

Lambert, Gavin. *On Cukor.* New York: Rizzoli International Publications, Inc., 2000.

Levy, Emanuel. *George Cukor: Master of Elegance.* New York: William Morrow and Company, Inc., 1994.

Madsen, Axel. *Stanwyck.* New York: Harper Collins Publishers, Inc., 1994.

McGilligan, Patrick. *George Cukor: A Double Life.* New York: Harper Collins Publishers, Inc., 1992.

McWilliams, Carey. *Southern California: An Island on the Land.* Santa Barbara, California: Peregrine Smith, Inc., 1973.

Morella, Joe and Epstein, Edward. *Judy: The Films and Career of Judy Garland.* New York: The Citadel Press, 1969.

Morin, Edgar. *The Stars*. New York: Grove Press, Inc., 1960.

Morley, Sheridan. *James Mason: Odd Man Out*. New York: Harper and Row, Publishers, Inc., 1989.

Overstreet, Richard. "George Cukor," in Robert Emmett Long, ed., *George Cukor Interviews*. Jackson, Mississippi: University Press of Mississippi, 2001, pp. 16-48.

Phillips, Gene D. "George Cukor: An Interview," in Robert Emmett Long, ed., *George Cukor Interviews*. Jackson, Mississippi: University Press of Mississippi, 2001, pp. 67-72.

Powdermaker, Hortense. *Hollywood the Dream Factory*. Boston: Little, Brown and Company, 1950.

Quirk, Lawrence J. *The Films of Fredric March*. New York: Citadel Press, Inc., 1971.

Riese, Randall. *Her Name is Barbra*. New York: St. Martin's Press, 1994.

Sarris, Andrew. *The American Cinema*. New York: E.P. Dutton and Company, Inc., 1968.

Selznick, Irene Mayer. *A Private View*. New York: Alfred A. Knopf, Inc., 1983.

Spada, James. *Streisand: Her Life*. New York: Crown Publishers Inc., 1995

St. Johns, Adela Rogers. *Some Are Born Great*. New York: The New American Library, Inc., 1975.

Thomson, David. *The New Biographical Dictionary of Film*. New York: Alfred A. Knopf, 2002.

Thomson, David. *Showman: The Life of David O. Selznick*. New York: Alfred A. Knopf, Inc., 1992.

Index

Aashiqui 2 269-70
Academy Awards 14, 40, 70, 72, 96, 98, 99, 103, 109, 115, 117, 121, 123-28, 136, 189-90, 192-93, 215, 222, 226, 240, 247, 258, 267, 270
Adorée, Renée 6-7
Aldrich, Robert 22, 25, 27
Alex in Wonderland 18
All About Eve 32, 44, 117
Allen, Gene 118, 171, 173-74, 194, 216
Allen, Jay Presson 222
Allen, Woody 2, 4, 35
Alperson, Edward 111-13
Altman, Rick 203, 232
Altman, Robert 14, 30, 222
American in Paris, An 126, 171, 186
Anderson, Eddie 46, 52
Arbuckle, Fatty 9, 11, 15
Arlen, Harold 111, 115-16, 125, 128, 170-71, 175, 183
Armstrong, Del 197
Arthur, George K. 10
Ascher, Kenny 225, 228, 240
Ashby, Hal 222
Astaire, Fred 115, 126, 135, 171, 186
Axelrod, Jonathan 220, 222
Ayers, Lem 118

Bach, Steven 114, 140
Bachelard, Gaston 242
Bad and the Beautiful, The 30-31, 36
Baldwin, Alec 35
Barefoot Contessa, The 23, 27-28, 33
Barrymore, John 66, 72, 100, 189, 198
Barstow, Richard 125-26, 129, 131, 170-71, 175, 193
Barton Fink 28

Bassey, Shirley 149
Beatty, Warren 218
Beavers, Louise 52
Begelman, David 272
Behlmer, Rudy 69-70, 102-03
Being John Malkovich 14
Bellamy, Earl 149
Bennett, Constance 40-42, 50, 56, 67, 149, 158, 263, 266-67
Bergman, Alan and Marilyn 226, 241
Berkeley, Busby 14, 18
Bern, Paul 109
Bernardoni, James 130, 137, 144, 150, 166, 170, 178, 185, 197
Bert, Malcolm 118
Bharatham 269
Bickford, Charles 120-21, 154, 191, 197, 265
Big Knife, The 27-28, 30, 32
Big Picture, The 34
Blandick, Clara 74
Blangsted, Folmar 215
Blondell, Joan 42
Boardman, Eleanor 24
Bogart, Humphrey 28, 31, 33, 115, 119, 173
Bogdanovich, Peter 217-18
Bologna, Joseph 222
Borgnine, Ernest 25, 28
"Born in a Trunk" 125-26, 152, 170-76, 195
Bow, Clara 18, 67
Bowers, John 109
Bowfinger 34-36
Branagh, Kenneth 20
Brando, Marlon 223
Brazzi, Rossano 28-29
Brenner, Marie 220, 222
Brooks, Louise 11
Brown, Clarence 55

Brown, Joe E. 12
Brown, Karl 12
Brown, Rowland 39, 264
Browne, Coral 25, 31
Burton, Richard 119
Buscemi, Steve 35
Busey, Gary 228
Butler, Jeremy 267, 269

Campbell, Alan 70
Cantinflas 13
Carlisle, Kitty 114
Carson, Jack 13, 120-21, 182, 207
Carson, Robert 70, 109, 185, 259
Casablanca 207
Cathcart, Jack 125
Chaplin 22
Chaplin, Charlie 6, 9, 15, 24
Cher 219
CinemaScope 111, 122-24, 128-29, 131, 144-45
Clark, Oliver 236
Clift, Montgomery 119
Cocoanut Grove, The 137-38, 142-44, 190-91
Cody, Lew 24
Cohn, Harry 29, 44, 66, 82
Colt, Sam 132
Columbia (Records) 220
Columbia (Studios) 13, 31, 33, 71, 128, 222, 264, 270, 272
Condon, Frank 12
Contempt 32
Coolidge, Rita 247
Cooper, Merian C. 103
Cortese, Valentina 25
Cosgrave, Luke 10
Countryman and the Cinematograph, The 2
Cromwell, John 32
Crosby, Bing 14
Cruze, James 9, 11, 271
Cukor, George 69-72, 78, 110, 228, 237, 241, 249-50, 252, 255, 262, 266, 271
  director, *Star is Born, A* (1954) 38, 50, 57, 91, 95, 111, 114, 116-18, 121-22, 124-26, 128-37, 140-42, 144, 148-54, 158, 162, 164, 166-70, 176-78, 181-85, 187, 189-91, 193-95, 197-98, 201-04, 206-09, 211-13, 215-16
  director, *What Price Hollywood?* 39-41, 43-44, 46-48, 50, 54-56, 58-60, 66-68
Curtiz, Michael 116

Dailey, Dan 14, 125
Dandridge, Dorothy 216
Daves, Delmer 12
David, Jacques-Louis 150
Davies, Marion 4, 6-7, 14
Davis, Bruce 216
Davis, Bette 12-13, 32, 117
Day for Night 18-19
Deal, The 34-36
Degas, Edgar 135
DeMille, Cecil B. 7, 9-10, 28, 36-37, 125, 221
DeNiro, Robert 35
Devine, Andy 79
Didion, Joan 75, 217-18, 220, 222, 238, 259, 271
Dietrich, Marlene 54, 87, 128, 161, 165
Dillon, Bob and Laurie 222
Dinklage, Peter 35
Dior, Christian 213
Dix, Richard 24
Donen, Stanley 15, 116
Donohue, Jack 193
D'Orsay, Fifi 14
Douglas, Kirk 30
Drown, Hope 9
Dunne, Irene 268
Dunne, John Gregory 217-20, 222, 259, 271
Dylan, Bob 223

Edens, Roger 170-71
Edison, Thomas 1-3
8 ½ 18-19, 35, 140
Edwards, Anne 222-223, 235, 243, 250
Edwards, Douglas 216
Englund, Robert 230, 248
Extra Girl, The 15

Fairbanks, Douglas 6, 9, 11-12
Falk, Rossella 25

Farrell, Glenda 25
Fay, Frank 109
Fellini, Federico 18, 140
Ferguson, Frank 203
Ferrer, José 25
Film Johnnie, A 15
Finch, Christopher 127
Finch, Peter 25
First Artists 217, 219, 222, 227, 259
Fleming, Victor 71, 78, 124
Flynn, Errol 189
Ford, Glenn 119
Ford, John 116, 124
Foreman, John 219
For Your Consideration 34, 36
Fosse, Bob 186, 222
Fowler, Gene 39, 264
Frances 22
Freed, Arthur 171
Fricke, Jonathan 126, 150

Gable and Lombard 22
Gable, Clark 41
Galatea 154, 163, 269
Garbo, Greta 25, 41, 80, 121
Gardner, Ava 23, 28, 165
Garfield, John 12
Garland, Judy 14, 49, 99, 110-17, 119-20, 123-28, 140, 147-50, 157, 161-62, 165, 169-73, 175-76, 186-89, 192-97, 211-12, 215-17, 229, 236, 238, 240, 246-47, 255, 263, 266, 269, 272
Gaynor, Janet 49, 71-72, 74, 92, 99, 106-09, 140, 149, 158, 161, 163, 190, 229, 246, 263, 266, 268
Geraghty, Thomas 12
Gershe, Leonard 170
Gershwin, George 115-16, 171
Gershwin, Ira 111, 115-16, 125, 128, 139, 170-71, 175, 183, 194
Get Shorty 34
Gilbert, John 6-7
Girl, The 20
Godard, Jean-Luc 32
Goddess, The 32
Going Hollywood 14
Goldwyn, Sam 44, 66, 78

Gone with the Wind 21, 40, 71, 88, 109
Goodman, Benny 14, 16, 125
Goodman, John 31
Gordon, Ruth 116
Goring, Marius 28
Gough, Lloyd 30
Graff, Wilton 213
Graham, Bill 233
Grammy Awards 240, 247-48
Granger, Stewart 119
Grant, Cary 32, 118-19
Grauman's Chinese Theater 25, 44, 77, 130
Greenstreet, Sydney 13
Guest, Christopher 34

Hagen, Jean 16-17
Haines, William 4, 6
Hamilton, Neil 52-53
Harburg, E.Y. 115
Harlow 22
Hart, Moss 91, 111, 113-15, 121, 140, 142, 148, 151, 158, 181-82, 197, 203, 209, 231
Hart, William S. 6, 9-10
Haver, Ronald 112-13, 116, 118, 120-21, 124, 127, 135, 141, 144, 150, 155-56, 171, 173, 192-94, 197, 215-16
Hayward, Susan (writer) 22, 24, 161-62, 267
Hayworth, Rita 116, 126, 128
Hearst, William Randolph 7-8, 39
Hedren, Tippi 20-21
Heflin, Marta 249
Heisler, Stuart 32
Heindorf, Ray 125, 178
Helton, Percy 203
Hemingway, Ernest 151-52
Henry, Buck 222
Hepburn, Audrey 216, 269
Hepburn, Katharine 49, 75, 80, 82
Hiller, Arthur 222
Hitchcock 20
Hitchcock, Alfred 20, 46, 67, 184, 200
Hoch, Winton 124
Holden, William 25
Holliday, Judy 117
Hollywood 9-12, 271
Hollywood Canteen 12-13, 37
Hollywood Ending 35

Hollywood Hotel 14, 16-17
Holmes, Rupert 225-26, 229-30
Hopkins, Anthony 20
Hopper, Hedda 31
Hoyningen-Huene, George 117-18, 171
Hughes, Rupert 24
Huston, John 49, 117
Hutton, Robert 13

I Could Go on Singing 115, 149
In a Lonely Place 31, 37
Independent Moving Pictures Company 1
Inside Daisy Clover 30

Jagger, Mick 219, 223
James Dean 22
Jenns, Elizabeth 80
John, Gottfried 25
Jones, F. Richard 15
Jones, Toby 20
Joplin, Janis 219, 235
José, José 149

Kael, Pauline 258
Kamelson, Benjamin 129, 215
Kanin, Faye 216
Kanin, Garson 116
Kaufman, George S. 113
Keaton, Buster 2, 4, 15
Keller, Marthe 25
Kelly, Gene 15, 17-18, 126, 171, 173, 186, 194
Kelly, Grace 111, 216
Kelly, M.G. 236
Kennedy, Edgar 77, 79, 86
Kern, Jerome 116
Keystone Studios 15
King, Barry 263, 266
Knef, Hildegard 25
Koehler, Ted 115
Korda, Alex 188, 265
Koster, Henry 116
Kramer, Stanley 124
Krasner, Milton 124
Kristofferson, Kris 219, 221, 223-24, 226, 228, 231-33, 235, 239, 241, 243, 247, 250, 253
Kulky, Henry 198-99

Lady Be Good 246
Laemmle, Carl 82, 265
Lambert, Gavin 66, 141, 197-98, 206, 212
Lancaster, Burt 266
Lane, Burton 116
Lane, Rosemary 14
Lardner, Ring Jr. 70
Laurents, Arthur 222
Lawrence, Florence 1
Lazar, Irving 115
Leavitt, Sam 124, 127, 144, 171
Legend of Lylah Clare, The 22, 24-25, 28, 31, 77
Legend of Valentino, The 21
LeGros, James 35
Lerner, Michael 28
LeRoy, Mervyn 24, 55
Leslie, Joan 13, 37
Levy, Emanuel 66-67, 119, 197
Living in Oblivion 35
Liz and Dick 22
Loggins, Kenny 226, 241
Loren, Sophia 32
Lorre, Peter 13
Louis, Jean 126, 128, 133, 145, 191, 213
Lubitsch, Ernst 18, 92
Luft, Sid 99, 111-14, 117-19, 126, 128, 171, 217
Lumet, Sidney 222
Lupino, Ida 13

MacDonald, Jeanette 268
Macy, William H. 34
Mankiewicz, Joseph 23, 32, 44
Manley, Charles 3
Mann, Daniel 116
"Man That Got Away, The" 123, 125, 128-29, 145-51, 154, 156, 162-63, 169, 178, 186, 215, 240, 256
March, Fredric 71-72, 92, 98-99, 103, 108-09, 134, 154, 190, 241, 247, 253, 266
Markson, Ben 39-40
Marlow, Lucy 130
Martin, Hugh 125, 147
Martin, Lloyd 125
Martin, Steve 34
Mason, James 50, 95, 110-11, 119-20, 134, 138, 144, 154, 189, 192, 198, 201,

Index • 281

206, 215-16, 229, 231, 238, 241, 247, 253, 261
Mastroianni, Marcello 18
Mayer, Louis B. 29, 99, 109, 161
Mayo, Frank 24
Mazursky, Paul 18, 236
McCormick, John 109
McDowall, Roddy 30
McGilligan, Patrick 67, 71-72, 117
McWilliams, Carey 15
melodrama 22-28, 30-33, 36-38, 250
Menjou, Adolphe 82-83, 112, 121, 155, 265
Mercer, Johnny 115
Merman, Ethel 149
MGM 6-8, 14-15, 18, 22, 30, 40, 55, 112, 116-17, 119, 125-27, 161, 165, 171, 184, 231, 246, 268, 272
Midler, Bette 219
Milland, Ray 119
Miller, Sienna 20
Minnelli, Liza 219
Minnelli, Vincente 30, 32, 55, 171, 186
Miranda, Carmen 157
Mirren, Helen 20
Mitchell, Millard 16
Mommie Dearest 22-23
Mondrian, Piet 173
Monroe, Marilyn 20, 32, 121, 128, 269
Montand, Yves 267
Moore, Colleen 109
Moran, Polly 5
Morin, Edgar 263
Morrison, Jim 228
Mowbray, Allan 17
Mulhall, Jack 24
Mulligan, Robert 30
Murfin, Jane 39-40
Murphy, Eddie 34
Murray, Mae 6-7
My Fair Lady 124, 215, 269
My Week with Marilyn 19

Neilan, Marshall 66
Never Give a Sucker an Even Break 33
Nichols, George 15
Nichols, Mike 218
Nitzche, Jack 225
Noonan, Tommy 120-21, 139, 147, 211-12

Normand, Mabel 15
Novak, Kim 24, 26, 77, 128
Nugent, J.C. 73-74
Nyberg, Mary Ann 126-28

O'Connor, Donald 17
Olivier, Laurence 20, 119
Ophuls, Max 46
Orlando, Tony 247-48
Osborne, Robert 270
O'Shea, Daniel 70
O'Toole, Peter 19-20
Overstreet, Richard 150

Pacino, Al 219
Palance, Jack 27
Pangborn, Franklin 86
Paramount 7, 9, 11-12, 33, 37, 209, 231, 268, 270
Parker, Dorothy 70
Parsons, Louella 6-7
Paul, Robert 2
Peck, Gregory 119
Penn, Sean 35
Pepe 13-14
Perry, Richard 225
Peters, Jon 217-23, 225-26, 231-33, 238-39, 242, 248, 253, 255, 258-59
Pfeiffer, Michelle 271
Phillips, Gene 144
Pickford, Mary 9, 11-12
Pidgeon, Walter 111
Pierson, Frank 222-23, 226-27, 232, 234-36, 239-42, 245, 248-50, 253, 259, 262
Player, The 14, 30
Plummer, Christopher 30
Plunkett, Walter 127
Porter, Edwin S. 2-3
Postcards from the Edge 33
Powdermaker, Hortense 261
Powell, Dick 14, 16, 31
Power, Tyrone 119
Preminger, Otto 124, 127
Presley, Elvis 219, 223
Puglia, Frank 142, 144
Pygmalion 154, 163, 269

Ralli, Paul 4
Ramone, Phil 233
Ratoff, Gregory 44-45, 67
Ray, Nicholas 31
Redford, Robert 271
Reed, Rex 256
Reid, Wallace 9, 11
Renoir, Jean 46, 212
Reynolds, Debbie 17
Riese, Randall 219-20, 225, 233, 236, 244, 256
RKO 39-40, 49, 70, 266, 270
RKO 281 21
Robbins, Tim 30
Robertson, Cliff 272
Robson, May 74-75, 104-05
Rogers, Roy 13, 79
Rogers, Will 9, 12, 21-22
Rosher, Charles 40
Ross, Diana 219
Rossen, Harold 170-71
Rudnick, Paul 45
Rush, Richard 18
Russell, Leon 226
Rydell, Mark 218-19

Sakall, S.Z. 13
Sargent, Alvin 222
Sarnoff, David 266
Sarris, Andrew 67
Scarlett O'Hara War, The 21
Schatzberg, Jerry 219-21
Schenck, Nick 184, 265
Schlesinger, John 239
Schulberg, Budd 70
Sedgwick, Edward 15
Selzer, Milton 25
Selznick, David 88, 94, 106, 113, 128, 183, 198, 248, 262, 266, 271
  producer, *Star is Born, A* (1937) 69-72
  producer, *What Price Hollywood?* 40, 66-68, 73, 101-03, 107, 109-10
Selznick, Irene Mayer 69, 72
Selznick, Myron 66, 72
Sennett, Mack 7, 15
Shadow of the Vampire 20
Sharaff, Irene 126, 170, 175
Shepherd, Dick 218
Sheridan, Ann 13

Sherman, Lowell 42, 45, 47, 49, 66-67, 72, 103, 154, 253
Show Girl in Hollywood 24
Show People 3-9
Shrine Auditorium 129-33, 137, 140, 145, 153, 160, 175, 188-91, 203, 208, 210, 212-14, 216, 229
Sidney, George 13
Signoret, Simone 267
Silent Movie 33
Simon, Carly 218-19
Simon, John 258
Sinatra, Frank 14, 119, 149
Singin' in the Rain 15-18, 131, 171, 175, 186, 194
Sirk, Douglas 204, 250
Sloane, Everett 30
S.O.B. 33, 37
Sothern, Ann 246
Souls for Sale 24
Spacey, Kevin 28
Spada, James 220, 222, 225-26, 233, 235, 256, 258
Springsteen, Bruce 235
Stander, Lionel 82-83, 121, 182, 200, 207
Stanley, Kim 32
Stanwyck, Barbara 12, 109
Stardust Memories 35
Star is Born, A (1937) 68, 153, 262-63, 266, 269
  production 69-72
  analysis 72-107
  reception 107-10
Star is Born, A (1954) 99, 111, 217, 228-29, 262-63, 266, 269
  production 112-29
  analysis 129-215
  reception and aftermath 215-16
Star is Born, A (1976) 263, 265, 269-70
  production 217-27
  analysis 227-56
  reception 256-59
Star, The 32
Steiger, Rod 28
Steiner, Max 40, 72-73
Sternhagen, Frances 25
Stevens, Warren 28
Stewart, Cal 3

Stewart, James 119, 162
St. Johns, Adela Rogers 39, 41, 45, 99
Story of Will Rogers, The 21-22
Stradling, Harry 123-24
Streisand, Barbra 217-26, 228-29, 232-33, 238-44, 247-51, 254-59, 263, 266, 269
Stunt Man, The 18-20, 36
Sturges, Preston 37
Sullivan's Travels 37
Sun Devil Stadium 232, 245
Sunset Boulevard 23, 25, 27, 30-31, 36-37, 82, 117
Surtees, Robert 226
Sutherland, Donald 18
Swanson, Gloria 7, 9, 23, 27, 117
Swimming with Sharks 28

Taylor, James 218-19
Taylor, Renée 119
Taylor, William Desmond 9, 62
Technicolor 78, 122-24
Terry, Ellen 152, 162
Thalberg, Irving 8
This is the End 14
Thomson, David 50, 66, 70-72, 85, 99, 107, 109
Todd, Ann 119
Travolta, John 34
Tropic Thunder 33, 36
Truffaut, Francois 18
Transcona Enterprises 111-13, 116, 216, 266
Turturro, John 31
20th Century Fox 32-33, 49, 115, 119, 122, 124, 171, 231
Two Weeks in Another Town 32, 36

Universal Studios 231, 264-65
Uncle Josh at the Moving Picture Show 2-3
Up Close and Personal 271

Valentino 21
Vidor, Charles 116
Vidor, King 3-5, 7
von Stroheim, Erich 49, 265
Vorkapich, Slavko 51, 62-63

Wagner, Robert 83, 270
Wag the Dog 33, 36
Walsh, Raoul 14, 39
Warner, Albert 123
Warner Bros. 12, 21, 40, 42, 72, 99, 112-13, 115-19, 121, 123-25, 129, 148, 156, 160, 170, 193, 215-20, 222, 226-27, 231, 235, 241, 259, 266, 268
Warner, Jack 29, 31, 113-14, 118-19, 121, 126-28, 171, 184, 193, 215
Warner, Harry 123, 129, 184, 215
W.C. Fields and Me 22
Weill, Kurt 116
Weiss, Donna 226
Welles, Orson 20, 46, 49, 130, 184
Wellman, William 70-73, 96, 99, 101, 106, 109, 181, 185, 198, 241, 248, 259, 262
What Just Happened 35
What Price Hollywood? 69, 71, 73, 80, 84-85, 93, 95, 103-04, 109-10, 169, 262-63, 267, 269
  production 39-40
  analysis 40-66
  reception 66-68
White, Alice 24
Wilder, Billy 23, 25
Williams, Michelle 20
Williams, Paul 225, 227-28, 235, 240
Willis, Bruce 35
Wizard of Oz, The 78, 112, 114-15, 171
Wood, Natalie 30
Wyman, Jane 12, 21-22, 216

Young, Robert 246

Zinner, Peter 250, 256
Zombieland 14
Zukor, Adolph 265